THE ART OF POETRY
1750–1820

THE ART OF POETRY

1750–1820

*Theories of poetic composition and style
in the late Neo-Classic and early
Romantic periods*

P. W. K. STONE

LONDON
Routledge and Kegan Paul Ltd

First published 1967
by Routledge & Kegan Paul Ltd
Broadway House, 68–74 Carter Lane
London E.C.4

Printed in Great Britain
by W. & J. Mackay & Co. Ltd
Chatham, Kent

SBN 7100 2934 9

Contents

Acknowledgements

I should like to express my gratitude to Professor Donald Davie for much helpful advice and criticism during the preparation of this book.

I should also like to thank the Master and Senior Tutor of Fitzwilliam College, Cambridge, Dr. W. W. Grave and Mr. R. N. Walters, whose kindness and interest made the undertaking possible.

Introduction

THE history of poetic theory in the period 1750–1820 has been often and, by now, very thoroughly investigated. Besides the accounts of the Romantic and 'pre-Romantic' eras to be found in general histories of criticism,[1] there exist several studies investigating in greater detail the origins and growth of Romanticism considered as a body of theoretical doctrine.[2] Yet these surveys, admirable in other respects, pay little attention to one interesting and, on the face of it, important topic: the theory, at this date, of poetic composition and style.

The topic seems important since, whatever the views of a theorist about the nature and function of literature, they must to a large extent be determined by his assumptions (if he makes any at all) about the aims and procedures of the writer. This part of his theory will be logically prior to the rest. To the student of critical history, interested in understanding and assessing the theories of a given time, it is naturally of the greatest value first to examine the fundamental conceptions upon which they are built. The whole may not be accurately interpreted unless due account has been taken of the most basic part.

The basis in this sense, however, of poetic theory during the period in question here has never yet been fully investigated.

The following study is, in its immediate aim, an attempt to make good the deficiency. It sets out to describe ideas current in the late Neo-Classical and early Romantic periods about the composition of poetry—about the 'art of poetry' in the traditional sense of the phrase, the practical principles upon which poetry is, or is held to be, written.

It is in the nature of the case, however, that this aim should subserve a further and more general one. It has not been very widely noticed, but is readily noticeable, that in the eighteenth century poetic theory was closely related to rhetoric.[3] Rhetorical ideas, on the other hand, play a conspicuously unimportant part in the work of the Romantic critics. The eighteenth-century 'art of poetry' is, in fact, largely derived from rhetoric, and is throughout founded upon presuppositions (about, for example, the nature of language or the relation of the writer to his audience) which have been taken over from rhetorical theory. This is not the case with Romantic theories of composition and style, which are based on assumptions not only different but hostile to those adopted by the rhetoricians. The two sets of ideas stand in sharp contrast to each other.

The fact is, apart from anything else, historically interesting. Nearly all recent historians of criticism have favoured the view that Romantic theory in England represents the culmination of a slow development over a period of at least half a century, that Romantic ideas about poetry were neither, at the time, unusually subversive in their implications, nor particularly new in themselves: in other words, that no 'revolution' occurred, merely a gradual 'evolution'.[4] Yet, as will appear in what follows, there is one department of poetic theory, a fundamentally important one, in which the Romantics did produce a radically new set of ideas. Their notions about the writing of poetry are indeed so much at variance with any hitherto entertained that they might almost be said to have invented a new conception of the art. It is notable that Wordsworth and Coleridge, and their fellow poets and critics, themselves asserted that in their lifetime a new sort of poetry had begun to be written on new principles.[5]

To show that these principles were genuinely new, and in what way, will be the larger aim of this study.

The question of 'pre-Romanticism' must figure largely in such an undertaking. It will be necessary to show that the concept is of extremely limited value in this particular field. It is true, no doubt, that many leading Romantic doctrines appeared first in the work of their eighteenth-century predecessors, and that most of those general tendencies which are normally cited as defining characteristics of Romanticism (e.g. the demand for originality and spontaneity, a preoccupation with the expression of emotion, with the individual and subjective rather than the general and objective) are likewise apparent at an earlier date. Nevertheless—or so it will be argued here—it is only by comparing such ideas and beliefs out of context that one set can be made to look convincingly like a 'foreshadowing' of the other. 'Pre-Romantic' ideas are always offshoots of traditional doctrine: re-formulated by the Romantics they appear in a different guise, in fact they become different ideas because they have been adapted to a different context of beliefs.

This argument would carry no weight, of course, unless it were established that authentically new ideas made their first appearance at a particular date. It will be postulated here that the revolution in poetic theory, though it was not accomplished at any given moment, did begin at a given moment, i.e. with the publication in 1800 of Wordsworth's Preface to *Lyrical Ballads*.

The Romantic 'revolution' will be described as an event in the history of poetic theory. Its characteristics will in fact be studied in one department of poetic theory. Though, since the changes effected there were radical ones, it will follow that a complete transformation of outlook must have accompanied them, this fact will not be presumed to throw any light upon the much-debated problem of 'Romanticism'. No new definition of Romanticism will here be mooted, and no attention paid, or reference intended, to the concepts of Romanticism or pre-Romanticism at large with all their aesthetic, philosophical, social, and even political implications. These concepts, though muddled, have their uses, but their introduction into the present study would thoroughly confuse every issue.

The relevant terms will be used instead purely as conventional labels. 'Romantic' will apply to the revolutionary school of theorists, 'Romanticism' to their views. Similarly 'Neo-Classicism' will denote only 'the theory of poetry current before 1800'. The term 'pre-Romantic' does not, of course, come into the same category since it implies not merely a period 'placing', but a tendentious historical judgment. Again, however, if its use is deprecated, it is the meaning 'precursor of the Romantic critics' which will be held objectionable, and no other possible implication of the term.

The dates demarcating the limits of this study have not been chosen altogether arbitrarily. 1750 marks accurately enough the beginning of a period of greatly increased activity in criticism, a period also of many new developments, inspired in part by the philosophies of Hume and Hartley which had recently come into notice.[6] By 1820 Romantic theory had received its fullest exposition, and was already on the way to being accepted as orthodoxy.

It will be the works largely of rhetoricians and literary theorists that are discussed below: among the theorists, however, a handful of aestheticians, psychologists and philosophers will be found included. At the same time 'theorists' will not be assumed to exclude those writers whose views were never set forth in extended and formal treatises. The critical literature of the period is vast, and the present study does not pretend to exhaustiveness, but it is hoped that all the important authors, and a sufficiently representative number of the less important, will have received due notice. An attempt has been made, too, not to ignore altogether the writers of non-theoretical or 'practical' criticism, who so often supply valuable clues to the theoretical assumptions of their time. Since the Romantic period saw less than the preceding one in the way of formal and systematic theorizing, more attention has been paid in the second than in the first part of this study to informal writings such as letters and memoranda. These often serve, in the case of the Romantics, to illustrate or complement ideas which may not be fully or clearly enough explained in their (contemporaneously) published works.

A part only of the theory of poetry will be fully treated in the ensuing pages, that part of it which relates to composition and style. Though obviously no clear-cut boundary can be laid down between this and neighbouring areas of investigation, the discussion has as far as possible been focused on a few leading topics which are clearly and obviously connected with the question: How is poetry written? Throughout the period philosophical and psychological speculation provides a basis and justification for answers to this question, and such arguments have been given their share of attention. Little direct notice, however, has been taken of another apparently relevant and, certainly at the time, important branch of inquiry. Aesthetics (in the strict sense of the term: theories about the nature of beauty, sublimity, and so on) has its bearing on the theory of composition, but it is not, during the eighteenth century at least, a close one. Though its principles may relate to the kind of subject a writer attempts, hence to the particular sorts of skill he must display, they do not directly apply to the more general problem of composition itself and how it proceeds.

Two topics of much nearer relevance have been left almost entirely out of account: the question of rhythm and 'music' in poetry and that of versification and metre. The justification, if any, for these omissions must be that treatment of these topics would have lengthened and complicated the discussion while contributing little of importance to the purpose in hand.

The division of this study will be partly chronological: Neo-Classicism and Romanticism will be discussed separately. Within these two main divisions, however, sub-divisions will follow a series not of successive periods or successive authors but of separate topics. The aim will be to present a general conspectus of the ideas current in either part of the period, rather than to trace in detail the development of these ideas, or to describe in full the particular views of individual critics. This method allows for a clearer and more comprehensive survey of the subject, and some care has been devoted to overcoming the concomitant disadvantage, namely that both Neo-Classicists and Romantics will be considered *en bloc*, a large number of writers coming under discussion with each topic. In a study of this scope minor eccentricities in individual critics must necessarily be ignored, but an effort has been made to take into account every marked divergence from views that are otherwise put forward as typical of a given time.

It remains only to say here that the argument in support of a Romantic 'revolution' will not be pursued entirely for its own sake. A correct historical perspective is necessary to a correct interpretation of both Romantic and Neo-Classical ideas, as well as to a just evaluation of them. The belief that Romanticism took its origins in the work of certain eighteenth-century critics has encouraged a historical confusion of some moment, since it involves seeing the Romantic achievement as the culmination of a development, the final re-attainment of a true understanding of literature which the previous age had been groping to regain. It is this sort of historical interpretation and evaluation which the present study may help to discourage if it succeeds in showing that Romantic theory differs sharply in kind, but not in degree of depth or completeness, from its Neo-Classical counterpart; that it is a new theory supporting a new kind of poetry, but not necessarily for that reason a more highly-developed one.

Part One: 1750–1800

1

Rhetoric and its Relation to Poetry

THE last thirty years or so have seen a marked resurgence of interest in rhetoric, more particularly in the use of rhetorical methods and devices in poetry. But this is a comparatively recent phenomenon. For over a century, that is from the Romantic era onward, no critic in the main tradition paid any more than cursory attention to the rhetorical aspects of composition and style, that is to the question of the effects of poetry and how they are achieved.[1] The Romantic view was, of course, that the subject did not warrant systematic investigation and analysis and was moreover, by its very nature, unamenable to it.

In point of fact, we have by no means entirely relinquished this view: even the new rhetorically-minded criticism seeks not so much to discover *how* poetry is, or may be, written, as simply to analyse its structure. It aims to describe what is there rather than ask why it is there. We find, it is true, critical studies of individual poems which not only define but ascribe a value to their structural characteristics, but rarely is any attempt made to generalize about methods and devices, their particular uses, their relative importance, their suitability in one context rather than another.[2]

In fact no such attempt could begin from present-day assumptions about the way poetry affects a reader. The effects of poetry are now understood as so extremely subtle and complex, so highly specific in each individual case, that any possibility of defining and classifying them, tracing them to their causes, and laying down principles of composition and style in accordance with the findings, is scarcely to be conceived. We are still really of one mind with the Romantics in believing the workings of poetry to be almost wholly mysterious.

Until the beginning of the nineteenth century, however, the critical attitude to these questions had been strikingly different. It was taken for granted that the methods of poetry could be isolated,

examined and described, and principles derived from them. Poetry
was an 'art', not in the modern sense of the word, or not only in
the modern sense, but also in that older sense (which still survives
in certain contexts) of 'craft', 'skill', 'know-how'.

It is well known that the critics and theorists of the Renaissance
regarded the writing of poetry as an 'art' in this sense.[3] Precisely
the same view survived into the last decades of the eighteenth
century, although the last treatise to employ the phrase 'the art of
poetry' in its title, at the same time attributing its traditional
meaning to the phrase, appeared in 1762.[4]

The theory of poetry as an 'art' had, during the Renaissance,
borne a very close resemblance to the theory of rhetoric. The
reasons are not far to seek. Though Aristotle maintained that
rhetoricians had originally learnt their skills from the poets, it was
in fact the former who took the lead in analysing and rationalizing
what might be called the 'artistic' use of language. It was rhetoric
from the first that legislated in this field. Hence Aristotle does not
find it necessary to discuss 'thought' and 'style' in the *Poetics:* he
refers the reader to his companion treatise.[5] The situation in the
sixteenth century is no different. Theorists of poetry borrow
wholesale from the rhetoricians for their stylistic maxims and
precepts. Indeed, as a consequence of their indebtedness they can
no longer draw any precise theoretical distinction between poetry
and its sister discipline.[6] Since they consider poetry as an 'art' and
rely, for defining an important part of their conception, on the
categories of a closely similar 'art', the result is inevitably a near-
identification of the two.

Poetry is still, in the later eighteenth century, regarded as an
'art', and still retains its connexion with rhetoric. However, before
we turn to examining the nature and implications of the relationship—the main purpose of this and succeeding chapters—it might
be as well to glance briefly at the fortunes of rhetorical theory itself
during the period. Whereas Neo-Classic theories of literature have
been thoroughly investigated, very little has been written on this
subject. It seems generally to be assumed, perhaps on the authority
of Croce's review of critical history in the *Aesthetic*, that the
theory of rhetoric reached the culmination of its development
during the seventeenth century and that its later history is accordingly of little interest or consequence.[7] Thus eighteenth-century
rhetoric has been almost completely neglected in histories of

literary criticism; furthermore no general account has yet been written of the continuous development of rhetorical doctrines in England from the Renaissance onwards, and of their constantly changing relevance to literature.[8] In view of this lack, some brief and very general indications of the status and function of rhetoric in the late eighteenth century will be useful in the present context and may at least suggest the directions that previous developments had taken.

A clear indication of the standing of rhetoric may be looked for in definitions of the term current during the period. Needless to say, no one definition is accepted by all rhetoricians alike. Even in Classical times definitions of rhetoric had been legion. Quintilian employs several pages in examining and rejecting a series of these before fixing on his own *'scientia bene dicendi'*.[9] But even the Classical definitions may be divided into two classes: one which assumes rhetoric to be the theory exclusively of public speaking, the other which considers the theory as applying indiscriminately to all forms of discourse. One might call them Aristotelian and Ciceronian respectively, after the authors of the earliest extant treatises in which they are represented. The two types of theory corresponding to these definitions naturally emphasize, on the one hand, argument and evidence as means of persuasion, and, on the other, structure and style as the means to obtaining every kind of rhetorical effect. They overlap, of course—the Aristotelian rhetorician does not ignore effectiveness of composition and style any more than the Ciceronian does logic and the selection of evidence—but the difference of emphasis is important. It is because the Ciceronian view of rhetorical theory was able, for various reasons, to gain wider acceptance, virtually ousting by late classical times the stricter Aristotelian conception, that, as long as the classical tradition lasted in literature, rhetoric was able to maintain a powerful influence in more 'purely' literary spheres. This type of rhetoric concerns itself with every kind of writing. The Aristotelians, who see rhetoric as applicable to oratory alone, have—at any rate in England since the Renaissance—constituted an uninfluential minority.

In England, then, we deal with rhetoric as primarily an 'art of speaking and writing'. During the Renaissance, indeed, a strong tendency developed to identify rhetoric with the study merely of style,[10] to the exclusion of other considerations. The so-called 'reforms' of Ramus, who achieved some influence in England, served only to strengthen the tendency.[11]

By the eighteenth century the balance has been restored. It is only exceptionally that rhetoricians devote themselves exclusively to style, and then with a consciousness that they are treating only a part of their subject. In fact the rhetorician's net, as we shall see, is now being cast wider than ever before, though the definition of rhetoric most widely accepted after 1750 is still the traditional Ciceronian one of 'an art of speaking and writing well'.

A new emphasis, however, is now placed on what was always implicit in Classical rhetoric: the principle that good speaking or writing consists in the perfect adaptation of means to chosen ends. This is stressed in some of the definitions offered during the period. Rhetoric is 'that art or talent by which the discourse is adapted to its end'. 'He who speaks, or writes, in such a manner as to adapt all his words most effectually to [his] end, is the most eloquent man'.[12]

For a few writers rhetoric still retains its orientation towards the platform and pulpit, and they offer appropriate definitions: 'Oratory is the art of speaking well upon any subject, in order to persuade'.[13] But these 'Aristotelians' make it clear that what they have to say must not be considered altogether irrelevant to other forms of discourse.[14] They are in any case a small handful, writing in the earlier part of the period.[15]

The more important writers define rhetoric as relevant to literature generally. Some who are not explicit in defining the bounds of their subject show in their works that they conceive it to have a very wide range. Not only do they run the whole gamut of traditional rhetorical concerns, invention, arrangement and style, they attack every kind of literary and aesthetic problem as well. They discuss the origins of the sublime and the beautiful, the doctrine of imitation, the psychology of literary invention. And these discussions are not merely incidental divagations, the result of an interest in the fringes of the subject. The very titles of some of these works—*Lectures on Rhetoric and Belles Lettres*, *A Course of Lectures on Oratory and Criticism*—indicate that their writers intend to effect a deliberate *rapprochement* between rhetoric and literary theory. The contents even of works which proclaim a concern with one of the two disciplines rather than the other make it clear that no precise de-limitation is implied by their titles: thus Campbell in his *Philosophy of Rhetoric* leads the reader as naturally into an investigation of the pleasures of tragedy as Kames in the *Elements of Criticism* into a rhetorical analysis of style.

The bounds of rhetoric were thus widened to the point where it could no longer be distinguished from literary theory. This great enlargement of scope was accompanied by a much more liberal and less pedantic approach to the subject. We may still find in treatises such as Ward's the rather lifelessly systematic method, the rigid categorizing and over-scrupulous cataloguing of the earlier textbooks, which are simply Cicero or Quintilian 'methodis'd', but even so early and (in other respects) conventional a work as Lawson's *Lectures concerning Oratory* reveals a much more flexible pattern. His procedure is not a mere running-through of the classical commonplaces in the approved order: he approaches the subject from a series of points of view, selecting topics to consider in a common-sense light rather than with a view to dissecting and tabulating. All the more sophisticated treatises of the later part of the century go further in adopting a philosophical method of approach: their interest is not in laying down a sequence of rules justified by little more than quoted examples of their application, but in developing a properly philosophical rationale for rhetorical theory, a system of principles which can be shown to be self-consistent and derived from reliable philosophical postulates.

Naturally, these writers do not favour the unsupported generalizations and arbitrary discriminations of earlier theory. The lists of tropes and figures so lovingly elaborated by Renaissance rhetoricians appear in their works (if they appear at all) in a much simplified and rationalized form, as do most of the other traditional sharp divisions and sub-divisions of rhetoric. They no longer, moreover, accept their doctrines, as had long been the practice, on the mere authority of the ancients. As is to be expected in representatives of the empirically-minded English Enlightenment, they require all their views to be experimentally justified: their precepts must find a basis in experience. They do, it is true, sometimes cling to time-honoured doctrines even when such empirical arguments as they are able to find in support of them are of a very implausible kind: one suspects very strongly that on these occasions the argument is a mere excuse, far from being as disinterested as the air it wears.[16] But on the whole their endeavour is as objective and honest as possible, and when they see the necessity, they have no compuction about discarding old-established views. Many important and widely-accepted rhetorical doctrines were attacked during the period on empirical grounds, and if they were not demolished, those who still defended them were thenceforth obliged to adopt more cautious and thorough justifications.

Since one of the most striking philosophical trends of the time was an attempt to remove psychology from the realm of speculation and establish it upon a properly scientific footing, it is not surprising to find the rhetoricians interested. Much of their argument from empirical data is still, like Burke's or Lowth's, the drawing of summary conclusions from personal discoveries or *ad hoc* observations, but there is a tendency increasingly noticeable after 1750 to attach rhetoric to systematic philosophy, to take over the concepts and the vocabularies of a Hume or a Hartley and apply them in the literary sphere. These philosopher-rhetoricians confessedly aim at placing the theory of literature upon a scientific basis.[17] However limited the success they achieved, it can certainly be argued that they instituted an original and potentially very fruitful movement in the study of literature.

One is tempted to add, though there can be little point in such historical regrets, that the movement was prematurely and too decisively cut short by the Romantics. It is true that much of this literary philosophizing or psychologizing is jejune and trivial. Abrams is quite right in maintaining that it often goes no further then the translation of a rhetorical vocabulary word for word into a philosophical one.[18] Kames, in particular, seems utterly unworthy in this respect of the reputation he achieved: when he is not being trite he is more often than not being merely silly.[19] But there are others such as Priestley, Ogilvie and Campbell who surprise the modern reader with the perspicacity and justice of their observations, observations which, some of them, seem to have caught the attention of their Romantic successors as well—who then, however, turned them to very different purposes.[20]

The mass of this body of empirical and quasi-empirical argument and speculation is no doubt, from our contemporary point of view, thin in intrinsic interest and of somewhat doubtful validity. But the results were by no means totally negligible, the methods employed were new and their potentialities seem even now not unpromising. There is still a great deal to be learnt from the empirical study of literature, at least about the nature and uses of literary techniques.[21] It is far from true, at all events, that, as received opinion has it, the eighteenth century marks a period of stagnation and decline in the history of rhetoric.[22] Under the aegis of empirical philosophy, and especially of the new-found science of psychology, a completely new theoretical enterprise had by the middle of the century got under way. Rhetoricians were no longer mechanically treading their predecessors' ground, but were occupied in re-mapping it and turning to the exploration of what lay beyond.

Within the sphere of rhetoric proper, the new point of view, the new methods of observation and analysis and new forms of argument, made on the whole little difference to the traditional foundation of the theory; the new approach left the old basis of doctrine for the most part unchanged. It may well be that the ideas and principles which had survived for centuries had done so precisely because they had in fact stood the test of experience: the more sophisticated rhetoricians of the late eighteenth century had little more to do with their new instrument of psychological analysis than confirm them. At all events it is still Quintilian, Cicero, Longinus who supply the axioms and first principles upon which every variety of theoretical superstructure is built. Their doctrines, as we have noted, are sometimes challenged, though not to any permanent effect; more often they are modified and elaborated. For example, Cicero's division of the process of composition into Invention, Disposition, Elocution is transformed into a complex psychological theory of literary invention, while broad generalizations such as Longinus' observation that figures are 'the language of passion' are carefully re-examined and re-stated with justifications, riders and reservations. The tendency is to extend the range and depth of discussion without disturbing the traditional framework: the few who are dissatisfied with one or more traditional ideas make no attempt to destroy the entire fabric. They seem, in any case, to stimulate their successors to a work of consolidating the weak points rather than widening the breaches.

Hence the marriage of classical rhetoric with empirical philosophy was, by and large, a harmonious one: the empirical outlook favoured the retention of ancient doctrines. While, however, the classical influence remained supreme, the body of classical thought on rhetorical subjects was much amended, modified and elaborated, and those rhetoricians most influenced by the philosophy of the

Enlightenment now re-stated it in entirely new terms. These writers, furthermore, extended their discussions far beyond the conventional bounds of their subject. Rhetoric was beginning to coalesce with, if not to absorb, the theory of literature. The Ciceronian meaning of the term—'the art of writing and speaking well'—was stretched at this period to its fullest possible extent.

But why and how was so little distinction maintained between rhetoric and other branches of literary theory, including the theory of poetry? We must turn for an answer to some examination of the kind of relationship thought to obtain between the two 'arts'.

It is not a blind *esprit de système* which classes oratory and poetry neatly under one head. It is a matter of observed fact to writers of the period that the two arts, with the same resources of language at their disposal, have certain ends in common as well; hence they share certain methods and techniques, the means of achieving those ends. They are 'sister arts'. Thus far the same rules and principles must apply indifferently to both, and rhetoricians and poetic theorists are justified in assuming a large extent of common ground.[23]

Where poetry is concerned, the Horatian maxim that it aims at pleasing, moving and instructing is still accepted doctrine, though the doctrine may now be couched, like so many others at this time, in psychological terms: poetry appeals to the fancy, the feelings, the judgment. Above all to the fancy: the emphasis at this period is overwhelmingly on pleasure as the chief and final end of poetry. By arousing feeling the poet contributes to pleasure, but 'moving', though it is often considered an essential part of the poet's task, remains usually a subordinate one. 'Instruction' as an end is often given merely incidental importance, if it is mentioned at all. This is, in general, the order in which the three ends of poetry are ranged, though individual views show variations in the tripartite scheme.

Johnson, for example, who is in many ways a reactionary, harking back to the ideas of an earlier age, stresses the element of 'instruction' in his well-known definition: 'Poetry is the art of uniting pleasure with truth.'[24] There are other writers who incline to a similar placing of emphasis; Lowth, for example, in his version of the familiar dogma about 'instruction' and 'delight'. For Lowth, as for others, 'moving' is a subordinate aim: '. . . by exciting the passions [poetry] more effectually attains its end.'[25]

Belsham takes up a similar position for reasons of his own. 'Of all the various inventions of literature, whose sole or principal object is to please, Poetry stands undoubtedly most conspicuous . . .'; however, '. . . when a man attains to maturity of judgment . . . works addressed exclusively to the imagination cease to please; and . . . he requires not only the imagination to be gratified, but the passions to be moved, and the understanding to be enlightened.'[26]

Nevertheless, it is a much simpler view such as Beattie's which is typical: '[the poet's] aim is, to please, by working upon your passions, and fancy . . .'[27] The end of 'pleasure', always recognized as a valid one, is here unequivocally given pride of place.

The aims of oratory are considered identical to those of poetry, except that to 'pleasing, moving, instructing' is added 'persuasion'. Persuasion is the orator's principal end, the others subsidiary, though never merely optional. A characteristic expression of opinion on this point is Ward's when he says that the orator must provide his audience with entertainment as well as convincing arguments, 'and unless both these are warmed and animated by a becoming pathos, the speaker may very probably miss of his end, in bringing his audience over to his sentiments.'[28]

The fact that oratory and poetry to a large extent share the same aims is frequently pointed out: '. . . the direct end of the [poet]', says Campbell, 'whether to delight the fancy as in epic, or to move the passions as in tragedy, is avowedly in part the aim, and sometimes the immediate and proposed aim of the orator.'[29] Thomas Sheridan, in a work which, it must be admitted, professes a nothing less than fanatical faith in the importance of rhetoric to education and the arts, goes so far as to say (of epic and tragic poets):

Their great ends are, *to move, to delight, to instruct;* and from whom could they learn the power of all this so effectually as from the orator, who must so far fail of his point, as he falls short in any of those ends, and whose constant practice pointed out the means by which those were to be attained?[30]

Some writers evidently feel that, apart from the distinct preoccupation of oratory with persuasion, there is a difference between oratory and poetry in the relative importance to either art of the three other aims they have in view. It is in this light, perhaps, that remarks such as the following are to be interpreted: 'Poetry sprang from ease, and was consecrated to pleasure; whereas Eloquence arose from necessity, and aims at conviction.'[31] According to Blair, again, the orator addresses himself primarily to the understanding, whereas the 'primary aim of a Poet is to please, and to move; and, therefore, it is to the Imagination, and the Passions, that he speaks'.[32] But there is no clear or generally-accepted opinion on the subject. It is not difficult to find views inconsistent with those quoted above, for instance Gerard's: '. . . the poet aims chiefly at pleasing, and the orator at moving'.[33]

The precise nature of the distinction held to obtain between rhetoric and poetry must be reserved for consideration in a later chapter.[34] For the moment it is enough to have observed that rhetoric and poetry are regarded as 'sister arts' sharing certain purposes. The implications and consequences of this view may now, in the next and succeeding chapters, be examined in detail.

No attempt will be made to trace the pattern of the relation-ship—which, as has already been indicated, was growing very much more complex in the later eighteenth century—in all its ramifications: this study confines itself to the theory of composition and style, the theory, that is to say, which applies directly on the one hand to the question of how poetry is written, and corresponds on the other to the traditional branches of rhetoric: Invention, Disposition and Elocution. It is here that the interrelationship between the two 'arts' is most interesting and revealing, in that it implies a series of fundamental and highly characteristic assump-tions about poetry which are never formulated and stated, and which have therefore for the most part been overlooked in histories of the period.

Even within these limits the system of ideas is a sufficiently wide-ranging and complicated one, and what follows will treat only the most important topics in any detail. Naturally no critic or theorist quoted will be assumed, on the strength of his conformity in one respect or another, to support the whole system in all its particulars; but, as much for the sake of intelligibility as brevity, the minor divergencies of individuals will be ignored while major areas of agreement are emphasized. Important reservations or con-tradictions will be noticed, but, since the purpose of the ensuing section is to present an over-all view of the thought of the period, no attempt will be made to account for these anomalies until a later chapter,[35] when arguments will be offered for considering the dissenting writers not as revolutionaries bent on breaking away from the traditional system but as experimenters working within its framework.

2

Rules and Principles

SINCE the aims of rhetoric and poetry are, for the most part, identical, it is assumed that little distinction can be drawn between the methods and technical devices appropriate to either art. We find it frequently pointed out that because both are arts of language they naturally employ the same materials, and exploit the same resources.[1] Such statements define the unexpressed beliefs of, for example, all those writers who, whether their subject is oratory or poetry, discuss style in one and the same set of terms, setting up the same ideals and laying down the same principles.

There are, it is true, those critics who maintain that poetry makes use of a 'diction' or 'language' distinct from that of oratory: '. . . though thoughts in poetry and prose differ but little . . . yet . . . the diction of poetry is very different from that of prose.'[2] But we shall see in a later chapter, when this point will be considered at greater length,[3] that in fact the distinction is simply a matter of the greater liberty of fancy and more lavish use of colour permitted the poet, and that there is never any question of his using a different set of resources.

Perhaps the most striking characteristic of the methods poet and orator assumed to share is that they are clearly, to some extent, deliberate. The orator *chooses* the means which are most fitted to encompassing his ends: as we have seen in the preceding chapter, rhetoric is often defined as predominantly a pragmatic art, a practical skill—'that art or talent by which the discourse is adapted to its end'. Language and style—to confine our discussion to this one aspect of the issue—are accordingly regarded as instrumental. We find a clear statement of the case in Reynolds.

. . . it is but poor eloquence which only shews that the orator can talk. Words should be employed as the means, not as the end: language is the instrument, conviction is the work.[4]

Precisely the same view of language and style characterizes discussions of poetry. In both arts the ultimate criterion of a good style is that it should be perfectly adjusted to producing the intended effect. All felicity of style consists in subordinating judiciously-chosen means to predetermined ends. The following extracts indicate the prevailing point of view. The writers are rhetoricians, but all three of them—including the first, who has previously stated that he considers poetry itself a branch of rhetoric —are talking about literature in general.

it is not ultimately . . . the justness either of the thought or of the expression, which is the aim of the orator; but it is a certain effect to be produced in the hearers . . .[5]

A writer, if he wish to succeed, ought always to have the reader in his eye . . .[6]

. . . all that can possibly be required of Language, is, to convey our ideas clearly to the minds of others, and, at the same time, in such a dress, as by pleasing and interesting them, shall most effectually strengthen the impressions we seek to make. When both these ends are answered, we certainly accomplish every purpose for which we use Writing and Discourse.[7]

Assumptions of this kind underlie all discussions of style, even where writers are concerned exclusively with the resources of poetry. When, as sometimes happens, these assumptions rise to the surface in observations such as the following, the occurrence does not strike one as odd or unexpected:

Great judgment . . . is required in the distribution of this figure ['description']. Whether it be intended to move the passions, or to please the fancy, it must answer the end proposed; and therefore it is never to be admitted but when some point can be attained.[8]

Again, in another work:

Well chosen images, *happily adapted to the purpose for which they are adduced*, if not too frequently employed, produce a fine effect in poetry.[9]

It is their conception of style and of the other resources of composition as instrumental, as means to ends, which justifies the theorists of the late eighteenth century in their affirmation of rules and principles. Since composition is, like so many other skills, an activity with practical aims in view, it may be assumed that its processes can be analysed, that connexions may be traced between causes and effects, and precepts laid down accordingly.

In the chapters that follow the more important of these principles and precepts will be examined in detail, so that no more need be said of them for the moment. But there are further aspects of the validity of the system as a whole, its validity, that is to say, in eighteenth-century eyes, that call for some attention.

We have already seen that there is a strong tendency among theorists in the latter half of the century to take over psychological doctrines as a foundation for their views, to displace rhetoric (in its widest acceptation as the 'art of writing') from its traditional basis of classical authority and common-sense observation and establish it on a properly philosophic foundation. The advantages attaching to this new mode of investigation were in one respect limited. As long as the rhetorical psychologists confined themselves to showing, by the analysis of mental and emotional reactions, *how* one literary effect will please and another will not, their arguments were plausible enough. But when they set their sights more ambitiously on discovering *why* this should be so the results were much less convincing. At least one contemporary critic was dubious about such attempts. With Kames's *Elements of Criticism* particularly in mind, William Belsham complains very justly of those theorists who claim to have discovered a rational explanation for literary preferences. It is, he says in effect, no solution to the problems of taste—as for example: why do we prefer 'musical and harmonious versification' to 'harsh and rugged numbers'?—simply to sanction the approved quality ('harmoniousness') by a rule based upon psychological analysis of its effect. However subtle the analysis, no objective grounds have been adduced for the superiority of this quality over the other. The problem has simply been transferred from the literary to the psychological realm: no real standard has been established.[10]

Belsham does allow, however, that the studies of Kames and his fellow-psychologists have some practical usefulness. Because taste, he holds, is to a large extent uniform in all men,

. . . it is both entertaining and instructive, by any fair process of induction, to point out the immediate, though we cannot trace the ultimate, causes of those uniform emotions of disgust and admiration, which is in effect to point out the means of avoiding or exciting them; or, in other words, it is to establish certain fixed rules of composition upon the authority of experience . . .[11]

Here is, in fact, a possible justification for the establishment of rules and principles on a basis of psychological data, even if those data can supply no fixed criterion of taste, and it is one that some critics are at pains to put forward: Blair, for example, who, assuming that the foundations of taste 'are the same in all human minds' and that it is 'built upon sentiments and perceptions which belong to our own nature', argues that criticism can therefore be an empirical science, proceeding by induction from observed phenomena.[12]

Some such argument must be understood to support and validate much of the theorizing on composition and style at this period. Whether or not the grounds of taste, as a few writers claim, can be rationalized, and general laws laid down which apply to the whole of aesthetic experience, it is accepted that a broad uniformity of taste exists in the educated class, that varieties of aesthetic experience which are common to educated readers can be distinguished and described and their connexion with certain literary qualities established. Because taste is uniform, and values are 'given', it is enough for the theorist to investigate typical reactions, and their causes, in order to arrive at a set of principles. The psychological method of approach proves practically useful, however little the pure aestheticians are able to accomplish with it.

The aestheticians, on the other hand, perhaps because they could make no headway with the method in one direction, were carrying it to dangerous lengths in another. Belsham had reproved Kames for trying to establish absolute standards on arbitrary grounds: such a proceeding made nonsense of the empiricist programme. But there were those aestheticians who came near admitting that there could be no grounds for any standards at all. They began, in other words, to find strong arguments against the all-important belief in a uniformity of taste. If aesthetics at this period was in difficulties, then rhetoric, which relied on the same methods of psychological inquiry, and to some extent at least was bound to accept the findings of the philosophers of Taste, must also have found itself on a very doubtful footing.

Those aestheticians especially who, like Gerard, Priestley or Alison, conducted their inquiries by the light of association theory found themselves in a dilemma. If aesthetic experience is simply a matter of associations, as these writers held, it must vary very widely from individual to individual. Each of us possesses a unique stock of associations, interconnected in a manner peculiar to ourselves. Where, then, are the data of induction? How is it possible to generalize? It might seem that eighteenth-century aesthetics, determined to base its conclusions on experience alone, had inevitably to lose itself, and was now lost, in a welter of discrete, unclassifiable particulars—the facts of personal and private reaction to literature. It has in fact been assumed that once the search for criteria of taste has been diverted from the objective to the subjective sphere, individualism and relativism were bound to follow, and did.[13] The empirical experiment had, in other words, failed, and it was left for Romanticism and Idealism to save the day.

This is some way from the truth. There is no sign at any time before the end of the century that rhetoricians or theorists of poetry lost confidence in their basic assumptions. Nor indeed did the aestheticians abandon all attempt at objective inquiry. If they were obliged to admit that the aesthetic experience must vary between individual and individual, they were still certain that each particular case must display universal characteristics and that these, in turn, could be traced to permanent and invariable principles in literature. Not one of them is to be found admitting that values are entirely a matter of personal preference or caprice.

For, wherever the associationists' arguments seemed to be leading, ultimately they had to take into account the empirical observation, as valid in their eyes as any other, that standards of preference were steady, if not fixed, that the majority of men at any one time and place appeared to like and dislike the same things on the same general grounds. They were satisfied, in other words, that aesthetic experiences run to type, and as long as so much remained self-evidently true there could be no question for them of relativism.

The recognition of a uniformity of taste is thus a key factor in eighteenth-century aesthetics, and it is accordingly of equal importance to the new methods of investigation in rhetoric and criticism. It is not only the initial justification for the psychological inquiry, by virtue of which the theorist's analysis of his own reactions may be offered as representative, it also protects the inquiry from pursuing its logic too far: what is purely personal and idiosyncratic in the theorist's experience must be acknowledged and discounted.

This 'uniformitarian'[14] doctrine is somewhat distorted by writers of an authoritarian cast such as Kames or Alison, who contend that since taste may be cultivated, and obviously improves with experience, the opinions of the best-educated and most widely-read should be regarded as prescriptive. But the usual formulation of the doctrine is based a little more persuasively on the argument that men living in the same country at the same period, to the extent that they share the same experience, must also share the same taste.

Thus Priestley, who does not believe taste to be entirely uniform, since men obviously differ in the strength of their sensibilities and in their various modes of associating ideas and feelings, makes a point of saying:

There seems, however, to be so great a similarity in our situations, as is sufficient to afford a foundation for a considerable *similarity in taste;* particularly in persons whose education and manners of life have been nearly the same. But a *standard of taste,* founded upon the similar influences which persons so situated have been subject to, cannot be applied to those persons whose education and manner of life have been very different.[15]

Within the sphere of 'similar influences' a standard of taste may be assumed, though even so it is no absolute and fixed standard: it is rather a set of empirically-discovered values collectively considered, a more or less steady but never finally established system of criteria. It is a standard of this kind implied in the following remarks of Blair, which sum up the most widely-held sentiments on the topic:

That which men concur the most in admiring, must be held to be beautiful. His Taste must be esteemed just and true, which coincides with the general sentiments of men.[16]

Hence we find it implicitly accepted by writers on composition and style that there is a sufficiently wide agreement about the sort of literature that is good: their procedure, as we shall see, is to

suggest what are the causes and conditions of favourable (or
unfavourable) judgment and to reveal the principles implicit in
them.

This procedure, however is open to yet another form of criticism
which will be worth examining since these writers often take pains
to defend themselves against it. It is a criticism not of the validity
of their methods, but of the utility of their results. Is there any
point in laying down rules for good writing? Is it not a matter of
talent or inspiration or both? Has a writer ever obeyed rules and
will obeying them help anyone to write well?

No rhetorician is, of course, naïve enough to claim that mere
obedience to the rules is sufficient guarantee of literary merit.
No one assumes that, if rules and principles are discoverable, good
writing is therefore merely a matter of training and skill. The
products of a highly sceptical age, these writers found no difficulty
in accepting limits to what they could know: they were quite
aware that a large, and essential, element in literary excellence is
inexplicable and can only be put down to talent—'original genius' in
the phrase of the day. All of them acknowledged that without native
ability no amount of assiduity in cultivating the rules could be of
any avail. Nevertheless they insisted, more often than not, that a
knowledge of rules was indispensable. It might be acquired through
the study of models and through imitative exercises rather than
from theoretical treatises,[17] but since rhetoric and poetry are 'arts'
with known and proved procedures for achieving their characteristic effects, total ignorance of their laws could not but prove a
handicap.

In his rather arid way, Lord Monboddo summarizes the
general opinion.

. . . there are three things absolutely necessary to fine writing.
First, Natural Genius, without which nothing truly excellent can
be performed in any art. *Secondly*, Various knowledge, which
furnishes the materials to work upon. And, *thirdly*, The knowledge
of the rules of the art.[18]

Young, in his celebrated *Conjectures*, attached very little importance
to the two latter requirements and placed an overwhelming
emphasis upon the first, yet he did recognize, too, an inferior
type of genius which does not rely wholly on original powers.[19]

Later writers are sometimes to be found echoing Young, in that they recognize a kind of 'original genius' which owes nothing to theoretical studies. On the other hand they assume that natural ability of this kind will arrive, though instinctively, at the same knowledge of 'art' which theory provides.[20] Their opinions, therefore, do not in the last analysis differ in substance from Monboddo's.

Talent is fruitless without a knowledge of the rules: inspiration, similarly, is useless without conscious skill. The function of 'art' however, is merely to assist 'nature': the formula is repeated in a dozen different ways.[21] Too much respect for the rules is stultifying since too strenuous an exercise of the judgment inhibits imagination and the play of natural faculties. 'In the arts', says Gerard, '. . . an uncommon acuteness of judgment is so far from constituting genius, that it will absolutely destroy genius, unless the imagination be as uncommonly comprehensive.'[22] Obviously with his eye on the contemporary scene, he goes on to repeat a comment which is not infrequently made:

It has been observed that, though systems of precepts in the arts direct and improve the judgment, they rather curb and restrain genius. They render men so studious to avoid faults, that they scarce aim at beauties. It is remarked that, when works of imagination have been brought to the utmost degree of correctness in any age or nation, there has been afterwards very little display of original or extensive genius.[23]

But this is a caveat against excessive deference to rule, and a criticism of the homage paid in some circles to an ideal of 'correctness': Gerard is not the only writer to drive the point home.[24] That he none the less considered judgment essential to art, thereby allowing the utility of precepts which 'direct and improve' it, is made clear elsewhere in the same work.[25] 'Art' must not overrule 'nature': it functions as an aid, though a necessary aid.

At least one writer, however, would regard this as an inadequate statement of the case. At the other extreme from Young, the champion of 'nature', stands Reynolds, the champion of 'art'. 'Every opportunity', declares the latter roundly,

. . . should be taken to discountenance that false and vulgar opinion, that rules are the fetters of genius. They are fetters only to men of no genius; as that armour, which upon the strong is an ornament and a defence, upon the weak and misshapen becomes a load, and cripples the body which it was made to protect.[26]

The point about genius is not that it can dispense with workaday rules, but that it can go beyond them, into a region where only its own rules apply. 'Genius', says Reynolds, 'begins, not where rules, abstractedly taken, end: but where known vulgar and trite rules have no longer any place.'[27]

In the general view, however, 'art', though essential, is merely ancillary to talent. The positive value of training and skill is thus limited—it is no guarantee of success. But it is typical of these eighteenth-century writers, with their concern not only for 'the sublime' but for standards of competence in the humblest literary enterprises, that they insist on a negative value as well. The rules may not ensure excellence, but, in the absence of talent, they are a safeguard against total failure: 'a needful aid to the lame', as Young calls them.[28]

Young is the only writer of the period who appears to consider that, where genius is concerned, the rules are superfluous. The rest recognize the importance, up to a point, of obedience to certain principles, for to ignore them is to make light of a fund of practical wisdom accumulated over centuries. One writer, defending in this instance the rules of oratory, puts the argument very clearly, if a little over-enthusiastically:

. . . all Art is not more, than a Method of employing most effect-ually the Powers of Nature, reduced into Rules by long Observa-tion and Experience: And whosoever rejecting the Aid of these in Oratory, chuseth to abandon himself to uninstructed Nature, acteth with the same kind of Prudence, as doth the Man, who in a dangerous Disease, persisteth in refusing the Assistance of Medi-cine . . .[29]

Some deplore the fact that attention to the rules encourages excessive 'correctness', but, apart from the fact that it is often the givers of rules themselves who by issuing the caution recommend a proper attitude, we shall see that in any case the more important of their principles set no definite standards which can be 'correctly' measured up to. The absolute dogmas of the previous age, such as, for example, the Unities or the rules of couplet-versification, are beginning to be recognized as accessory conventions of only temporary validity, distinct from the fundamental and necessary rules of art.[30] Probably much of the distrust of rule and system expressed in writings of the period stems from a failure to make this distinction between two types of rule, and is directed in fact at such arbitrary fancies of the preceding period as still have a hold on conservative minds.

This seems the more likely in that the system of essential rules leaves, as will appear, plenty of room for the irrational and the spontaneous, for liberty of imagination and feeling, indeed pre-supposes that these are important factors in all good writing. A system which allows so much latitude cannot, by its very nature, demand rigid obedience. It is a system, in fact, of working principles, scarcely of 'rules' at all in the earlier sense. Authority or logic are rarely invoked to back it up: the appeal is above all to the evidence of common experience. Since the system itself disclaims total authority, there seems little reason why writers, recognizing its value within limits, should make guarded reservations about its ultimate usefulness.

Before leaving this topic it may be worth recalling the premise underlying the ideas and opinions discussed above. If it was considered possible to contruct a system of principles, based on empirical data, to apply to the writing of poetry, this could only be because poetry was considered as essentially a practical art, and as such a sister to rhetoric. It will be necessary before con-sidering the principles themselves, to examine some further assumptions involved in this assimilation of poetry with rhetoric, assumptions which are of great importance to the correct inter-pretation of individual precepts.

3

The Theory of Composition

BOTH rhetoric and poetry were regarded during the later eighteenth century as arts which, proposing to themselves certain aims, may adopt known methods, defined by rule, to effect those aims. Supplementary to this view of art as a matter largely of means-to-ends is a view of composition as governed by design.

The simplest and clearest formulation of the eighteenth-century conception of composition would take the following form: a plan is conceived appropriate to the purpose in view, the main lines of the subject are laid down; the plan is then elaborated in detail and the whole presented in a style which must be adapted both to subject-matter and purpose so as to achieve the desired effect (moving, pleasing, etc.) This conception of composition, sometimes set forth much as it has been above, sometimes rather more subtly and less matter-of-factly, is common to both rhetorical and poetic theory.

In rhetoric the position is clear. The orator's first necessity is to define and elaborate his subject. Given that he has a definite purpose in view, he is expected to collect the materials—arguments, examples, observations—which are germane to that purpose, and arrange them in the order he judges most effective, finally to set them forth in an appropriate style.

Classical rhetoric recognized three distinct stages in the process of composing a speech and had evolved a complex system of aids to the aspiring orator in making his way through them. The elaboration of the subject (*Inventio*) was governed by rules relating to the finding and exploitation of various types of argument. A scheme of 'topics' of invention (borrowed largely from the topics of Aristotelian logic) helped the orator to amplify his basic ideas. The next step was the arrangement of this material (*Dispositio*), governed again by rules and directions as to the division of the speech into parts and the proper management of exordium, narration and peroration. To the third and final stage of the process, the clothing of this material in suitable language (*Elocutio*), applied a body of principles relating to style.[1]

As we have seen, few late-eighteenth-century rhetoricians produce treatises written to the systematic classical pattern; nevertheless, most still follow classical precedent in postulating three divisions of rhetoric, corresponding to three separate stages of composition.

Ward makes a point, in theory, of reducing the divisions of rhetoric to two. 'All discourse,' he says, 'consists of *things* or ideas, and *words* the signs of those ideas, by which they are expressed to others.'[2] Invention and disposition he classes together as relevant to things, elocution and pronunciation as relevant to words. However, for practical purposes, he maintains the traditional sub-divisions. He offers separate discussions of invention and disposition, conducted on classical lines.[3] The bulk of his work is devoted to a study exclusively of elocution or style.

Priestley, in similar fashion, proceeds from Invention (the process of amplification and the use of topics) to Disposition, about which he has some novel suggestions to make, thence to style.[4]

A later, in some respects more sophisticated, rhetorician such as Campbell may insist that the schematic divisions of rhetoric are more determinate in theory than in pratice:

The art of the rhetorician, like that of the philosopher, is analytical; the art of the orator is synthetical. The former acts the part of the skilful anatomist, who, by removing the teguments, and nicely separating the parts, presents us with views at once naked, distinct, and hideous . . . the latter imitates Nature in the constructing of her work, who, with wonderful symmetry, unites the various organs, adapts them to their respective uses, and covers all with a decent veil, the skin. Thus, though she hide entirely the more minute and the interior parts, and show not to equal advantage even the articulations of the limbs, and the adjustment of the larger members, adds inexpressible beauty, and strength, and energy to the whole.[5]

Nevertheless, he is not in the main denying the validity of the traditional distinctions, as the design of his book, with its separate treatment of subject-matter and style, goes to show.[6]

Other 'advanced' rhetoricians of the period, more interested in aesthetic and stylistic matters than in the art of composition as such, nevertheless take for granted its traditional basis.[7]

The same distinctions in theory between invention, arrangement and expression are made in the case of poetic composition; the same three stages are recognized in the construction of a poem as are recognized in the construction of a speech. It is true that, whereas in the department of *Elocutio* rhetorical principles are adopted wholesale for poetry, no such close identity with rhetoric is possible in respect of the other two divisions of the Art.[8] Nevertheless, the three processes are recognized, and the broad distinctions between them admitted: given the poet's purpose or design, he 'invents' a subject, arranging and ordering it suitably, finally clothing it in appropriate language.

Contemporary speculations on the psychology of literary creation are based on these assumptions. Since it is, in fact, in works of this kind that basic presuppositions about method are most clearly and fully in evidence, it may be convenient to examine them first.

Their authors accept by and large the psychological commonplaces of the time, the parcelling out of mental activity to various faculties, the derivation of all mental content from sense impressions and the relics of sense impressions in memory, and they all make use to some extent of the theory of association of ideas which, originating in Hobbes and Locke, had by this time been fully developed by Hume and, especially, Hartley.

Generally speaking, imagination, the most characteristic function of which is to combine ideas and images into new and original forms, is regarded as the fount of invention. Judgment keeps watch over the operations of imagination and is the final arbiter of order, coherence, propriety. 'Invention'—in the rhetorical sense, the finding of material—is the province of imagination, 'disposition' largely the work of judgment. 'Elocution' receives separate attention, as will be seen, as an activity of the faculties working in combination.

According to John Ogilvie, imagination is the inventive faculty *par excellence:* 'that which strikes out happy imitations, forms new and original assemblages of ideas'.[9] It is productive of images, incidents, characters,[10] and even 'sentiments'.[11] The role of judgment (which for Ogilvie is identical with 'understanding') is:

. . . the discovery of a theory or hypothesis; the disposition of parts in the plan of a work in such order as most effectually promotes an ultimate purpose; the comprehension of this plan as adapted fully to the subject of whatever kind; and finally [the maintenance of] a certain propriety of sentiments and of illustration . . .[12]

Two other faculties make their contribution. Memory supplies materials to the imagination, while Discernment, a faculty which partakes of both understanding and imagination but differs from either, 'without carrying on any regular process, comprehends as it were instantaneously the proper manner of treating any subject, by fixing upon the points that are of principal consequence . . .'[13]

Plainly Ogilvie regards the writer's task as one primarily of elaborating and organizing a subject-matter. He emphasizes the fact in his definition of composition as 'that ART by which the several *parts of a subject* are so justly fitted to each other, as to form a proportioned and beautiful whole'.[14] The expression of this subject-matter in language is a separate consideration: a separate consideration of the author's as well as the critic's. Talent for composition, Ogilvie says, is 'accompanied in *every case* with a *propensity* to place such ideas as occur to it in lights at the same time happy and diversified, to range these in just and perspicuous disposition; to express them in suitable words which are selected with facility. . .'[15] He assumes that the author will have paid separate attention to each of the three requirements.

In the same year as Ogilvie's *Philosophical and Critical Observations* appeared Alexander Gerard's better-known *Essay on Genius*. Gerard is more interesting, he penetrates further into his subject, but in essentials his theory is no different. He assumes (with the exception of 'discernment') the same mental faculties, all of them depending ultimately on Sense; and to each of the faculties he attributes more or less the same sphere of operation. But there are some differences of approach. Gerard relies more heavily, and more overtly than Ogilvie on association theory.

At this point, however, it should be emphasized that in Gerard's theory of invention, as in all others of the time, a strictly limited role is allotted to the association of ideas. Association is not by itself considered responsible for the genesis of the poetic or other subject; it comes into play within the limits fixed by a preconceived plan or design. Genius, as Gerard explains:

. . . implies such *comprehensiveness* of imagination as enables a man, on every occasion, to call in the conceptions that are necessary for executing the designs or compleating the works in which he engages . . . No sooner almost is a design formed, or the hint of a subject started, than all the ideas which are requisite for compleating it, rush into his view as if they were conjured up by the force of magic.[16]

The 'magical' force is that of association. But it is neither self-impelled nor self-directed,[17] nor is it entirely free in other respects. Judgment plays an almost equal role with imagination, necessary 'to correct and regulate its suggestions'. 'Without judgment, imagination would be extravagant. . .'[18] Judgment is a critical and selective faculty, subordinate in its turn to design: Gerard sees the materials of imagination as submitted to the poet's *choice*,[19] and the exercise of choice presupposes a conscious criterion, a purpose.

Disposition is similarly the work of imagination and judgment; in fact, Gerard finds that disposition and invention proceed simultaneously.

. . . to collect the materials, and to order and apply them, are not to genius distinct and successive works. This faculty bears a greater resemblance to *nature* in its operations, than to the less perfect energies of *art* . . . the same force of association which makes us perceive the connexion of all the ideas with the subject, leads us soon to perceive also the various degrees of that connexion. By means of it, these ideas, like a well-disciplined army, fall, of their own accord, into rank and order . . . The most strongly related unite of course in the same member, and all the members are set in that position, which association leads us to assign to them, as the most natural.[20]

Nevertheless he does not conceive of this process as entirely spontaneous:

Fancy forms the plan in a sort of mechanical or instinctive manner: judgment, on reviewing it, perceives its rectitude or its errors, as it were scientifically; its decisions are founded on reflection, and produce a conviction of their justness.[21]

A consciously formulated design, in any case, remains the

ruling factor; and it should be noted that for Gerard, too, the execution of a design consists in the combining of parts into a whole.[22]

Expression remains for separate consideration. The last section of Gerard's work draws distinctions between, and attempts to account for, various types of genius. One characteristic of artistic genius is that it 'implies, in every case, not only the power of invention, but also the power of *execution*'.[23] This power depends on clarity of conception and skill in adapting means to ends (abilities characteristically demanded by rhetorical theory, as will later be shown) and is ultimately traceable to psychological processes very much like, but—this is clear—not coincident with, those of invention.

The power of expression, so far as it differs both from mechanical dexterity, and from knowledge acquired by study,[24] consists perhaps entirely in a capacity of setting objects in such a light that they may affect others with the same ideas, associations and feelings, with which the artist is affected. This capacity arises chiefly from such force of imagination as at once renders the conception of things precise and definite, and leads a person to foresee readily what effect every touch in the expression will produce, or to conceive quickly the proper means of producing any desired effect. This is obviously resolvable into association, and therefore will, in every art, be found to spring from the same principles of the mind, which form the source of invention in that art.[25]

Ogilvie's and Gerard's treatises may be taken—in so far as we are concerned only with the general principles of invention—as representative of late eighteenth-century views. Duff's earlier treatise follows the same broad lines,[26] but his treatment of the subject is very much more superficial than Gerard's. In Beattie's essay *On Memory and Imagination*, occurs an analysis of genius and its powers which follows Gerard in the main. Beattie introduces a distinction between Imagination and Fancy, but this seems to serve no purpose. 'They are, indeed, names for the same faculty; but the former seems to be applied to the more solemn, and the latter to the more trivial exertions of it.[27] He, too, stresses the importance of judgment and good sense in order to combat the opinion, he says, 'that Genius, especially poetic genius, is nothing more than a certain warmth of fancy, or enthusiasm of mind, which is all-sufficient in itself . . .'[28]

The devotees of 'enthusiasm' do, it is true, minimize the importance of order and design[29]—without, however, disputing the whole theory of invention, or attempting to replace it with another: they merely reject one part of it, retaining the rest.[30] Some accept it *in toto*.[31] The extreme rationalists, not surprisingly, give it whole-hearted support.[32]

The theory, as we have seen, hinges on a distinction between three stages of composition. The first two—invention and disposition—are sometimes regarded as concurrent. In any case, that the three stages are *successive* is not always insisted upon; three separate activities, however, separate at least in kind, are recognized, all of them controlled and modified by some preconceived purpose. The mental faculties employed in composition, poetic or otherwise, are described and defined as engaged in one or other of these activities. The parallel with the traditional rhetorical scheme of 'Inventio, Dispositio, Elocutio' is very close.

The poet, it follows, is conceived of as pursuing a specific aim, inventing, elaborating and ordering a subject-matter in accordance with that aim, then clothing his notions in suitable language. This view of the matter, where it is not made explicit, is everywhere implicitly accepted—in the arguments of theoreticians as in the *obiter dicta* of practical critics.

A famous pronouncement of Johnson's may be allowed to represent the very voluminous evidence:

Pope had, in proportions very nicely adjusted to each other, all the qualities that constitute genius. He had *Invention*, by which new trains of events are formed, and new scenes of imagery displayed, as in the *Rape of the Lock*; or extrinsick and adventitious embellishments and illustrations are connected with a known subject as in the *Essay on Criticism*. He had *Imagination*,[33] which strongly impresses on the writer's mind, and enables him to convey to the reader the various forms of nature, incidents of life, and energies of passion . . . He had *Judgment* which selects from life or nature what the present purposes requires . . . and he had colours of language always before him, ready to decorate his matter with every grace of elegant expression . . .[34]

Johnson says nothing of 'disposition', which indeed it might have taken some equivocation on his part to extol in Pope,[35] but his implied allegiance to the views outlined above is clear.

The eighteenth-century conception of composition, involving as it does a belief in the necessity of deliberate design[36] and a theory of invention as a putting-together of parts, was scorned by the Romantics. They dubbed the theory 'mechanical'.[37] It is liable to strike us unfavourably too. It seems made to encourage or excuse, woodenness, artificiality and insincerity.

The merits and defects in general of the theory will be discussed in a later chapter,[38] but it may be as well to notice at this stage that eighteenth-century critics were themselves very conscious of the disadvantages incidental to their views. We have seen that they made a point of deprecating excessive 'correctness'. Even more often did they condemn artificiality and affectation. No later criticisms of rhetorical bombast and frigidity are harsher than theirs. Campbell speaks for a great many when he says that 'affectation is always a deadly sin against the laws of rhetoric'.[39]

That his was a very common attitude, and that in fact it was partly imposed by the theory itself, will be confirmed when we turn to the investigation of principles of style. Before, however, embarking upon that part of the inquiry some attention must be given in the next chapter to a further important *idée reçue*, one that forms a necessary link between the main theory of invention and composition and the subsidiary one of style.

4

Thought in Rhetoric and Poetry

THE close dependence of rhetoric on logic was recognized from the first. The power and efficiency of a speech must often derive very largely from the cogency of the arguments it develops. Thus Aristotle, in opposition to what he regarded as the corrupt teaching of his day, insisted that proof (or 'apparent proof') was strictly the first and proper business of the orator—though other means of persuasion need not be neglected; and in the schemes of such classical rhetoricians after Aristotle who pretend to comprehensiveness, questions of argument and evidence are invariably given first consideration.[1] The structure of rhetorical discourse, in fact, was regarded from the first as argumentative, soundness of knowledge and clarity of thought as its necessary basis. The arguments of oratory need not, of course, be entirely explicit, nor entirely abstract: recourse to narration and description, for example, could scarcely be avoided in forensic or ceremonial oratory.

England in the sixteenth century had inherited a rhetoric which was already much less interested in techniques of argument and proof, and much more in the techniques (especially of style) which Aristotle had regarded as non-essential to the art, though belonging to it.[2] In the latter half of the eighteenth century, though rhetoricians are no longer so exclusively preoccupied with style, they still pay comparatively little attention to the nature of the evidence and arguments appropriate to oratory, and a great deal to the more 'literary' aspects of the art.

It is understood, none the less, that argument is the primary concern of the orator. A speech must make its appeal first to the understanding; through the understanding it may strike the imagination and move the passions.

Thomas Gibbons, for example, (though he is, in fact, concerned as a rhetorician exclusively with style), says:

Let our discourses be founded upon reason, and let us establish every thing we advance with solid and convincing arguments. We are first to labour to enlighten the understanding and inform the judgment, and then introduce our *Figures* to affect and engage the passions, and thereby secure a complete triumph over our audience.[3]

Narration and description are no less the province primarily of understanding: they are, in other words, types of 'argument'. The orator, when he narrates or describes, is before all else stating facts.

Priestley sums this up:

All the kinds of composition may be reduced to two, viz. NARRA- TION and ARGUMENTATION. For either we propose to relate *facts*, with a view to communicate information, as in *history*, natural or civil, *travels* &c., or we lay down some *proposition*, and endeavour to prove or explain it.[4]

The propositions, the facts may be so embroidered, so arranged and so interlarded with interrogations, exhortations, apostrophes and other devices as to stimulate the imagination and evoke an emotional response; nevertheless, the body of a speech, its bone and sinew, must be a series of discursive—in the sense 'intellectual' or, conceptual'—ideas.

It is fairly obvious that so much would be, and was, required of a speech: it is less obvious that it was also required of a poem. Poetry too, had had since the sixteenth century its necessary relation with logic.[5] The relation was still being assumed after 1750. This is not to suggest that the three 'arts' of Logic, Rhetoric and Poetry were deliberately brought into line with each other. It was simply taken for granted that in the nature of things certain important connexions obtained.[6]

Given that the subject-matter of poetry, like that of rhetoric, is 'invented' to fill out a preconceived plan or elaborate a design, it follows that, as in rhetoric, a series of separate but connected elements, methodically arranged, is envisaged as the result: in other words the 'thoughts', 'sentiments' and 'images' (in the eighteenth-century sense, i.e. 'pictures') which are so often spoken of as the stuff of poetry.

These 'thoughts' are discursive: as much so as the 'thoughts' of the orator; they are logically formulated and most often considered to be logically interrelated as well. It would be fairly easy to substantiate this were one to call to witness only the extremer rationalists among the critics of the time, for example John Scott of Amwell who says bluntly that 'sentiments that have no foundation in fact, or in reason, can have no merit . . .'[7] or Vicesimus Knox who, deploring the degeneracy of contemporary literature, throws the blame partly on the depraved taste of readers who will tolerate divagations from the path of reason. 'In truth, unconnected thoughts . . . are congenial to minds unaccustomed to accurate thinking . . .'[8] This author cannot entirely bring himself to approve of Gray's Churchyard Elegy, which he finds 'to be no more than a confused heap of splendid ideas, thrown together without order and without proportion'.[9] Even Joseph Warton, one of the champions of 'enthusiasm', persistently, in his celebrated *Essay on Pope*, singles out sense and sentiment to be criticized by standards of justice and truth, in a way which would now be considered inappropriate except in the case of some obviously discursive form of writing. Johnson's opinions are so familiar that they scarcely need rehearsing again to show that he, too, expected a sense from poetry that would satisfy the demands of rational scrutiny.[10]

That the thoughts in poetry should be logically interrelated is not, however, always insisted upon and in certain circumstances it may be very positively denied. Lowth, for instance, the archpriest of 'enthusiasm' during the period, asks:

For what is meant by that singular frenzy of poets, which the Greeks, ascribing to divine inspiration, distinguished by the appellation of *enthusiasm*, but a style and expression directly prompted by nature itself, and exhibiting the true and express image of a mind violently agitated? When, as it were, the secret avenues . . . of the soul are thrown open; when the inmost conceptions are displayed, rushing together in one turbid stream, without order and connexion?[11]

He says again, on the same subject:

The language of Reason is cool, temperate . . . The language of the Passions is totally different: the conceptions burst out in a turbid stream, expressive in a manner of the internal conflict; the more vehement break out in hasty confusion; they catch (without search or study) whatever is impetuous, vivid, or energetic.[12]

Nevertheless, while Lowth is claiming that the expression of passion or enthusiasm necessarily takes the form of a diffuse and disordered series of ideas, he does not say that these 'conceptions' are of any special non-discursive kind. He is in fact as concerned as anyone else to emphasize the function of 'understanding' in elaborating the structure of thought in poetry:

The first object [in composition] is . . . to perceive and comprehend clearly the reasons, principles, and relations of things . . .[13]

Few critics take so extreme a view of the confusion and incoherence that must result from the expression of passion. It is more usually maintained that even when poetry is at its most passionate an order of ideas may still be discerned, though the connexion is concealed.[14]

Other critics are content to say that there is always a connexion, but that it is a connexion established naturally by the association of ideas.[15] This, however, must not be taken to mean 'free association under the influence of emotion'. Emotion may cause abruptness and disconnexion in the flow of thought,[16] but since a *specific* emotion, 'such an emotion as is produced by some one particular cause, and directed to some one determinate object',[17] is always presupposed, a specific subject to which it is attached remains the principal determinant of structure. The conscious will and judgment, in other words, are never assumed to lose control entirely over the course of association.[18]

In any case none of the writers who assume that the expression of emotion is essential to poetry considers that poetic thought is of a specially intuitive kind. They talk of 'thought' in poetry without distinguishing it from any other variety.

The theories of invention discussed in the previous chapter bear this out. (As we shall later have occasion to notice, these theories take full account of the importance of emotion to poetry.) Artistic imagination proceeds on exactly the same principles as scientific or philosophic imagination. Whatever the field of thought, invention 'can be accomplished only by assembling ideas in various positions and arrangements, that we may obtain uncommon views of them'.[19] The connexion between imagination, which combines ideas, and judgment, which corrects and regulates the operation, is 'so intimate, that a man can scarce be said to have invented till he has exercised his judgment'.[20] Judgment is by definition a critical faculty, perceiving relations, rejecting what is false, improper and superfluous.[21] There is no doubt that well-defined, clearly and consciously formulated ideas are in question here: indeed philosophy and science will hardly admit of any other kind. And poetry is not distinguished from them in this respect.

The difference between artistic invention and other kinds lies entirely in the peculiar object the artist proposes to himself. 'Scientific genius addresses its discoveries to the understanding; their end is information: genius for the arts addresses its productions to taste, and aims at pleasing by them.'[22]

The mention of taste brings us to the preoccupations of a group of critics who hold that poetry appeals, as do the other arts, to aesthetic sensibility. Their point of view is no different for that reason. The appeal of poetry to taste is not assumed to imply a form of thought in poetry of an esoteric kind. The contrary is true, for taste, though it is a complex of capacities and susceptibilities, is supposed to depend primarily on understanding. Beattie emphasizes that lively imagination and distinctness of apprehension are necessary ingredients of true taste. Liveliness of imagination 'qualifies one for readily understanding an author's purpose; tracing the connection of his thoughts; forming the same views of things which he had formed; and clearly conceiving the several images or ideas that the artist describes or delineates'.[23] Blair discovers that poetry derives its power to please taste and imagination largely from its capacity to imitate and describe: and description, he maintains, can be effective only when the ideas transmitted are lively and distinct.[24] The same idea is to be found in Kames and Lowth,[25] among many others. Perspicuity and Vivacity are indeed the stylistic ideals *par excellence* of the period: they are ideals of clearly and precisely formulated thought, ideals universally acknowledged as applicable to poetry in exactly the way they are applicable to prose.

Perspicuity, the clear presentation of ideas so that they may be grasped without effort by the understanding, is for most critics the *sine qua non* of an effective style,[26] though here and there a dissenting voice is raised. Priestley thinks that a writer may call for some exertion on the part of the reader 'provided it be not the *chief* exercise he gives our faculties . . . However, in the generality of compositions, it is indisputable, that the proper medium of excellence is much nearer the extreme of perspicuity than of obscurity'.[27]

The sublime or impassioned style is sometimes supposed to involve necessarily a certain obscurity.[28] Lowth's remarks on enthusiasm quoted above will indicate the kind of argument that supports this belief. But here is an exception which proves the rule, for 'obscurity' is a lack of prespicuity: it is defined negatively in terms of its opposite, rather than positively as a distinct form of thought and expression.

In the case of Burke, who opposes 'obscurity' to 'vivacity' rather than 'perspicuity', this is not altogether so. He considers it very improbable that poetry is capable of raising lively images in the mind of the reader, and contends that the dim and indistinct images it *is* capable of raising are one means by which it achieves its end of moving the passions.[29] Obscurity in this sense is obviously a positive factor in poetry. Burke's very original views will be more fully described in a later chapter:[30] for the moment it is enough to note that he is alone in his opinion. 'Clear and distinct images' are universally required of the orator and poet.[31] Vivacity is everywhere regarded as an essential attribute of the good style. Moreover, when reviewing the factors that contribute to 'liveliness', critics repeatedly urge the discrimination of particulars, the use of distinct, determinate terms[32]—evidence again that they are presupposing, and indeed recommending, clearly-defined 'discursive' thought.

Yet further indications of what they mean by 'thought' are provided by their descriptions of the subject-matter of poetry. Art is said to employ the materials of *knowledge*. 'Knowledge and science must furnish the materials that form the body and substance of any valuable composition.'[33] Though the language of poetry is often characterized as highly and peculiarly figurative, there is no one to suggest that metaphor and symbol are the very stuff of poetry. The content of poetry is typically described, on the contrary, as facts, incidents and images[34] or action, sentiments and descriptions.[35]

Occasionally a type or types of thought are specified as especially congenial to poetry. *The Art of Poetry on a New Plan* lists the grand or sublime, the beautiful or agreeable, the delicate, and the brilliant. 'Elevated' thought is very frequently stated to be a characteristic of the best, and sometimes essential to all true poetry. Discussions of the sublime are, as is well known, legion: so indeed are disquisitions on beauty, grace, elegance, wit, ridicule, etc. None of this speculation, however, is of immediate relevance here. It is in part concerned with types of subject-matter in poetry, that is with forms of idea and image which produce certain aesthetic effects; and in part with varieties of style and structure.[36] What makes, it is considered, the 'thought' in poetry aesthetically effective is its content, or its formal deployment, or perhaps its appropriateness in a formal scheme: it need not be, and is never, assumed that 'beautiful' or 'elevated' thought differs radically from thought of the ordinary kind.[37]

Of the generally accepted views on thought in poetry perhaps enough has been said. Only one critic of the period, it appears, offers them any challenge. According to John Ogilvie, imagination alone, unaided by understanding or judgment, may be the source of poetic sentiment.[38] He seems a little shocked by the discovery, and expects the reader to be incredulous. 'Sentiment! (will some reader exclaim) of what sentiment is imagination the parent?—This important province is considered as occupied wholly by the understanding . . .'

'That sentiments,' he readily agrees, 'in order to have either propriety or connection with each other, must be such as the understanding hath approved, is a truth which no man will call in question.' Nevertheless, there are sentiments

. . . which in consequence of indicating a certain wildness which we consider as a criterion of imagination; of being thrown out with promptitude rather than with accuracy; of being placed in loose arrangement; of presenting in short, upon the whole, ideas which the mind rather contemplates as brilliant, with a transient satisfaction, than dwells on as just with fixed attention . . .

can originate only in imagination.

There are . . . pieces that please upon the whole as imitations of nature, in which a lively fancy appears to have delineated objects just as they occurred, and to have coloured so highly thoughts that indicate quickness rather than depth of conception, as to merit the appellation of having suggested them.

These we must observe with very little attention to be the peculiar and immediate provinces of imagination; which, instead of proceeding by slow and deliberate gradations in its process, making every step in the scale of evidence lead naturally to another, is characterised by its combination of dissimilar ideas, associated from points of resemblance extremely remote, but whose union, when once formed, is by this very circumstance rendered striking and uncommon.

This is sufficiently unconventional in its recognition that an irrational process may by itself produce something at least striking and uncommon. But what follows is even more extraordinary: one senses that Ogilvie is attempting clumsily to open up a vein of speculation that thirty years later Coleridge was to discover and exploit.

In the series of thoughts . . . arising in this manner from various exertions of the inventive faculty, some will no doubt appear to have been immediately derived from the different external forms of nature. Others on the contrary, wholly subordinate to, and incidentally rising as it were from the former, will grow out from the principal subject, which like a vigorous plant will thus appear surrounded with shoots, which from the native strength and fertility of the root from which they sprung. Of these, the former constitutes a vein of sentiment purely original, and require a very large proportion of what is denominated plastic or creative imagination:—the latter are only considered as the consequences of being thrown into a certain track, in which when a man of no uncommon genius is once set out, he may either improve upon, or add to the discovery of the original inventor.

However, this train of thought is neither very clear nor very far-reaching, and Ogilvie, in any case, immediately repudiates what he has said.

In whatever light . . . we view imagination as the parent of new and ingenious sentiment, it must be acknowledged extremely hazardous to submit to its guidance in this delicate exertion . . . its vivacity will lead us to be diffident of the clearness and comprehension of its theory; its versatility, of the justness and symmetry of its proportions; its power of seizing remote points of resemblance will induce us to call in question the accuracy of imitation; and the unusual combinations which it presents to the mind will very naturally infuse a suspicion of their solidity and truth. Coherence and proportion are never to be regarded as the native offspring of imagination.[39]

We are returned to clarity, accuracy and coherence. As Ogilvie is so anxious not to deny, 'sentiment' is really the province of understanding.

The contention that in the eighteenth century 'poetic' thought was regarded as no different from thought of any other kind would require little support if critics and theorists of the time had made any attempt to define, or even loosely indicate, what they meant by 'thought' or 'sentiment' in poetry. Literary critics, however, are probably not to be blamed for begging philosophical questions, and indirect evidence as to what they did mean is not lacking.

The final proof must be a negative one. It was the critics of the early nineteenth century who first spoke in England of a specifically poetic thought,[40] and defined it. No late eighteenth-century critic, with the only just admissible exception of Ogilvie, reveals any remotely similar conception, or says anything to suggest he might be entertaining such a conception.[41]

The next chapter, which takes the analysis a step further to the consideration of some leading ideas about style, will offer further confirmation of this fact.

5

Language as the Dress of Thought

WHAT might be called the fundamental principle of the Neo-Classic theory of style is the doctrine that language is 'the dress of thought'. Though it is not clear when the idea was first embodied in this particular metaphor, it almost certainly originated in Classical rhetoric.[1] During the Renaissance the formula was frequently repeated,[2] and in the latter half of the eighteenth century there are few among theorists of literature who do not recur to it in one context or another.

The early Romantics rejected the belief it implies as pernicious, and we should probably go further to dismiss it as absurd. How can language be distinguished from the thought it expresses? Clearly they are one and the same thing. Yet until 1800 even the most clear-sighted and critical take this dualistic view of speech and writing, and even where less estimable writers are arguing the opinion or illustrating it by example we cannot feel that they are defending a total fallacy. There is obviously something in what they say that corresponds with the facts.

Kames, for example, maintains that there is a difference between beauty of thought and beauty of expression:

. . . these beauties, if we wish to think accurately, must be distinguished from each other. They are in reality so distinct, that we sometimes are conscious of the highest pleasure language can afford, when the subject expressed is disagreeable . . .[3]

He might with the same justice—as other writers did—have argued that a beautiful thought may be given disagreeable expression.[4] This sort of argument of course begs important questions, which we must consider below, but it is not entirely indefensible.

The same argument is offered by Johnson in slightly different terms:

[Truth] owes Part of her Charms to her Ornaments, and loses

much of her Power over the Soul, when she appears disgraced by a Dress uncouth or ill-adjusted.[5]

Underlying these statements is, of course, an assumption that the same thought may be expressed in a variety of ways, and often the assumption is explicitly defined: '. . . it is plain that a different choice of words makes a very great difference in the stile, where the sense is the same'.[6] What is more, a practical demonstration of the principle is frequently provided as confirmation of it. Thus Monboddo composes three prose versions of the first speech in *Paradise Lost* Book II, each more elaborate and figurative than the last, each approaching more closely, though still remote (as Monboddo modestly admits) from, the 'copiousness' and 'nervousness' of the original.[7] Harris also adduces a concrete example:

Take then the following—*Don't let a lucky Hit slip; if you do, belike you mayn't any more get at it.* The *Sentiment* (we must confess) is exprest clearly, but the DICTION surely is rather *vulgar* and *low*. Take it another way—*Opportune Moments are few and fleeting; seize them with avidity, or your Progression will be impeded.* Here the DICTION, tho' *not low,* is *rather obscure.* The Words are *unusual, pedantic* and *affected.*—But what says SHAKE-SPEARE?

> There is a TIDE in the affairs of men,
> Which, taken at the flood, leads on to fortune;
> Omitted, all the Voyage of their life
> Is bound in shallows—[8]

These illustrations have a genuine point to make. Considered in this light the 'dress-of-thought' conception of language appears less naïve, though naturally everything depends on the precise way in which the key-terms 'dress' and 'thought' are understood. In fact, as will appear, the meanings attached to these words make perfectly good sense of a doctrine in which the modern reader, with a different set of concepts, is likely to find very little virtue.

The first impression, however, may well be one of confusion. The fact is that two distinct definitions of 'dress' appear to be current, distinct at least in our eyes, though not entirely so at the time.

The first of these definitions assumes that there may be an exact correspondence between words and ideas. 'Dress' means simply 'external guise'. Language is the outward form of thought, its objective equivalent. This is the point of view adopted in statements such as the following, though their authors, for reasons of emphasis, have here chosen variants of the usual metaphor:

Thoughts are the images of things, as words are the images of thoughts, and they are both, like other pictures and images, to be esteemed or despised, as the representation is just and natural, true or false.[9]

or again:

. . . there are two things in every discourse which principally claim attention, the sense and the expression; or in other words, the thought, and the symbol by which it is communicated. These may be said to constitute the soul and the body of an oration, or indeed, of whatever is signified to another by language.[10]

It is this view of language, implying an exact correlation between words and ideas, which supports certain of the principles of style discussed later in this chapter: that of perspicuity especially, and to some extent those of vivacity and propriety as well. It will be noticed that on this interpretation of the 'dress' maxim no one assumes an identity of language and thought, such that both spring spontaneously and simultaneously into being. They are thought of as separate ('there are *two* things in every discourse') but the one may, and should, be accurately adjusted to the other. As long as the maxim implies no more than that words should be carefully and judiciously chosen, there are perhaps no strong objections to raise against it.

The other conception of 'dress', much the more common, is never explicitly distinguished from the idea outlined above, though the difference is plain. The two conceptions are not even complementary; each, complete in itself, indicates a separate approach to the question of how language expresses thought.

The second conception of 'dress' derives from a presumption that one and the same thought may be expressed in a variety of different ways: language is said to 'dress' thought in that it may present it under different guises. Tropes and figures are regarded as especially appropriate to this purpose. The chief consideration here is not accuracy, but effectiveness: the choice of such language as will serve best to present a given thought in a certain light.

Objections will immediately occur to the modern reader's mind. If a thought has been dressed in an elaborate rhetorical garment, has not the thought itself been, *ipso facto*, elaborated? By the same token, tropes and figures cannot be merely the clothing of thought: if they are not themselves 'thought' they are nothing.

But such objections would be based on a misunderstanding. The meaning of 'thought' in this usage is clearly confined to something like: 'the main idea a writer intends to express—which may be elaborated or varied according to the particular force or colour he wishes to give it'. The assumption is of a core of clearly-expressible meaning which can nevertheless be presented in a variety of different lights depending on the writer's ultimate purpose. And this assumption must rest on two anterior suppositions. First, that the basis of every writer's thought is conceptual, for it would not make sense to speak of 'dressing' an idea of the 'poetic' or 'intuitive' kind: such thinking is ideally one with its expression. Secondly, that the details of 'dress' which are not strictly necessary to the straightforward expression of an idea (and this includes whatever may be required of figurative language) are *accessory* to the idea, and not a part of it.

Both 'dress' and 'thought', therefore, are intended to convey a narrower meaning than may at first sight be apparent. 'Language', furthermore, is undoubtedly an unfortunate choice of word in the context. For it need not be choice of language alone which is responsible for the particular 'dress' of an idea: it may also be the syntactical form in which it is presented, and the accessory ideas—in the shape, for example, of tropes or figures—which are assimilated with it. This particular piece of confusion is perhaps to be traced back to the classical rhetoricians who on occasion define tropes and figures as *linguistic* devices.[11] They invariably, in any case, consider figurative language under the head of 'style', not, as would very often be more logical, under that of 'invention'. Other traces of this wrong-headed approach are to be found in eighteenth-century theory (tropes, for example, are still sometimes defined as *words*), though the psychologists at any rate consider figurative language as a product of invention, and there are other writers who seem more or less successfully to have extricated themselves from the muddle.[12]

Vaguely and inaccurately phrased though it may be, however, the much-quoted doctrine does allow of the interpretation outlined above, and it is the only possible one where the formula 'dress=

outward form' is obviously not intended. This interpretation is certainly required by the many passages, referred to above, in which writers aver that the same thought may be expressed in different ways. It is also clearly indicated in other contexts where attention is drawn to the relation of style and thought. Here is Lowth's argument for the necessity of 'dress':

. . . we are all of us in some measure fastidious: we are seldom contented with a jejune and naked exposition even of the most serious subjects, some of the seasonings of art, some ornaments of style, some splendour of diction, are of necessity to be adopted; even some regard is due to the harmony of numbers, and to the gratification of the ear.[13]

And here Gibbons illustrates the point that figurative language fulfils an accessory, though vivifying, function:

If we would have a distinct and full idea of the beauty of a Trope, let us substitute the natural expressions in the room of the tropical, and divest a bright phrase of its ornaments, by reducing it to plain and simple language, and then observe how much we abate the value of the discourse.[14]

It is noteworthy that a lessening of effectiveness, not a falsification of meaning, is what Gibbons considers demonstrated by this exercise. The 'thought' of the passage will not have changed.

This view, then, of the relation of style to thought, confirms what was maintained, but on other grounds, in the previous chapter: that rhetoricians and literary critics, when they speak of 'thought' in literature, mean by it a basis of discursive thought: a kind of thought which may be elaborated, but without any intrinsic change, by the procedures of style.

It *must* in fact nearly always be elaborated. Where a writer's aim is merely statement he need do no more than express his ideas in so many words. But a vital factor in rhetoric—how much more necessary to poetry—is the artful colouring and shaping which is to appeal to imagination and emotion. It is here that the powers of style come into play. Style is understood as a way of *presenting* ideas so as to make them as effective as possible for a given purpose.

It is the function of style to attract attention, to interest, to charm the reader or auditor.[15] Its function is also, as there will be occasion later to notice in more detail, to arouse feeling. However, though style may be looked upon as a presentation of subject-matter in attractive and appealing garb, there is no trace left at this period of the Renaissance tendency to regard 'ornament' as some-thing extraneous and artificial with which subject-matter can, as it were, be overlaid.[16] The term 'ornament' is still very widely used, and 'ornaments' are still understood as accessory details, but they are not for that reason regarded as arbitrarily chosen or as mere decorative appendages to the matter in hand.

Some writers, in fact, insist that the ornaments of style be so intimately connected with the subject that they grow naturally out of it.

It is [says Blair] a very erroneous idea which many have of the ornaments of Style, as if they were things detached from the sub-ject, and that could be stuck to it, like lace upon a coat . . . the real and proper ornaments of Style are wrought into the substance of it. They flow in the same stream with the current of thought.[17]

Others, indeed, make a more general application of the same idea. Language at all times, they believe, should spring spontan-eously from thought;

As words are intended to express our thoughts, they ought to grow out of them. Since the most natural are the best, and proper ex-pressions are generally connected with the ideas themselves, and follow them as the shadow does the substance.[18]

These statements are not entirely typical in their stress on spontaneity, but they do illustrate, by carrying it to an extreme, a general tendency. 'Rhetoric', in its modern pejorative sense of the artificial, bombastic and high-falutin finds no favour in the eyes of the time.

It may seem, however, as though there must have been some conflict of opinion between a few writers who favoured 'spon-taneity' in the matter of style and the rest who favoured 'art'. But no real contradiction is to be supposed, as long as there is a valid distinction to be made between 'art' as the conscious *acquisition* of skill and 'art' as the conscious *application* of it. It never occurs to the writers who are dubious about the latter that the former may also be dispensed with.[19]

Thus Blair is not being inconsistent when he says:

Propriety and beauty of Speech, are certainly as improveable as the ear or the voice; and to know the principles of this beauty, or the reasons which render one Figure, or one manner of Speech preferable to another, cannot fail to assist and direct a proper choice.[20]

The other supporters of 'spontaneity' make, in their own way, the same assumptions about 'art'.[21] Knowledge and skill are pre-requisitions of a spontaneity which is not the absence of 'art', but a result of the perfection of 'art' to a point where it has become 'natural'—a spontaneity, in other words, of trained intelligence, taste and ingenuity, and not of mere impulse.

These discussions of spontaneity seem all to be inspired by a conviction of the importance of certain principles of style, especially that of propriety (the most 'natural' language will be the most proper). We ought briefly to consider the more important of these principles, all of which illustrate that, if for some writers spontaneity is the ultimate ideal, at a more practical level style is invariably discussed as a means, a means of presenting ideas so as to produce an effect.

The last chapter gave some account of one of these principles, perspicuity: the basic condition of a good style, since ideas to produce any effect at all must first be clearly presented and understood. Closely related to the principle of perspicuity is that of precision, which demands the curtailment of all superfluities. 'The human mind', as Blair says,

can never view, clearly and distinctly, above one object at a time. If it must look at two or three together, especially objects among which there is resemblance or connection, it finds itself confused and embarrassed . . . The same is the case with words.[22]

Ogilvie sees a lack of precision as detracting from 'force',[23] another principle of the same class. Campbell has it that brevity contributes energy to expression,[24] but force is also the result of syntactical devices—the economical use of connectives,[25] the suspension of sense in a periodic sentence.[26]

These are principles which relate to the impact of style on the understanding: ideas must be clearly and strongly impressed on the mind. Others have a more purely aesthetic bearing. Of these the most frequently mentioned is purity: a good style will be free from neologisms, barbarisms, solecisms, and other departures from established usage.[27] 'Elegance' one might suppose to have been an interesting and fruitful topic of speculation at this period, but the writers who bring up the subject have disappointingly little to say. Ogilvie refers vaguely to 'natural graces' and 'ease'; Beattie says elegance is proof of a writer's learning and taste; we get no further than a *je-ne-sais-quoi*.[28] Campbell, who promises a discussion of this quality, and who would, one imagines, have discussed it thoroughly, apparently forgets about it when the moment arrives.[29]

The musical properties of style come in for much discussion: harmony or sweetness (mellifluous combinations of words or the avoidance of harsh combinations);[30] rhythm or measure;[31] sound as an echo to sense.[32] About the latter, however, critics are sceptical.

As Campbell says:

. . . examples serve to evince rather how little than how much can be done in this way, and how great scope there is here for the fancy to influence the judgment.[33]

There are, too, those principles which are more relevant to subject-matter than style—uniformity and variety, novelty, contrast, etc.—though they are sometimes adduced to account for stylistic effects. These are aesthetic principles of more limited applicability and, in the interests of concision, will here be left aside.[34]

Very much more important than any so far mentioned, with the exception of perspicuity, are the principles of vivacity and propriety. These three principles are almost universally agreed upon as the fundamental laws of good writing.

It is probably as well to distinguish two senses of the term 'propriety', though the first, and less important, is in fact a derivation from the second.[35] In this sense propriety is closely akin to perspicuity: it consists in the apt correspondence of words with ideas:

the selection of such words in the language, as the best and most established usage has appropriated to those ideas which we intend to express by them.[36]

Much more frequently the term has a wider application, and at the same time a more specific meaning: it denotes a nice accommodation of style to the writer's situation and intentions and to the social and emotional level of his subject. 'If the matter be high, so ought also the words to be . . .'[37] Beattie says that natural, i.e. 'proper', language must be suitable to the condition of the speaker, meaning by the word *condition*, not only the outward circumstances of *fortune, rank, employment, sex, age,* and *nation,* but also the internal temperature of the *understanding* and *passions,* as well as the peculiar nature of the *thoughts* that may happen to occupy the mind.[38]

Propriety is especially important in the use of ornament.[39] But it is a principle of the widest application, relevant to invention as well as style:

The thoughts . . . as well as the style, must be suitable to the subject, or the writer will ever miss of his aim.[40]

More than one writer points out that the end of composition cannot be answered without it: any impression of incongruity must disgust a judicious reader. Ward sees in propriety the very essence of style: Burke, too, with his very different approach to the whole question of language, considers it of cardinal importance. Beattie includes it among the essential rules of all art.[41]

The third main principle of style, vivacity, is to some writers almost as important as propriety is to those cited above. To Kames, for example, who calls the effect of vivacity 'ideal presence':

Upon the whole, it is by means of ideal presence that our passions are excited; and till words produce that charm, they avail nothing . . .[42]

Vivacity has to do with the representation of clear, life-like images, and it would seem to be a principle of invention rather than of style. However, in so far as style is assumed to include the invention of accessory detail, it is partly understandable that vivacity is invariably discussed under this head.[43]

Various methods are suggested for achieving vivacity, chief among them being an avoidance of literalness and minuteness in favour of the few striking particulars which create a strong impression;[44] secondly an avoidance of generalities in favour of words which have precise and characteristic meanings.[45]

Tropes and figures are naturally highly conducive to vivacity. Their functions will be considered in the next chapter, but it is worth noting in the present context that the Renaissance idea of 'illustration' is still alive—the idea that a figurative style, even where no aim of description is in view, is a sort of 'painting', enlivening ideas by converting them into pictures.[46]

Though the three main principles of style can be fairly clearly distinguished, it remains to be said that they are also closely interrelated and that the relationship may be differently conceived by different writers. Ogilvie, for example, sees vivacity as a means to perspicuity; Blair considers propriety serves the same end; while Ward makes propriety a first principle to which the others are subordinate.[47]

The particular purposes assigned to each of the three principles remain much the same from writer to writer. Perspicuity is necessary to understanding, propriety to the satisfaction of taste and judgment. Vivacity, first and foremost, pleases the imagination.[48] But it is also essential in fictitious writing, for its capacity to induce belief;[49] and some theorists consider it of vital importance to a writer whose aim is to 'move'.[50] Justifying this last claim is the belief that lively, accurate description works on the emotions only less powerfully than sensation itself.[51]

Thus each of these principles exemplifies a pragmatic outlook on style. Each subserves an end, or ends, and the overall aim is effectiveness, not the 'natural' flow of the writer's thought. They must be seen therefore as principles entirely of 'presentation', principles governing the 'dress' of thought. As such—without attempting to categorize too precisely—perspicuity is more relevant to dress as 'external form': the choice of clear and appropriate language at all times; while vivacity and propriety have more bearing on dress as 'ornament': the choice of subsidiary detail, the turn of thought or phrase.

The relevance of these principles to 'the dress of thought' in one sense or the other—though of course no hard-and-fast rules about their applicability in this connexion were, or, could be, thought necessary—is made very clear in discussions of the 'kinds' of style. For the low style no more is required than an attention to perspicuity, the one indispensable requirement for every kind of writing. As Ward says:

. . . pure nature, without any colouring, or appearance of art, is the distinguishing mark of the low stile. The design of it is to make things plain and intelligible . . .[52]

Blair distinguishes between a 'dry' style, which need be no more than perspicuous, and a 'plain' style, at which level propriety is also called for.[53] With the middle style (subdivided by Blair into 'neat' and 'elegant') vivacity becomes a requisite, and propriety even more necessary, for now excess becomes a danger:[54] 'all the ornaments of speech, and beauties of eloquence have place here'.[55]

Much of the groundwork sustaining the late eighteenth-century theory of composition and style has now been reviewed, and in every department of the theory its practical bias has become apparent. Its analyses and speculations, its axioms and principles, are all products of the same pre-occupation: an interest in discovering and defining the means proper to the ends of writing. The theory, with its inevitably strong emphasis on discrimination and skill, applies as much to poetry as to prose—and, in spite of the importance attached by some writers to the intuitive judgment of Taste or Discernment, and by others to the spontaneous exercise of 'art', so rational a prescription for the writing of poetry might strike us now as providing only for arid and uninteresting *tours de force*. But the personal element in literature did not—as how could it?—go unrecognized. Neither rhetoric nor poetry were conceived of as matters exclusively of 'wit and will'. They never had been, but now more than ever was importance attached to the expression, especially in poetry, of personal feeling.

The next chapter, accordingly, brings us to the final stage of the analysis. This and the following chapter will examine the last of the important presuppositions which support Neo-Classic views about writing: certain assumptions about feeling and the role it plays in literary creation.

6

Tropes and Figures

NEO-CLASSIC tenets about the expression of feeling are
so closely bound up with opinions about figurative language
and its function that the two questions cannot easily be separated.
Hence the best introduction to the topic of feeling will be by way
of a postscript on the subject of style.

Tropes and figures are regarded as *par excellence* the 'dress' of
thought. They are the chief instruments of style, the chief means
of varying a thought or elaborating a subject so as to present it in a
particular light.

> Simple Expression just makes our idea known to others; but Figura-
> tive Language, over and above, bestows a particular dress upon
> that idea; a dress which both makes it be remarked, and adorns it.[1]

To some extent, however, the function of figures differs from
that of tropes, so that there will be some advantage in beginning
with a separate consideration of each.

Classical rhetoric customarily defined tropes as words which are
used in a context foreign to their normal one. In the new context
they convey a new meaning, but there is always some ground of
relationship between this new meaning and the original one: in
the case of metaphor, for example, the relation is one of analogy.
It is a compressed simile.[2] This naïve form of explanation, little
more than a description of obvious characteristics, is still repeated
by most eighteenth-century rhetoricians.[3] But the more enlightened now offer analytical definitions, which attempt to account in
psychological terms for the effect of tropes.[4] Kames compares the
use of tropes to the use of harmony in music, and, incidentally,
confirms the point emphasized in the preceding chapter that
writers at this period regard the ideas which are introduced into
discourse by figurative language as subordinate to the main
'thought' conveyed:

. . . a word used figuratively . . . has the effect to present two objects; one signified by the figurative sense, which may be termed the *principal object;* and one signified by the proper sense, which may be termed *accessory:* the principal makes a part of the thought; the accessory is merely ornamental. In this respect, a figure of speech is precisely similar to concordant sounds in music, which, without contributing to the melody, make it harmonious.[5]

Kames's interpretation, however, of the function of tropes is peculiar to himself: in general their purpose is understood much as the Classical rhetoricians had understood it. Firstly, tropes supply the defects of language. They are useful in defining ideas for which no proper terms exist.[6] Indeed it is, by this time, a commonplace of linguistic theory that language owes its development largely to the metaphorical turning of existing words to new uses.[7]

This doctrine, however, is supplied with a corollary: since language has now developed to its full extent, the invention of new metaphors must be, on the whole, superfluous. Hence some writers feel that, though they may (on other grounds) be discreetly used in poetry, there is no longer any real necessity for original metaphors.[8] It is the extended comparison which they offer far more confidently as the appropriate device for illustrating, defining, elucidating.[9]

A second function of tropes is that they contribute to 'vivacity', especially those which define abstract ideas in concrete terms. Personifications (which are, strictly speaking, 'figures', though they frequently involve a tropical use of language) and metaphors are especially singled out for 'liveliness'.[10] Campbell, among others, gives a detailed analysis of the ways in which tropes may enliven discourse.[11]

Closely related to their 'enlivening' function is the capacity of tropes to 'amplify'. Like their other uses, this one derives from a suggestion of analogy or some other relation, but here the implied comparison works a subtler effect. Not only a concept, but its connotations as well, are associated with the matter in hand, and the result is a dignifying or embellishing of the subject. The writers of this time, however, did not understand the connotations of tropes (as opposed to their denotations which are of use in defining or 'enlivening') as we should certainly be inclined to do.

Connotations are thought to be connected exclusively with judgments of approval or disapproval, *ideas* of dignity or beauty and
their opposites.

Priestley's explanation of amplification is worth quoting in full
since it makes clear the rather narrow conception that he and his
contemporaries entertain of the evocative power of words. Connotation is not the entire 'aura of suggestiveness' around a trope;
it is limited to the value-associations it carries. To use a banal, but
conveniently illustrative, trope for our own purposes: it is the
social or aesthetic *cachet* of words which is exploited in amplification.

The advantage of using metaphors is, that we can borrow a name
from a thing which contains the quality we mean to express, in a
greater degree than the subject to which we ascribe it, and by this
means can often suggest a stronger idea of a quality than any terms
originally appropriated to our subject could convey. Besides, along
with the name, other ideas, as of dignity or meanness, agreeableness
or disagreeableness, and the like, will be transferred to the object
to which it is applied. So that, by means of the complex ideas which
accompany the names of things, we can give just what size and
colour we please to any thing we are describing.[12]

Other descriptions of this function of tropes are closely similar
and bear out the conclusions that may be drawn from Priestley's.
It is no more than associations of dignity or beauty which are
operative in amplification: there is no question of sensuous associations or of those vaguer emotional connotations of metaphor which
serve to define subtle and intuitive impressions.[13] Amplification
exploits the language of evaluation rather than the language of
sensibility.

Tropes may also contribute to 'vivacity' in a slightly different
and more general sense—a variety of ancillary images diversifies
and brightens discourse.[14] Many writers also point out that tropes,
apart from their primary functions, give added pleasure because of
their very nature as devices of language: we enjoy perceiving the
resemblances they draw, or, as some critics have it, discovering
uniformity in variety.[15]

Classical rhetoricians, with a few exceptions, attempted to maintain a clear distinction between tropes and figures. Whereas tropes
were words put to some other than their normal use, figures were

either unusual syntactical constructions (figures of language) or else turns of expression which convey their meaning by implication rather than statement (figures of thought).[16] This distinction could not be completely satisfactory: if allegory, for example, is a trope the argument for categorizing personification as a figure cannot be altogether convincing. Irony, again, is obviously both a trope and a figure. But the classification had its uses and part of its significance lay in the fact that a special function was reserved for figures alone: that of expressing and arousing feeling.[17]

The more conservative rhetoricians of the later eighteenth century still preserve the division of figurative language into two categories, and still ascribe expressive power to figures only.[18] Ward explains the difference of function between tropes and figures in terms of their origin in different needs:

. . . if we consider the nature of speech, we shall easily perceive, that as mankind must have been under a necessity very early to introduce the use of Tropes, for supplying the want of proper words, to express their simple ideas; so the like necessity must have put them upon the use of *Figures* to represent their different passions.[19]

On the whole, however, the distinction is no longer emphasized. The passage from Kames quoted above, which discusses metaphor as a 'figure of speech', is extracted from a chapter entitled 'Figures'. This terminological vagueness has invaded the writing of even those rhetoricians such as Blair who yet make a point, when it suits their argument, of distinguishing the two categories. As to the expressive function of figures, it has in many instances been re-assigned to figurative language generally,[20] though, as we shall see in the next chapter, tropes and figures cannot be supposed to fulfil this function in precisely the same way.

The next chapter will show, too, that in expressing feeling figurative language also arouses it in audience or reader: they are correlative aspects of the same process. Here we need only notice that, since figurative language is discussed indifferently in terms of its capacity to express or its capacity to move,[21] and since one is invariably assumed to involve the other, there is never any question in these writers' minds of expression as an end in itself. The emphasis is always pragmatic: if figurative language is a means of expression, it is *ipso facto* a means to the end of 'moving'.

None the less, a striking contradiction seems to be inherent in these discussions of figurative language and its connexion with feeling. In spite of the constant references to the *uses* of tropes and figures, both individually and collectively considered, it is very widely held that figurative language occurs spontaneously to the mind in a state of emotion.[22] This might still leave room for deliberation and choice, for the 'art' that is elsewhere the basic rule, but some writers maintain that *only* those tropes and figures which arise spontaneously are of any value.[23]

On the other hand, the emphasis on their practical function is strengthened by a number of subsidiary precepts. The strictest rules of propriety must apply to the use of figurative language: we find warnings on this score issued on every hand. The most important are: (1) that an excessive use of metaphor has a fatiguing, if not obfuscating, effect;[24] (2) that over-elaborate or far-fetched tropes invariably strain a reader's complaisance;[25] (3) that extended comparisons and 'studied' metaphors (the caveat is sometimes extended, as it is by Kames, to apply to *all* metaphors) are incompatible with the expression of strong emotion.[26] Intense feeling, it is said, leaves the mind no leisure to seek out the affinities and analogies which are the basis of the 'comparative' tropes.

The apparently conflicting points of view become still more difficult to reconcile when we discover writers explaining the whole relation of feeling to figurative language as one of propriety. The use of figurative language is justified only by genuine emotion. The writer must therefore be careful not to simulate the style of a passion which he does not feel, nor to express a feeling in language incongruous with its nature.[27] This principle recommends neither spontaneity nor deliberation, but contrives to favour both.

It is, in fact, more often than not the same writer who will speak both of the spontaneous origin of tropes and figures and, in the next breath, of their uses, to which various rules apply. Could these writers be supposed to have reconciled such seemingly opposed opinions? The spontaneity in question here is not one of trained judgment and skill; it is the spontaneity of irrational feeling. If they consider feeling alone as the source of one important element in style, are they not succumbing to confusion of mind when they assert that this same element must also be subject to judgment and control in the interests of a purpose?

It does not, of course, inevitably follow. There need be no

irreconcilable contradiction between spontaneous feeling and the exercise of judgment. Nor, in fact, did the rhetoric and poetic theory of the period commit itself to untenable views on this score; the reason why, however, will not become fully apparent until two further elements in the theory of expression have been examined: one, a conception of the role that feeling plays at large in the process of composition, the other, a particular view of the way in which language must express emotion in order to move an audience.

7

The Role of Feeling in Composition

WE found in the last chapter that in the Neo-Classic period figurative language was considered—no less than it was in the succeeding age—an important, if not the most important, means of expressing, hence of arousing, feeling. But why and how should it fulfil this function?

The answer given before 1800 is in one respect surprisingly definite and clear, and in every respect differs entirely from such explanations as the Romantics felt able to offer.

Figurative language may be connected in two ways with the end of 'moving'. In the first place, tropes (and certain figures such as personification) are a means to 'vivacity', and 'vivacity', as we have seen, is a quality valued partly for its emotive power. This aspect of expressiveness will be considered in more detail below.

A more important method of expressing feeling, one which receives a larger share of these writers' attention, is also a highly indirect one. Classical rhetoric had recognized it in pointing out the effectiveness of figures (properly so-called) in arousing emotion, and it is in fact from classical discussions of the use of figures that we gain the clearest indication of the principle involved.

No more than a brief examination is needed of the various expressive figures listed in a Classical rhetoric to reveal why they are considered effective. Figures are obviously useful only as they *demonstrate* feeling: they are signs of a state of mind in the speaker which his audience will readily interpret, and instinctively react to. Such figures of thought as exclamation, interruption, apostrophe and the rest, such figures of language as asyndeton or tautology,[1] clearly cannot convey feeling by exploring and defining it: they are merely indications of its presence in the speaker.

Figures of this class are still listed by eighteenth-century rhetoricians as important means of showing, and hence arousing, feeling.[2] By this time, however, certain tropes, more especially metaphor and hyperbole, are also being recommended as effective for the same purpose, and in the same way.[3] This is a natural extension of the principle since the use of tropes may be, as well as that of figures, the mark of vivid feeling. (And here, perhaps, is one reason why the line of demarcation between the two categories of figurative language has by now been all but obliterated.)

The principle which supports the classical conception of the moving power of figures, the principle, that is, that reader or audience reacts to a *demonstration* of feeling on the part of writer or speaker, may now serve to account in general for the moving power of literature. 'Sympathy', the concept so important to eighteenth-century ethics, is the crux of the matter here. It is through sympathy that an audience, recognizing the signs of emotion, is moved to participate in it.

Thus Campbell—who accounts as follows for the effect of repetition and tautology in an oration:

The hearer perceiving [the speaker], as it were, overpowered by his subject, and at a loss to find words adequate to the strength of his feelings, is by sympathy carried along with him, and enters into all his sentiments.

—also generalizes from such examples. 'Sympathy', he says, 'is one main engine by which the orator operates on the passions.' Several other rhetoricians agree.[4]

Theorists of poetry, too, think along the same lines. Lowth, who believes that the essential function of poetry is the expression of feeling, considers that poets express passion by *imitating* it, that is to say by exhibiting its effects. We are moved because we respond instinctively to such imitations, recognizing the signs without any effort of understanding: 'the object [of imitation] is clear and distinct at once.'[5] Burke, though he denied imitative powers to poetry, would undoubtedly have allowed it to be an imitation in this sense. The principle involved is central to his views:

. . . we take an extraordinary part in the passions of others, and . . . we are easily affected and brought into sympathy by any tokens which are shewn of them; . . . there are no tokens which can express all the circumstances of most passions so fully as words . . .[6]

That Lowth, among other writers who make similar statements,

means by 'imitation of passion' not an analysis of the state of mind
it induces, but a dramatic display of its effects, is revealed by
references to *figures* as one means of imitation. Figures, says
Lowth, 'new and extraordinary forms of expression',

... are indeed possessed of great force and efficacy in this respect
especially, that they in some degree imitate or represent the
present habit and state of the soul.[7]

Figures elsewhere are compared to gestures and the force of
the analogy with dramatic imitation becomes even clearer:

Figurative speech . . . is indicative of a person's real feelings and
state of mind, not by means of the words it consists of, considered
as *signs of separate ideas*, and interpreted according to their common acceptation; but as circumstances naturally attending those
feelings which compose any state of mind. Those figurative expressions, therefore, are scarcely considered and attended to as
words, but are viewed in the same light as *attitudes, gestures*, and
looks, which are infinitely more expressive of sentiments and feelings
than words can possibly be.[8]

Feeling is expressed, therefore, in at least one important way by
a demonstration of its symptoms or an imitation of the forms in
which it is characteristically manifested. Figurative language, and
especially the figures properly so-called, are a principle means of
accomplishing this. But tropes and figures are not the only significant marks of feeling: just as effective are the connexion of a
writer's thoughts and the particular colour he gives them or, to
look at the same thing from another point of view, the precise way
in which he handles and elaborates his subject. This class of
'symptom' will be considered in more detail below. For the
moment it is simply necessary to see that even in this much more
general way feeling is considered to be expressed and aroused by
imitation appealing to sympathy:

The affections that prevail in the author himself direct his attention
to subjects congenial, and give a peculiar bias to his inventive
powers, and a peculiar colour to his language. Hence his work . . .
will exhibit a picture of his mind, and awaken correspondent
sympathies in the reader.[9]

Thus the phrase 'expression of feeling' in one area at least of its application bears a very restricted sense. It means, in the first place, no more than 'expression of the marks or symptoms of feeling'—the order and complexion of thoughts and the rhetorical forms which are the typical concomitants of emotion. The term 'expression' is in fact misleading. We are accustomed to using it, at least in literary discussions, in what might be called the Romantic sense: to express feeling is to convey its precise quality, to communicate all the subtle impressions which are its constituent elements. We have here to do with something different: what would perhaps be more accurately described as 'display' since, on these principles, language and the ideas it conveys do not evoke feeling directly, but function as signs from which an unconscious inference is drawn; they move, but only as a form of highly and immediately persuasive *evidence*.

The term 'display' implies, moreover, a deliberate aiming at effect, a determination to create an impression—and this is precisely the idea that is never far from the surface in most eighteenth-century discussions of emotional expression. References are numerous to the *efficacy* of figurative language in arousing feeling,[10] to the *means* of moving at an author's disposal,[11] to his *purpose* of affecting readers or hearers.[12]

Display involves an element of control: it is by no means that 'spontaneous overflow' for which the only rule is sincerity.

This being so, it is clear that 'feeling' as well has a more limited meaning in these discussions than we should naturally be inclined to attach to the term. For not every kind of feeling can be effectively displayed, but only that range of comparatively strong and unsubtle emotions which are part of a dynamic, as opposed to a reflective, response to experience—and not to vaguely-defined areas of experience, but to specific objects or persons or situations. The eighteenth century referred to these feelings, which are further characterized by being easily recognizable and distinguishable (Grief, Love, Anger, Indignation, and so on), as 'passions'.

Kames, for example, contrasts emotion and passion. Emotion he defines as simply an impression of pleasure or pain: passion on the other hand, is emotion accompanied by desire. It prompts to action, whereas emotion is 'quiescent'. Lawson, too, stresses the dynamic nature of passion, which is an impulsion to act. He finds little to distinguish passion from will.[13]

Gerard reveals another aspect of the difference between passion and emotion:

A passion in strict propriety means only such an emotion as is produced by some one particular cause, and directed to some one determinate object.[14]

Obviously 'passion' in this sense is the only kind of feeling which may readily be displayed in a histrionic way. Oratory indeed, concerned as it is exclusively with the life of action, could have little interest in any other kind of feeling, nor could it usefully adopt any other mode of expression. Rhetoricians, therefore, recognize none, and theorists of poetry, in this as in other connexions, see no reason to differ.

The Romantics saw that passion could operate on sensibility (in so far as it became the source and subject of meditation);[15] for them passion became 'expressible'. But no eighteenth-century critic conceived the possibility of formulating feeling in language in a way comparable to that in which thought is defined. Passion could be represented only through the effects of which it is the cause. Twining, for instance, says:

In a strict and philosophical view, a *single* passion or emotion does not admit of description at all. Considered in itself, it is a simple internal feeling, and, as such, can no more be *described*, than a simple idea can be defined. It can be described no otherwise than in its *effects*, of *some* kind or other.

He goes on to say that these effects may be either internal ('the operation of passion on the mind'), or external, arriving finally at much the same position as other writers referred to above, except that, since his interest is focused on the drama, he views the external effects principally as actions.[16]

Feeling, however, has internal effects as well. It is considered to influence both the order of the thoughts that arise in a writer's mind and their particular colour or complexion, so that to this extent his thoughts themselves will strike a reader as signs of his emotion. Can we be certain that a different sort of feeling is not in question here, one that is nearer to what the Romantics were to call 'sensibility'? The answer will perhaps be clearer if we examine the two kinds of effect, and what is said about them, separately.

It is a favourite idea of the late-eighteenth-century critics that strong feeling results in abruptness and incoherence in the sequence of thought. That this in turn can serve as no more than 'evidence' of the feeling in question is clearly demonstrated in all accounts of the phenomenon. In fact what disconnectedness amounts to is the consistent, though perhaps varied and irregular, use of one rhetorical figure: asyndeton. As such it is no more than an extended figurative 'token' of feeling. It is almost equally obvious that only 'passion' can be thus expressed, since the disconnectedness is quite naïvely assumed to appear as disconnectedness, and not as a subtle form of connexion. But here are some typical pronouncements which make this clear:

Joy, grief, and anger are most naturally expressed by exclamations, sudden starts and broken sentences . . .[17]

The language of enthusiasm, and of all those passions that strongly agitate the soul, is naturally incoherent . . .[18]

It is . . . observable that these affections [the more violent affections of the heart] break and interrupt the enunciation by their impetuosity; they burst forth in sentences pointed, earnest, rapid, and tremulous . . .[19]

The psychological explanation of this phenomenon must remove any remaining doubt. Gerard provides an elaborate analysis of it in the course of which he distinguishes more than one of the processes of association and dissociation likely to result in abruptness, but the following represents clearly enough his line of demonstration:

Every passion often occasions an abruptness of thought; this is one cause of that abruptness; different ideas being connected with the passion, in different respects, but with almost equal closeness, the passion introduces them all, or several of them at least, in alternate succession.[20]

Passion is presumably a sensation distinct from the ideas with which it is associated, and which it calls up 'in alternate succession': this is not implausible as the description of an agitated state of mind, and as such it stands in the sharpest contrast to the unanalysable unity of feeling and thought which the Romantics discovered in the mind of the poet. Clearly Gerard is preoccupied with a totally different sort of feeling.

An explanation of the second way in which feeling influences thought may also be found in Gerard. Feeling arouses only such associated ideas as are congenial with itself.[21] But since it is regarded, in the first place, as attached to some definite central idea, in other words as having been aroused by a given subject (just as, outside literature, 'passion' requires a determinate object), this influence of feeling on invention is not unlimited: it is confined, in fact, to 'enlivening' or 'amplifying' the matter in hand.

'Sensibility' is again out of the question. The following passage from Gerard makes it clear that the working of fancy is an effect of which emotional impulse is the cause: invention is not conceived of as somehow co-terminous with feeling itself. Compare Romantic remarks on the coalescence of feeling and thought, feeling and image.

Every artist must often excite the passions: they are excited chiefly by being well expressed [through tokens]: they are excited also by strong representations of their objects and their causes [vivacity]; but it is the fancy, excited by the lively conception of the passion, running into the same thoughts which the passion, if really working, would suggest, and placing the artist in the situation in which he would then be, that puts it in his power to imagine, and consequently to represent, its causes and its objects in a way proper for infusing it into others.[22]

Here Gerard is assuming that passion will be simulated, but the point to notice is that he has in mind a feeling which has a cause and an object and *suggests* thoughts which are plainly subsidiary to the main idea. Feeling does not determine the subject; on the contrary it is itself determined by 'its causes and its objects' which *are* the subject to be represented.[23]

If we leave psychological abstractions for more particular descriptions of the way in which feeling influences invention we find that, since it is only details which are affected, as distinct from the subject proper, the process may be reviewed equally well from the standpoint of style. Feeling results in a choice of such details as 'amplify' the objects to be described. From this point of view it may be seen as accounting for the 'dress' of thought. 'The mind', says Lowth,

with whatever passion it be agitated, remains fixed upon the object that excited it; and while it is earnest to display it, is not satisfied with a plain and exact description; but adopts one agreeable to its own sensations, splendid or gloomy, jocund or unpleasant. For the passions are naturally inclined to amplification . . .[24]

Similarly, Kames:

. . . a man, when elevated or animated by passion, is disposed to elevate or animate all his objects: he avoids familiar names, exalts objects by circumlocution and metaphor, and gives even life and voluntary action to inanimate beings. In this heat of mind, the highest poetical flights are indulged, and the boldest similes and metaphors relished.[25]

According to some accounts of amplification we are to understand not so much that objects will be 'exalted' by the language in which they are described, as that the conceptions of feeling, themselves 'exalted', will receive definition in an appropriate form of words. But the difference of approach has little significance: in essence these accounts are no more than alternative versions of the explanations quoted above. An example will make this clear. Blair believes that

Under the influence . . . of any strong emotion, objects do not appear to us such as they really are, but such as passion makes us see them. We magnify and exaggerate; we seek to interest all others in what causes our emotion; . . . Hence, in congruity with those various movements of the mind, arise those terms of expression [figurative language] . . .[26]

Amplification, like other means of expressing and arousing feeling, is also, it seems, considered effective partly because it is a sign of feeling appealing to sympathy. There are a few writers, at all events, who imply as much, if they do not make a point of saying so.[27] But more often the explanation takes a different turn.

It cannot be said that any one writer is absolutely clear and consistent in his views on the subject, in fact few seem interested in investigating it, but from such comments as are made two fairly definite ideas emerge.

It is plain enough that some writers consider an 'amplified' imitation to be effective in precisely the same way as any representation is effective, except that here the representation is particularly vivid and forceful, it may even be a 'sublime', one.[28] The writer's 'passion' in this case is expressed not through its effects but through its cause. It is the conceptions which roused the writer's feelings that, being faithfully reproduced, move the reader as well. The cause-and-effect relationship between feelings and what is presented is still the most notable characteristic of the process, which constitutes a form of expression just as indirect as 'display-through-tokens', and one which might equally well be described as 'display'.

At this point it might be as well to consider the function of 'vivacity'—the one important factor in the theory of expression which remains to be discussed—since 'vivacity' produces its effect in a closely analogous way. Several writers insist on the importance to the end of 'moving' of clear, life-like representations:[29] as we have seen, vivid images are believed to affect the mind only less powerfully than sensation itself. Here again the writer is assumed to represent the *object* of emotion: the principle is the same, the difference lies only in the fact that in this case he will aim at verisimilitude rather than elevation or dignity.[30]

A third approach to amplification ascribes its power to the effect of the emotional connotations which are transferred to a description by tropes. 'Vivacity', in so far as it is not merely 'vividness' but 'colourfulness', may also be effective for the same reason. From this point of view, in fact, it would be impossible to differentiate between the two principles, and no distinction was attempted. 'Illustration' and 'illumination'—terms which are everywhere associated with 'vivacity'—are also employed to denote the result of amplification.[31]

Though the cumulative effect of connotations attached to a subject may conceivably express 'passion' in so far as they elevate the subject, yet the effect of the connotations attached to figurative language cannot, by itself, be regarded as 'passionate'. Clearly another kind of feeling is conveyed which, since only two broad categories are in question here, must be classed with 'sensibility'. Needless to say eighteenth-century writers were aware of the fact that our reactions to imagery are of the 'emotional', not the 'passionate' kind. The following extract from an analysis of the first stanza of Gray's Elegy is one of the many passages which are clear enough witness to this:

... the supposed tolling of the curfew, just as the sun was leaving the horizon, is not wholly destitute of analogy to the tolling of what is called the passing bell for the deceased. The mention of a knell, naturally recalls this idea, and spreads a solemnity over the mind, which prepares it for the sentiments which follow.'[32]

How did writers of the time account for this effect in a theory which associates 'moving' exclusively with 'passion'? Above all, what did they think a writer was 'expressing' through such effects, since it is plainly not 'passion'?

Clear answers to these questions would be looked for in vain, since they were never apparently framed in precisely this way. But the following considerations may at least indicate why.

The connotations carried by imagery are thought to consist exclusively of ideas which prompt value-judgments: ideas related to dignity or beauty and their opposites, for example the 'solemnity' referred to above. Their function therefore in amplified descriptions, which aim at representing and, as it were, justifying the causes of passion, needs no special explanation. Their use in 'enlivened' descriptions would result not in 'feeling' but 'pleasure', the 'pleasures of the imagination', the 'emotions of Taste'—and this phenomenon receives a great deal of attention. But the amplest explanations take account of no other than abstract associations as the origin of 'pleasure': the sensuous associations of imagery, and the whole range of emotional associations which has no influence on judgment or opinion but rather on 'feel', 'impression', 'intuition', these never caught the attention of the eighteenth century.[33]

As to 'expression', it might reasonably be argued that, even with this very narrow range of resources, an author, in arousing 'emotions of Taste', must also have felt them and intended to convey them, that Neo-Classic theory must in fact have recognized the expression of sensibility, however indirect and limited the means it allowed.

But any such conclusion would be false, if not entirely so. The aims of a writer are clearly conceived: to please by an attractive presentation of his subject, to move by (among other means) an 'amplified' representation of it. It occurs to no one that a writer will set out to express the reactions of his sensibility for their own sake. His sensibility (in so far as that word is our equivalent for 'Taste') will merely help him choose the appropriate detail at the appropriate time in accordance with his other purposes.

Taste, in fact, is considered, in the writer, as a kind of judgment, a faculty of discrimination. There are some writers who do not recognize its existence, and some who positively deny it. Lawson, for example, says:

If . . . the known Faculties of the Mind suffice to [the] End which is ascribed to Taste, why should we suppose the Existence of this latter? We must reject it as altogether imaginary.

The function of Taste is part, Lawson believes, of the operations of Understanding. To the objection that Taste is, on the contrary, a sentiment, he answers:

. . . what are all these, distinguished by the fashionable name of *Sentiments*? The Understanding approveth or disapproveth: To those Acts, Nature hath annexed certain Degrees of Pleasure or Pain: But these Consequences follow so closely, that we cannot distinguish between them and their Causes; and the *Feeling* being the stronger Impression, we drop the preceding Act of the Understanding, and name the whole, *Sentiment*.[34]

But the many later writers who differ from Lawson in considering Taste a 'sense' or a 'sentiment', do so only in this one respect. They still believe that, whatever its nature as a psychological phenomenon—and as a response to representations in literature it is found to be fairly complex—it functions during the act of composition as a kind of intuitive judgment, directing aesthetic choice.[35]

Hence no one thinks of 'taste' or 'sensibility' as a feeling to be expressed in literature, and no one imagines that such appeal as (in theory) can be made to the reader's sensibility may be a part of 'moving'. The 'emotions of Taste' are 'pleasure': whereas the emotive function proper to literature is the expression of 'passion'.

Another characteristic of the Neo-Classic theory of expression, which may indeed be deduced from all that has been said about it above, is that the expression of feeling is clearly considered ancillary, if not always to a design (since such writers as Lowth, for instance, appear not to favour formal construction), at least to the exposition of a subject-matter, which is the cause or object of the feeling.[36] Since all the means of expression are demonstrative ('tokens', 'abruptness', 'amplification') they can only make an effect if the reason for, or the object of, the demonstration is at the same time defined.

One has to assume that, with this necessity uppermost, and furthermore because demonstrations of feeling are by definition deliberate attempts to create an impression, writers are expected to exercise as much 'art' when expressing their emotions as at any other time.

Hence the many recommendations of spontaneity to be found scattered through late eighteenth-century rhetoric and poetic theory, injunctions to ponder Horace's maxim, '*Si vis me flere, dolendum est primum ipsi tibi*',[37] may be intended to stress the importance of spontaneous, in the sense of 'genuine' and 'unforced', feeling but they cannot be incitements to the writer to throw off all restraint.

The primary importance of the subject, and consequently the subsidiary role of feeling, is very well illustrated by some variations of Horace's precept. Certain critics allow the possibility of self-induced feeling: cases in other words when a subject is already present to the author's mind before he rouses himself to suitable emotion. Nevertheless, it must still be genuine emotion, and to do this requires a special temperament. 'The pathetic', says Gerard,

can be expressed only by the person whose sensibility of heart enables him to conceive the passion with vivacity, to catch it as by infection, and whose imagination immediately receives an impulse from it, and pours in the ideas . . . of those effects . . . by which each passion naturally shows itself.[38]

And Kames agrees:

To awake passion by an internal effort merely, without any external cause, requires great sensibility; and yet that operation is necessary, no less to the writer than to the actor; because none but those who actually feel a passion, can represent it to the life.[39]

At least one writer finds difficulty in believing that genuineness of feeling can be combined with sufficient control. Lawson advises the orator to 'seem to feel the Passion he would excite' but not to succumb to its influence. An actor, he says, could never convey a passion he really felt. 'Why? Because the Strength of the Passion would disable him from expressing it.'[40]

The analogy with acting is very apt since the eighteenth-century theory of expression is so largely preoccupied with dramatic display; nevertheless, Lawson's conclusions do not altogether represent his contemporaries' views, and there is an obvious flaw in his argument. Whether actors do so or not, and it appears some of them do, most people are able when they choose to display strong and geniune emotion while retaining perfect command of themselves.

As long as the 'introspective' emotions are not in question, and as long the purpose in view is not absolute fidelity to the inner experience, there is no contradiction between genuineness of feeling and the exercise of 'art' in expressing it. If this can be accepted as self-evident, the apparently paradoxical views of the period about figurative language, met with in the last chapter, can be seen as entirely logical. As the means of 'display', figures may be intentionally exploited for effect, and judgment may be exercised in choosing and disposing them; on the other hand, in so far as they are suggested by feeling they may be seen as its 'natural' outcome.[41]

An everyday analogy will make this clearer. We express doubt on occasion by a shrug of the shoulders. To the extent that we decide to communicate our uncertainty, and have chosen this signal from among others less suitable to the occasion or the strength of our feeling, we are acting purposefully. Nevertheless, the gesture might also be regarded as spontaneously produced: whereas shrugging has no connexion with the great majority of other states of mind and emotion, it is 'natural' to a state of doubt.

8

The Distinguishing Characteristics of Poetry

THE preceding chapters have indicated that the theory of composition and style in the later eighteenth century borrowed its principles, and the assumptions upon which they are based, from rhetorical theory. Methods are considered as means to external ends, composition regarded as regulated by design, and determinate 'discursive' thought as the material of poetry. Style is looked upon as the 'dress' of thought, figurative language as the means by which feeling is displayed. Feeling itself is spoken of in terms which identify it with the extroverted 'passion' of the orator. Since the process of poetic composition resembles that of rhetorical composition in every essential respect, how was it thought possible to maintain any valid distinction between the two arts?

There is, of course, the obvious fact that poetry is written in 'numbers'; and though verse is not universally acknowledged by these critics as necessary to poetry, when it is not, the occasion is marked only by more or less profitless quibbling.[1] On the whole no one denies Dr Johnson's laconic definition in the Dictionary, 'Poetry: metrical composition'. Metre, rhythm, versification and other formal and external features are much discussed, and their importance in the art of poetry fully acknowledged.

But the question frequently arises whether poetry can be given a characterization less outward than this, its nature distinguished more fundamentally from that of prose, and, while there is no lack of glib solutions to this problem, the more conscientious theorists betray that they are perplexed by it.

There are many attempts at analysis and classification. One prominent group of critics support the view that passion or enthusiasm is an essential of poetry, and that poetry is *par excellence* a form of passionate utterance.[2] Allied to this view, and often conjoined with it, are the doctrines that poetic imitation is always 'heightened', 'lively', the manifestation of a 'warmed' or 'enlivened' imagination, and that consequently it appeals chiefly to the imagination and emotions of its audience.

Blair may be taken as one representative of this group. He does, it is true, reject imitation as a *distinguishing* factor in poetry, but concludes, in accordance with the general opinion of the school, that poetry 'is the language of passion, or of enlivened imagination, formed, most commonly, into regular numbers'. This implies a 'peculiar elevation' of style. It is also *to* imagination and passion that the poet speaks.[3]

Beattie, from a slightly different point of view, finds that 'what distinguishes *pure* poetry from other writing, is its aptitude, not to sway the judgment by reasoning, but to please the fancy, and move the passions, by a lively imitation of nature'.[4]

There is no contradiction, of course, between these two critics who subscribe to the same theory while placing their principal emphasis on different elements in it, Blair on the straightforward expression and communication of feeling, Beattie on the power of 'vivacity' to move.[5] A variety of other critics, too numerous to quote, offer the same or very similar views.[6]

Occasionally older and simpler definitions are repeated: 'elevation of thought' and 'heightened imitation' are still put forward *per se* (isolated from emotional origins and effects) as defining characteristics of poetry.[7]

Minor, and less persuasive, distinctions are sometimes made. A highly figurative style is, of course, considered peculiar to poetry. Figures, however, are by common consent so much implicated with the expression of feeling and the appeal to imagination that they can hardly be classed by themselves as a distinguishing feature. One critic does attempt to do so.

Though versification be one of the criteria that distinguish Poetry from Prose, yet it is not the sole mark of distinction. Were the Histories of Polybius and Livy simply turned into verse, they would not become Poems; because they would be destitute of those figures, embellishments, and flights of imagination, which display the Poet's Art and Invention.[8]

After elaborating the idea, however, that poetry 'has a language of its own', he is obliged to contradict himself:

Tropes and figures are likewise liberally used in Rhetoric . . .
But these figures must be more sparingly used in Rhetoric than in
Poetry, and even then mingled with argumentation, and a detail
of facts altogether different from poetical narration. The Poet,
instead of relating the incident, strikes off a glowing picture of the
scene . . .[9]

He is not really distinguishing between two kinds of language, but
between two kinds of subject-matter and approach, the poetic
kind making its appeal to emotion and imagination. (His previous
characterization of poetic language has in fact been entirely
coloured by the idea that it speaks 'feelingly to the heart' and
'pleasingly to the imagination'.)[10]

Another ingredient of poetry sometimes, though not often,
brought up as especially characteristic of it is its diction. Lowth,
for example, says 'it is the nature of all poetry . . . to be totally
different from common language; and not only in the choice of
words, but in the construction, to affect a peculiar and more
exquisite mode of expression'.[11] What has caught Lowth's attention, however, is evidently no more than an unusual vocabulary
and syntax: 'words pompous and energetic . . . composition
singular and artificial', as he phrases it elsewhere.[12] For Beattie,
poetic diction is entirely a matter of vocabulary. He classifies
various types—archaic words, 'poetical' words, abbreviations,
compound epithets—and adds:

. . . the influence of these words in adorning English verse is not
very extensive. Some influence however they have. They serve to
render the poetical style first, more melodious; and secondly,
more solemn.[13]

It seems, therefore, that poetic diction—in the sense either of a
specialized vocabulary, or of typical syntactical configurations—
may be classed, along with versification, as an external characteristic of poetry, an indication of its superficial traits but not of its
substance or function.

With these external characteristics belongs, too, the element in
poetry of 'music' or 'melody' that is so often singled out for remark.
As Kames says, 'verse is more musical than prose, and its melody
more perfect'. The difference is analogous to that between song
and recitative.[14] Kames however is suggesting no more than that

the rhythm of verse is regular, smooth and 'sweet': this is the point at which all eighteenth-century discussions of 'music' in poetry stop. Hence these discussions take the definition of poetry no further than the requirement of verse, for poetry is accounted more mellifluous than prose because it is written in verse.

'Figurative language', 'diction', 'music' are evidently notions of no great service to the critic in search of a definition of the essential nature of poetry. No more convincing, though less obviously pointless, are the more elaborate proposals of the critics cited above who find in 'imagination' and 'passion' the determining factors they are looking for.

Some of them admit it. 'The truth is', Blair says, 'Verse and Prose on some occasions, run into one another, like light and shade. It is hardly possible to determine the exact limit where eloquence ends, and Poetry begins . . .'[15] Another critic allows that the essential difference between prose and verse can only lie in 'measure', and very reasonably asks: 'if we admit such perform- ances as Selemaque [*sic*] or Fingal into the class of poems, how is it possible to draw any precise line between the two species of composition?' Even 'measure', in this critic's opinion, may be barely enough to establish a noticeable difference. Blank verse 'has so near an affinity to prose, that it requires the most consummate skill and judgment in the arrangement of the periods, as well as the utmost force and elevation of language to preserve the distinc- tion between them'.[16]

A more uncompromising thinker, Campbell, goes further and dismisses the distinction of 'measure' as superficial and empty.

Poetry indeed is properly no other than a particular mode or form of certain branches of oratory . . . the same medium language is made use of, the same general rules of composition, in narration, description, argumentation, are observed; and the same tropes and figures, either for beautifying or invigorating the diction, are employed by both. In regard to versification, it is more to be con- sidered as an appendage, than as a constituent of poetry. In this lies what may be called the more mechanical part of the poet's work, being at most but a sort of garnishing, and by far too unes- sential to give a designation to the kind.[17]

Between the severe rationalism of Campbell, assimilating poetry entirely to rhetoric, and, on the other hand, the loose and compendious characterizations of poetry which are rather panegyrics than definitions, there is a middle way to the settlement of the point, clearly the only practicable one at the time, which neither arbitrarily ignores, like Campbell's, all difference between poetry and prose, nor seeks, like that of other critics, an absolute difference where there is none. This course, though there are other critics who incline to it, is mapped out most clearly and in greatest detail by Thomas Barnes in his essay 'On the Nature and essential characters of Poetry, as distinguished from Prose'.[18]

Barnes examines all the conventional definitions of poetry and finds them wanting. His objections to them, given the presuppositions of the time, are unanswerable. He considers first the definitions that hinge upon fiction or imitation or the aim of pleasure. These are easily disposed of: '. . . it is evident, that *fiction, imitation*, and *pleasure*, are not the properties of poetry *alone*'.[19] He then considers the remaining alternatives, asks whether the essence of poetry is to be looked for in metre on the one hand, or in elevation of thought, imagery and ornament on the other, and presents the arguments for both views. Elevation of thought and a heightened style are interrelated. 'Does not elevation of sentiment of itself produce *modulation* of language? The soul, inspired with great ideas, naturally treads with a lofty step.'[20] But, then, are compositions in the 'low' style, e.g. *Hudibras*, to be denied the name of poetry? Moreover, 'elevation of sentiment, imagery, and creative fancy, are not to be found in POETRY alone. They often belong as much to the Orator'.[21]

So much for this view. According to the other, metre and rhythm are the only true defining characteristics of poetry.

If we might argue from the *name*, POETRY, we should naturally conclude, that the ancients themselves understood by the term, not those *irregular* modulations, which *naturally* arose from the impulse of strong and impassioned feelings . . . but something more *artificial* and *elaborate*; something, which demanded more ingenuity to *form*, than merely arose from the effusions of a glowing heart.

On these grounds language without metre or rhythm 'may be indeed *poetical*, but can never be, POETRY ITSELF'.[22]

Having outlined these conflicting opinions, Barnes professes himself reluctant to decide between them, but in fact does offer a judgment of his own, which seems the only feasible compromise in the circumstances.

To FINISHED AND PERFECT POETRY, or rather to the HIGHEST ORDER of poetic composition, are necessary, elevation of *sentiment*, fire of *imagination*, and regularity of *metre*. This is the *summit* of PARNASSUS. But, from this sublimest point, there are gradual declinations, till you come to the region of prose. The *last line* of separation is, that of *regular metre*.[23]

No other definition of poetry was strictly possible before the advent of the Romantics and their total disengagement of poetry from rhetoric. The preceding chapters will have evinced the justice of Barnes' claim: that 'lively imitation', 'emotion', 'imagination', and the rest were as characteristic of rhetoric as of poetry, and in precisely the same way. They could not be made to serve as defining characterictics of the latter art.

As we have seen, one critic at least whose definition of poetry depends primarily on an idea of it as emotional utterance is obliged to admit that no hard-and-fast distinction is possible between poetry and eloquence.

'Nor is there any occasion', he continues, 'for being very precise about the boundaries, as long as the nature of each is understood.'[24] And this seems a very just statement of the case. No clear dividing line can be drawn, except for the obvious, and usually recognized, one which sets poetry apart in its mould of verse and 'numbers'. It cannot, with any pretence to logic, be distinguished from rhetoric by virtue of a kind of thought, feeling or language proper to itself. A distinction may, of course, be drawn by emphasizing the relative importance to either art of various aims and methods. Poetry, for example, might be characterized, though it could not be finally defined, by its predominant aim of giving pleasure: an aim which accounts for its typically vivid and imaginative content, its highly figurative style and (partly, at any rate) its passionate accent.

There are, besides, formal characteristics other than its metrical construction which distinguish poetry from rhetoric, namely its typical configurations of subject-matter: the 'kinds'. The latter, it is true, may themselves be given a rhetorical rationale,[25] but the line of argument on such occasions plainly has no relevance to rhetoric proper.

The 'kinds' are still, during this period, a live topic in criticism: discussions of epic and tragedy, ode and elegy are frequent and sometimes very interesting. But to enter upon any detailed account of them would, since this inquiry concerns the foundations rather than the superstructure of poetic theory, take us too far afield.

One or two general features, however, of this part of Neo-Classical theory will be worth noticing, since they are directly connected with the fundamental ideas discussed in preceding chapters, and since they reveal a further aspect of the influence of those ideas upon contemporary conceptions of poetry.

The theory of composition in the late eighteenth century encourages above all pictorial representation and the dramatic expression, or display, of feeling. Because it is believed that vivid description will please and move only less powerfully than sensation itself, descriptive poetry is very highly thought of: in fact, pictorial representation is sometimes considered to be of the very essence of poetry.[26] Even the concept of poetry as 'imitation' has come in certain quarters to imply no more than this.[27]

Equally striking is the frequent association of poetry with the expression, or display, of feeling. In this connexion it is the poetry of invocation and declamation that is mentioned with respect: the Ode and other lyrical forms of a dramatic cast.[28]

These tendencies in favour of the picturesque and the lyrico-dramatic appear to be the natural consequence of contemporary assumptions about the way in which poetry is conceived and written, though it is true that in all surveys of the 'kinds' conventional pride of place is still reserved for the epic and the drama.

The analysis contained in the above chapters of the Neo-Classic theory of composition and style, though by no means complete (details of great interest have been unavoidably excluded), has shown that the main tenets of late eighteenth-century theorists, and the assumptions they are founded on, constitute what might be called a 'rhetorical' conception of poetry. Before demonstrating that the 'reforms' carried out by the Romantics involved a complete rejection of this view, some special attention must be given to the views of those critics, the so-called 'pre-Romantics', who are supposed to have anticipated Romantic doctrines, and who certainly (as quotations from their works in the above chapters have indicated) did not subscribe wholly to orthodox opinion.

9

'Pre-Romanticism'

THE term 'pre-Romanticism' is used by historians of critical thought to denote an anti-classical trend in literary theory, generally considered characteristic of the last half of the eighteenth century, though its origins are sometimes discovered in an earlier period.[1] No very precise meaning can be attached to the term: it is applied in various ways according to the views of individual historians. Nevertheless, their use of it has very clear implications, for, in calling a certain class of theories 'pre-Romantic', they necessarily suggest not only that such theories display Romantic tendencies, but also that, for this reason, they are best understood as prefigurations of Romantic theory itself. It will be the object of the present chapter to argue that the application of this term to any theory of the later eighteenth century is misleading. Needless to say, there are historians who canvass 'pre-Romanticism' without actually using the term: to their views the following objections must equally apply.

We shall see that the so-called 'pre-Romantics' cannot be said to have developed anything approaching a new theory. Their work is invariably solidly based on traditional views, and if their more daring departures from orthodoxy impress one, when considered apart from the rest of their ideas, as quintessentially Romantic, nevertheless, to judge the whole of their work by these few striking anomalies can only result in gross misinterpretation. For their 'Romanticism' assumes a very different complexion when considered in context: it is never a striking out along a new path; it is never more than the desertion of one of the old ones, in favour perhaps of an extension elsewhere.[2]

There will be no need here, in view of the preceding analysis of Neo-Classical theory, to demonstrate that a critic's insistence on 'imagination', 'emotion', or 'spontaneity' as important requirements in the poet is not necessarily, in itself, evidence of his

'Romanticism'. It is not on these grounds that we can regard such writers as Blair or Gerard or Beattie as 'pre-Romantics'. We have seen that such ideas were an integral part of Neo-Classical theory. The theory of rhetoric had indeed from its very inception recognized the importance of irrational elements in style and composition.

There are certain writers, however, who, apart from their non-rationalist bias, are markedly antagonistic to other elements in traditional theory. It will be worth examining in some detail the views of the most prominent among them, so as to judge of their claims to being considered pioneers of revolutionary change.

Of these writers the best-known and most extraordinary (though judged on his intrinsic merits as a theorist, the least interesting) is Edward Young.

Young is sometimes acclaimed as the first of the Romantics, the first critic entirely to abandon the rationality and system of Neo-Classicism and to assert the necessity of freedom, spontaneity and untrammelled individuality in literature. But this view of his achievement is over-enthusiastic: it can only be justified as long as, by concentrating on selected passages, the main bearing of the essay upon which it is based, the celebrated *Conjectures on Original Composition*, can be ignored.

Young's principal theme is, in fact, a rhetorical one. It is not a plea for Romantic poetry: it is an elaboration of the traditional rhetorical debate as to whether an author should rely more upon his natural resources than upon imitation of the established classics:[3] and Young offers the traditional answer: 'imitate; but imitate not the *Composition*, but the *Man*'.[4]

Young has, of course, nothing against imitation in the other sense. He is entirely orthodox in believing literature to be representative. Imitation of nature (as opposed to the imitation of other works) he regards as the distinguishing characteristic of original composition.[5]

By 'originality' Young quite simply means 'the expression of new ideas'. If we disregard, for the moment, his many flowery, hence potentially misleading, remarks on this topic, and examine some of the plainer statements, this becomes sufficiently obvious:

. . . thoughts, when become too common, should lose their currency; and we should send new metal to the mint, that is, new meaning to the press.

[Originals] extend the republic of letters, and add a new province to its dominion. *Imitators* only give us a sort of duplicate of what we had, possibly much better, before; increasing the mere drug of books, while all that makes them valuable, *knowledge* and *genius*, are at a stand.[6]

So that, up to this point, Young is not propounding a new theory of poetry, merely exhorting writers to extend the field of their endeavours, to acquire 'new provinces' for their 'dominion'. For a few pages of the essay, however, he adds to the main contrast between 'originality' and 'imitation' a further contrast between 'genius' and 'learning'.[7] To some extent Young uses the new pair of concepts to support much the same thesis: the genius is original in producing new subject-matter, the learned writer is an imitator. The genius may succeed without book-learning, since his knowledge is acquired from nature. Young, in fact, defines the faculty of genius as a 'power of accomplishing great things without the means [i.e. erudition] generally reputed necessary to that end'.[8]

There are, however, passages elsewhere in this section which imply something bolder. 'Learning' is associated with a knowledge of the rules of art, 'genius' with innate skill. We are told that, whereas learning is 'a great lover of rules, and boaster of famed examples', genius can go beyond 'authorities and laws' to achieve 'unexampled excellence'.

There is something in poetry beyond prose-reason; there are mysteries in it not to be explained, but admired . . .[9]

So much might again be construed as no more than the repetition of a Neo-Classical commonplace: art is only an aid to nature, and nature (genius) may, ignoring the rules on occasion, 'snatch a grace beyond the reach of art'. Young, however, goes further than this to state, or so it seems, that genius may dispense with rules altogether.

Genius can set us right in Composition, without the rules of the learned; as conscience sets us right in life, without the laws of the land . . .[10]

We are reminded of the earlier remark that an 'original'

may be said to be of a vegetable nature; it rises spontaneously from the vital root of genius; it *grows*, it is not *made*. *Imitations* are often a sort of *manufacture* wrought up by those *mechanics, art* and *labour*, out of pre-existent materials not their own.[11]

It is in these passages, if anywhere, that Young is anticipating Romantic doctrine; that is, if he really means that poetry is not always an 'art', that the poems of genius are not made, but 'grow', that to them no technical rules and principles need apply.

But what he really means can only be determined by reading these passages in their context. And to do so is to discover that their drift is much less extraordinary than it can be made to seem.

In the first place, if Young decries the rules, he appears to have in mind for the most part not the essential principles of Neo-Classical art, but the adventitious conventions once (and still in some quarters) regarded as binding. One may note that the only rule he singles out for explicit condemnation is Horace's dictum that a drama shall be divided into five acts. 'So says Horace', Young comments, 'so says ancient example. But reason has not subscribed.'[12]

When it comes to the *method* of classical composition, he positively recommends it. We need not, he says, go in awe of the ancients.

Have we not their beauties, as stars, to guide; their defects, as rocks, to be shunn'd; the judgment of ages on both, as a chart to conduct, and a sure helm to steer us in our passage to greater perfection than theirs?[13]

The rules, besides, are not to be dismissed altogether. There is an inferior type of genius which must rely upon them, and for writers of more modest talents they are indispensable.[14]

If the genius, moreover, can ignore the precepts of art, it is not suggested that he will proceed upon different principles. Young nowhere puts forward any positive theoretical statement on this point which might be interpreted as a depature from conventional doctrine. On the contrary, he makes statements of the opposite bearing such as can only confirm his adherence to traditional views.

It is possible, he says, to be original and yet *mistaken:* hence, 'as nothing is more easy than to write originally wrong; Originals are not here recommended, but under the strong guard of my first rule—*Know thyself*'.[15] To know himself the writer must explore

and understand his own capacities, 'excite and cherish every spark
of intellectual light and heat', assemble his thoughts, then allow
his genius (if he have any) to 'rise . . . as the sun from
chaos'.[16]

In case the last image should suggest a process unlike the one
usually described in Neo-Classical theory, one ought immediately
to compare this passage with a later one in which Young enumerates
the faculties he understands as necessary to composition. He is suggesting here that modern literature may not only equal but surpass
that of the ancients. The possibility, he maintains, is quite con-
ceivable since

a marvellous light, unenjoy'd of old, is pour'd on us by revelation,
with larger prospects extending our *understanding*, with brighter
objects enriching our *imagination*, with an inestimable prize setting
our *passions* on fire, thus strengthening every power that enables
composition to shine . . .[17] (My italics.)

His meaning here is clear, his ideas precisely those accepted by
his contemporaries: 'understanding' is the basic intellectual requirement, 'imagination' the image-making faculty, 'passion' that
kind of emotion which is associated with desire and will. With
notions such as these Young cannot at the same time be entertaining any new conception of literary psychology or literary method.

Elsewhere his discussion reveals, too, that the 'original genius',
however natural and untutored, will still be a genius on the Neo-
Classical pattern. His poetry will contain 'wit', 'thoughts', 'sense',
'knowledge'. It will be representative, an imitation of nature.
When Young refers to poetic feeling he calls it 'pathos'.[18]

Thus there is not a single statement in the *Conjectures* which
may be construed as 'pre-Romantic' in any positive sense. The
famous comparison of original production with organic growth is
no exception. Commentators tend, here especially, to overlook the
context in drawing their conclusions about the force of Young's
observations. The passage occurs in the early part of the essay
which considers originality in the sense exclusively of 'newness
of subject-matter'. The analogy with growth is clearly intended to
contrast novelty of content—which can only be of natural and
spontaneous origin—with the second-hand and artificial results of
imitation. The analogy is general enough; it is one that Young
repeats elsewhere with the same significance:

Thyself so reverence, as to prefer the *native growth* of thy own mind to the richest import from abroad; such borrowed riches make us poor.[19] (My italics.)

Clearly no reference is intended in either instance to the actual process of composition: so unusual an idea would have required an emphasis and elaboration which these isolated remarks never receive. Their bearing is different: the ideas of an original belong to him alone, they have 'grown' in his mind, whereas the imitator's thought has been 'wrought up' out of materials purloined from others. Young is saying no more than this, and in saying this is saying what is neither very interesting nor in itself very original.

His essay is interesting for other reasons. It cannot be understood as a new experiment in critical theory, but it may be read as symptomatic of a (not entirely new) trend in literary taste. Shakespeare is lauded, in spite—it should be noted—of his 'faults'; Pope decried.[20] Other writers are suitably aligned, according as they are 'originals', 'imitators' or show signs of being both. Longinus, the mentor of so many of the later Neo-Classicists, is looked to for arguments which sanction a reversal of the values predominant in the earlier part of the century;[21] and it is clearly against these values, against the slavishly conventional classicism of the Augustans, rather than against Neo-Classical beliefs in general, that Young's elaborate polemic about originality and imitation, genius and learning, is directed. The tone, one cannot fail to notice, is throughout rhetorical, sometimes exaggeratedly so. Restored to their proper place in this scheme of persuasion and exhortation, Young's assertions about the free and independent genius can be seen for what they are: scarcely novel and carefully-considered theoretical dicta, but certainly an incitement to throw off the stultifying prejudices of the previous age.

This is not to deny what appears to have been thoroughly substantiated, that Young's more colourful pronouncements played an influential role in the development of Romanticism in Germany and that they ultimately returned, by way of the Germans, to form part of English Romantic doctrine.[22] But meanwhile they had been more or less deliberately misunderstood; moreover, had been given a philosophical justification—that is to say had acquired a theoretical status which Young (given the Neo-Classic assumptions about literature everywhere apparent in his essay) could not possibly have given them, nor even, we may reasonably assume, have wanted to give them.

There is no evidence that his contemporaries and immediate successors in England took him as seriously as did the Germans, although, as we have already noticed, the discussion on the topic of 'art' versus 'nature' continued throughout the century.[23]

Two years before the publication of Young's *Conjectures* had appeared Burke's *Philosophical Enquiry into the Origin of our Ideas of the Sublime and Beautiful*. One of the most noteworthy features of this work is an attack on the cherished Neo-Classical belief that poetry appeals to imagination (hence moves the feelings) by, as it were, painting pictures. Poetry, Burke argues, can convey images but imperfectly. On the other hand, it can move the passions without conveying images at all.

The images raised by poetry are always on [an] obscure kind; though in general the effects of poetry, are by no means to be attributed to the images it raises . . .[24]

. . . as to words; they seem to me to affect us in a manner very different from that in which we are affected by natural objects, or by painting or architecture . . .[25]

To explain the power of language over the emotions, Burke has recourse to what would now be called a behaviouristic theory of language. There is a type of word which arouses no concrete image, or even clear idea, e.g. the class of abstract terms such as 'virtue', 'honour'.

Such words are in reality but mere sounds; but they are sounds, which being used on particular occasions wherein we receive some good, or suffer some evil, or see others affected with good or evil . . . they produce in the mind, whenever they are afterwards mentioned, effects similar to those of their occasions. The sounds being often used without reference to any particular occasion, and carrying still their first impressions, they at last utterly lose their connexion with the particular occasions that gave rise to them; yet the sound without any annexed notion continues to operate as before.[26]

Burke does not deny that certain classes of words may raise images in the mind, but he believes that even these words derive their chief force, not from any picture they convey, but from the 'affection of the soul' produced by them—'by having from use the same effect on being mentioned, that their original has when it is seen'.[27]

These ideas may seem to take Burke a considerable way towards a Romantic theory of style. The Romantics were also interested in the occult connexion of words with feeling, though they would not, perhaps, have been interested in so rational an explanation of the phenomenon. An important and necessary factor in their theory, however, is certainly this view of words as 'foci' of emotional associations rather than as labels attached to clearly-defined ideas.

For Burke, however, his discovery of the 'Romantic' properties of language does not open up the possibility of exploiting them for new purposes in a new kind of literature. In the first place, he is still only aware of the kind of emotional associations which the eighteenth century already thoroughly understood—associations aroused by, or by way of, judgments of beauty or value. He draws his principal illustrations of the process he is analysing from, precisely, the class of what he calls 'compounded abstract' words (e.g. 'virtue', 'honour'); while his discussions in general imply no consciousness of the power of sensuous associations or of emotional associations of another kind.[28] His theory of poetic language goes no further, in the last analysis, than to deny the importance customarily attributed to 'vivacity', while emphasizing that of the technique employed in 'amplification'.

Another unusual feature of the *Enquiry*—Burke's stress on 'obscurity' as a source of the sublime—implies an exactly similar standpoint. Burke is at variance with accepted doctrine in so far as he sees 'obscurity' not as an incidental result of poetic 'enthusiasm' but as a positive factor in composition: it may be a means to the end of moving. On the other hand, he has in mind not the obscurity of subtle thought or of a difficult style, but an obscurity which is the opposite of 'vivacity': an absence of definition in the 'picture' the poet paints. He believes, of course, that poetry is normally obscure in this sense. Hence the vagueness of image which contributes to an effect of sublimity must be effected by exaggeration, by a deliberate process of 'amplification', as the following remarks reveal:

No person seems better to have understood the secret of heightening, or of setting terrible things . . . in their strongest light by the force of judicious obscurity, than Milton. [There follows a quotation from *Paradise Lost*, II, 666–73.] In this description all is dark, uncertain, confused, terrible, and sublime to the last degree.[29]

In other respects Burke is entirely conventional. He subscribes to principles of design and propriety. He combines his own theory of the emotive power of language with the accepted idea that the impassioned style is analogous to impassioned gesture, and is effective becaue of our instinctive, sympathetic reaction to tokens of emotion.[30] He has little or nothing to say of other aspects of composition and style, but the general trend of his thought is clearly orthodox. His is an interesting development of traditional theory, but in no sense preliminary to a new one. Coleridge, it is interesting to note, thought the *Enquiry* a 'poor thing',[31] and Burke's successors seem not to have paid it much attention.[32]

Lowth, who has been often cited in preceding chapters, diverges from orthodoxy in another direction. An extreme representative of the Longinian school, he believes true poetry to be the offspring of passion—as such, highly figurative, rhapsodical, disconnected, diffuse, 'the true and express image of a mind violently agitated'.[33] His views entail the rejection of a whole group of Neo-Classical ideals: design, order and propriety. Yet Lowth—if he seriously intends his definition of poetry to be an exclusive one—is merely narrowing the limits of poetry, and of the theory supporting it. He is far from recommending a radical change. Though he clearly favours vatic effusions, it is equally clear that they are to be of the traditional, rhetorical kind. His arguments are everywhere, and explicitly, conducted in rhetorical terms. His remarks on figurative language, on the importance of 'vivacity' and 'perspicuity', on language as the dress of thought,[34] and particularly on the mode in which style expresses feeling,[35] leave one in no doubt that his 'poetry of passion' is a far cry from the 'spontaneous overflow' required by the Romantics.[36]

Lowth is merely one exponent, if perhaps the most uncompromising, of the 'emotionalist' variety of Neo-Classical theory. There are of course 'rationalists' who are biased in the opposite direction: John Scott of Amwell is a notable example, and in this group one might even place—though he is by no means an extreme case—Johnson himself.

We need not here consider, or reconsider, a group of writers who base their theories on an aesthetics of Taste, though it is often these writers who are regarded as *par excellence* the 'pre-Romantics'.[37] We have seen that the aestheticians by no means abandon Neo-Classical empiricism in favour of a Romantic subjectivity.[38] They understand and analyse the aesthetic experience as a wholly subjective one, but they consider it as the experience of spectator or reader, his reaction to aesthetic qualities in natural objects or in art. It does not occur to them that this reaction may itself constitute the subject-matter of poetry: Taste, and its emotions, are for the poet merely a guide in his task, which is one of producing *objects* of Taste.[39] None of these writers abandons the fundamental tenets of Neo-Classicism.

The possible exception is Alison, among the latest and most 'advanced' of the eighteenth-century aestheticians, and of them all the one who comes nearest to deserving the title of 'pre-Romantic' since in some respects he displays so markedly idealistic a bias. Yet even Alison, as we shall see, cannot be said to have taken any decisive step in a new direction.

Alison claims to be a Platonist, a successor to Shaftesbury, Hutcheson and Akenside. But this seems to be a correct description of himself only on the rather general grounds that he believes 'matter is not beautiful in itself, but derives its beauty from the expression of MIND'.[40] Something more definitely Platonic is implied in a passage towards the conclusion of his *Essays on Taste*:

The forms, and the scenery of Material Nature are around them [i.e., artists], not to govern, but to awaken their genius; to invite them to investigate the sources of their beauty; and from this investigation to exalt their conceptions to the imagination of forms, and of compositions of form, more pure and more perfect, than any that Nature herself presents to them. It is in this pursuit that Ideal Beauty is at last perceived, which it is the loftiest ambition of the artist to feel and to express . . .[41]

But the main body of Alison's arguments is far less coloured by Platonism than this extract suggests. His thought might perhaps be broadly reconciled with Platonic doctrine but, in view of the fact that he depends on a materialist psychology (associationism), the reconciliation could not be a very happy one.

Unlike most other late eighteenth-century aestheticians, Alison is scarcely, if at all, interested in the aesthetic properties of structure and style. He appears to consider it the exclusive aim of the imitative arts to represent natural objects; it is these representations (or, of course, the objects themselves) which arouse what he calls the emotions of Taste. Thus Alison constantly alludes to poetry as *description*.[42] He refers to Beattie's essay 'On Poetry and Music' for a fuller illustration of his general canons of art[43]—and Beattie, as we know, believes 'lively imitation' to be the chief aim of the poet.[44]

According to Alison, however, objects, or representations of them, whereas they may by themselves arouse simple emotions, can give aesthetic pleasure (that is to say arouse the complex emotions of Taste) only in so far as they are signs of 'mental qualities'. Alison explains, on the usual lines, how objects become associated with these 'qualities' as their signs (e.g. by cause-and-effect, resemblance with other signs, etc.) but what the 'qualities' actually consist in remains extremely doubtful until, as he approaches the end of his work, it occurs to Alison to define them. The 'qualities' are divided into two classes: active (mental powers) and passive (affections, 'which we love, or with which we are formed to sympathize').[45] This is sufficiently clear, but helps not at all to dispel the confusion of the earlier part of the book. It would be impossible, in terms of the above classification, or indeed of any simple classification, to rationalize the following lists of 'qualities', both excerpted from Alison's first volume:

Dexterity . . . Taste . . . Convenience . . . Utility . . . Peace . . . Danger . . . Plenty . . . Desolation
      Strength . . . Delicacy . . . Coldness . . . Modesty . . . Old Age . . . Youth . . .[46]

No more is ultimately clear than that Alison believes objects will give aesthetic pleasure only when they are associated (whether consciously or subliminally) with abstract notions ('mental qualities') which are emotionally charged.

The painter is obliged to imply the 'mental qualities' which make his representations beautiful, but language allows the poet much freer scope: he can *confer* these qualities upon the objects he describes:

All the sublimity and beauty of the moral and intellectual world are at his disposal; and, by bestowing on the inanimate objects of his scenery the characters and affections of Mind, he can produce at once an expression which every capacity may understand, and every heart may feel.[47]

At first blush, this might seem an extraordinarily bold departure from the usual literal-minded imitation theory, and one which prefigures Romantic views about the creative Imagination, but we have to dismiss any such interpretation on recalling that the 'qualities of Mind' are merely general notions associated with the objects described, so that the poet in 'bestowing' the quality is merely describing the object in such a way as to make the association clear. That Alison thinks the 'bestowing' may be effected by the device of 'personification'[48] further indicates that the process he has in view is not the Romantics' imaginative recreation of experience. On the contrary, the poet aims at *representation*, and he is even at some disadvantage in this respect, compared with the painter: though language gives him greater freedom, his images are not so clear and precise.[49]

In any case, Alison still regards poetry as an 'art'. The passage quoted above, among others, clearly implies that the poet consciously seeks the means to his chosen ends.[50] Neo-Classical notions of composition are everywhere implicit in Alison's work, so that the conferring of 'mental qualities' may be seen without distortion as a rhetorical principle of invention and style—though perhaps a rather eccentric one.

Above all, Alison never suggests that the poet's purpose is to express his subjective experience—what the Romantics were to call 'sensibility'. This is all the more striking in that his description of the emotion of Taste as a reaction to nature and art bears, in some ways, a close resemblance to Romantic definitions of poetic thought and feeling.

The emotion of Taste is a complex one. It consists of a train of ideas and images 'analogous to the character or expression of the original object'[51] and arises out of a simple emotion which is the immediate reaction to the object. Critical attention inhibits this feeling.

It is then, indeed, in this powerless state of reverie, when we are carried on by our conceptions, not guiding them, that the deepest emotions of beauty or sublimity are felt.[52]

It is the initial simple emotion which influences the whole chain of associations.[53] Hence the necessity of unity in a work of art. Since

those trains of thought which attend the Emotions of Taste, are uniformly distinguished by some general principle of connexion, it ought to be found, that no Composition of Objects or qualities in fact produces such emotions, in which this Unity of character or of emotion is not preserved.[54]

Plainly, however, Alison regards this unity not as the *product* of the emotion of Taste (as the Romantics were to regard 'organic unity' as the product of Imagination) but—from the rhetorical point of view—as a means to *producing* it. The nature of his approach is clearly indicated in a remark immediately following the passage quoted above, which simply refers the reader to accepted doctrine:

This proposition also may be illustrated from the most superficial review of the Principles of Composition, in the different arts of Taste.

Alison's principle of unity is thus really a variation of the rule of propriety. He relates the emotions of Taste to the processes of art not as the experience which determines them—such would certainly be a Romantic or quasi-Romantic idea—but as the effect at which they aim. He is so firmly Neo-Classical in this and other respects, so clearly does not anticipate what is really original in, and characteristic of, Romanticism, that there can be no valid reason for regarding him as a 'precursor' of the Romantics.[55] He is more accurately classified as one of those writers—of whom we have now, perhaps, considered a sufficiently representative selection—who are developing the traditional theory in new directions. At best these writers can be seen as indirectly preparing the ground for Romanticism, since they canvassed notions which the Romantics were later to exploit—but the Romantics gave these ideas a very different significance, and were only able to do so because they had entirely abandoned traditional views.

The term 'pre-Romantic' is of little service to critical history. There is in fact only one document of the period to which it could reasonably be applied: Wordsworth's Preface to *Lyrical Ballads*.

The Preface undeniably breaks with traditional theory on all the important issues. Wordsworth's ideas—unlike those of other supposed 'pre-Romantics'—find little support in the rhetorical theory of composition and style, which indeed he is at some pains to reject. Yet the Preface is by no means a complete outline of Romantic doctrine.

As a theoretical statement it is not easy to analyse. For all the novelties Wordsworth propounds, he is in many lesser ways conservative in his views and it is not always immediately clear how he is reconciling the old ideas with the new. His prose style often baffles where we should most like it to be lucid. Further obscurities result from the fact that he is writing both an apology for the particular sort of poetry contained in *Lyrical Ballads* and a manifesto of his beliefs about poetry in general: we often cannot be sure (when the point seems material to a proper understanding of what he is saying) which of these two purposes is uppermost in his mind.

But this last circumstance suggests what is probably the most useful clue to the meaning of the Preface as a whole: Wordsworth seems so little conscious of his dual purpose, that perhaps we are wrong to draw so sharp a distinction between one aim and another. It is at any rate possible to find a connected and consistent argument in most of the Preface if we read it as primarily a rationale of the ballad genre, extended in certain important passages to account for poetry as a whole.

There seems little doubt, at least, that it is because Wordsworth has the ballad-form in mind that he is so often content to repeat traditional ideas. Thinking in terms of narrative poetry of a peculiar kind, he talks of poetry in general as representative, dramatic, 'pathetic'. He has by no means dismissed the Neo-Classical theory of imitation: he speaks of 'the most valuable object of all writing, whether in prose or verse; the great and universal passions of men, the most general and interesting of their occupations, and the entire world of nature . . .', and these 'objects' are to be 'described'.[56] This is the language of any eighteenth-century theorist.

So, too, (with an important reservation, to be noticed later) when he speaks of figurative language as the language of 'passion'.[57] Significantly, it is more than once dramatic 'passion' he is concerned with in these passages, 'where the Poet speaks through the mouths of his characters'.[58] Where Wordsworth discusses the

poet's own feelings he may still refer to 'passion'—perhaps only
in defence to the traditional cliché, but he has much more in
mind than the cliché implies. 'Passion' finds itself in company
with 'thought', 'feeling', 'moral sentiment', and above all 'sensation'.[59] We shall consider his views on this topic in more detail
below.

If it is because Wordsworth has to take into account the narrative and dramatic aspects of the ballad-form that he retains
certain Neo-Classical notions, it seems equally probable that
another markedly eighteenth-century feature of the Preface can be
put down to a similar cause. It is, in other words, not unreasonable
to suppose that a preference for the characteristic plainness of the
ballad-style prompts Wordsworth's refusal to discriminate between
the languages of poetry and prose.

Ostensibly Wordsworth was reacting *against* eighteenth-century
ideas of a special diction reserved for poetry. But though the practice of eighteenth-century poets may have given him valid grounds
for dissatisfaction, he was not really disagreeing in the main with
eighteenth-century theorists, who although they permitted, and
even in certain instances favoured, 'poetic diction' (in the sense
either of 'a special vocabulary' or 'an elevated style') did not
regard it as essential to poetry.[60]

Wordsworth's departure here from accepted views is revealed
in certain other aspects of his argument which we must reserve for
consideration below. It is worth noting, however, that when the
argument involves him in justifying metre as a 'superadded' asset
to poetry, his ideas are once more entirely consistent with Neo-
Classical opinion.[61]

Just as the conservative features of the Preface may be connected
with Wordsworth's predilection for the ballad form, so the original
features of his thought may be understood as arising from an
attempt to find a convincing theoretical support for it. Wordsworth
does in fact state—though not until the 1802 version of the
Preface—that his arguments are directly relevant to an understanding of the poems contained in *Lyrical Ballads*, poems which—if
they are not ballads in the pure sense—are yet (with the obvious
exceptions, such as *Tintern Abbey*) plainly inspired by traditional
examples of the form. It is also interesting that Wordsworth
believes his ideas to be new—'a practical faith in the opinions I
am wishing to establish is almost unknown'—and not only new,

but revolutionary: they will, if accepted, alter the entire complexion of contemporary critical thought. [62]

The peculiar character of the ballad as a literary form cannot be wholly accounted for in terms of Neo-Classical theory. It does not fit neatly into the category of dramatic narrative: it cannot be explained as a variety of the epic. Some of its most striking features derive from the fact that it is really a type of *lyric* poetry, and these features Neo-Classical theory is quite unfitted to explain.

In the first place its narrative connexions are rarely strictly logical: the pattern is surprising and strange, the succession of ideas disjointed and elliptical. Apparently unimportant details are curiously emphasized, large sections of the 'argument' simply left out. The whole gives no impression that an objective plan has been conscientiously worked out: the effect is rather of an un-studied narration, in which the sequence of ideas has been deter-mined not by preconceived intention but by the free associations of the poet's feeling. This feeling moreover, is clearly not 'passion', but something in the nature of an imaginative re-living of the story: a feeling *of* rather than *about* it.

The principles of composition suggested by Wordsworth in the Preface are very well suited to justifying this kind of poem. He says more than once that what chiefly interests him is 'the manner in which we associate ideas in a state of excitement'. [63] These passages are a little ambiguous in that they refer to his *characters'* associations as though they existed independently of his own, but the celebrated passage on poetry as the 'spontaneous overflow of powerful feelings' makes his general drift quite clear. Firstly, composition must be spontaneous. Wordsworth says he writes without any 'distinct purpose formally conceived'. Secondly, the materials of poetry are clearly not to be discursive, a series of logically interrelated ideas and images. And thirdly, though the first two requirements might by themselves be compared to those of some eighteenth-century Longinian, Wordsworth's 'powerful feelings' have nothing in common with the Longinian 'passion'.

Wordsworth's description of what is expressed in poetry, in the way both of thought and of feeling, suggests something much nearer the 'emotions of Taste' of the aestheticians. The poet's feeling proceeds from 'organic sensibility'—no 'passion' is in question here. It could not be, since 'influxes of feeling are modified and directed by . . . thoughts, which are indeed the representatives

of all our own past feelings'. The poet contemplates 'the relation of these general representatives to each other' until, if he
is 'originally possessed of much sensibility', habits of mind are
produced which he has only to obey 'blindly and mechanically'.[64]

Poetry, moreover, though it may be written in the language of
prose, no longer expresses prose thoughts. It is opposed to Science
(to 'Matter of Fact, or Science', as Wordsworth later elucidates).[65]
In the 1802 edition of the Preface he elaborates the distinction:
the truths of poetry, unlike the 'individual and local' truths of
science, are such as we feel 'carried alive into the heart by passion'.[66] The poet's knowledge is intuitive: he moves in an 'atmosphere of sensation'. He may one day deal in the discoveries of
science, but only when they 'shall be manifestly and palpably
material to us as enjoying and suffering beings'.[67]

The intuitions of 'sensibility' have replaced 'discursive thought'
as the stuff of poetry; the Poet's feeling is no longer 'passion', but
an inward feeling, stemming from sensation and bound up with
thought; the act of composition is no longer directed by any
deliberate impulse or external plan.

Though Wordsworth's wider-ranging philosophical disquisitions (contained for the most part in the 1802 additions to the
Preface) are largely irrelevant to any rationale of the ballad form
we may see these basic ideas as developed to justify the kind of
poetry he is interested in writing. For in the very midst of his
assertions about 'sensibility' and 'spontaneity' he is likely to speak,
since he still has a partially 'objective' genre in mind, of—for
example—'descriptions of such objects as strongly excite [the]
feelings'.[68]

A further characteristic of the ballad is possibly relevant to the
particular course of Wordsworth's thinking. Apart from the peculiar nature of the emotion the ballad expresses, an inner excitement
which generates an 'atmosphere' rather than an outwardly-
demonstrated feeling which invites the reader's sympathy, it seems
to take its very origin in this emotion and to derive all its force from
expressing it. At all events, its emotional effect cannot be fully
explained in terms of its plot, which is generally far too meagre to
be the important factor. As Wordsworth says of his own ballads,
it is the feeling 'therein developed [which] gives importance to the
action and situation, and not the action and situation to the
feeling'.[69]

Eighteenth-century theories, as we have seen, attributed an important role in composition to feeling as 'passion'. In Wordsworth, feeling assumes overwhelming predominance. It is the very source of poetry, which 'takes its origin from emotion recollected in tranquility'.[70] The poet is characterized almost entirely in terms of his intense sensibility, his unusual capacity for feeling,[71] and this capacity is not merely, as for the eighteenth century, a particularly keen susceptibility to emotion:[72] though it is that as well, it is also a propensity to 'rejoice in' feeling, to value it for its own sake and contemplate it with pleasure.[73]

Wordsworth's originality in this respect may at best be conjecturally related to his concern with the ballad. What seems again almost certain, however, is that it was the 'plain style' of the ballad which, as it led him to deny any difference between the language of poetry and prose, interested him in a poetry employing only the 'real language of men'. On this subject he is once more breaking entirely new ground.

The topic has been very often discussed, and there will be no need here to examine the whole of Wordsworth's argument. Its importance, for our purposes, lies in the fact that, since he rejects the view of style as 'presentation', a means to 'effectiveness' of one kind or another, he dismisses the whole of Neo-Classical thought on the subject. His criteria are realism ('language which the Poet himself [has] uttered . . . or which he [has] heard uttered by those around him'); and sincerity ('The earliest poets . . . generally wrote from passion excited by *real* events').[74] He will acknowledge no other considerations, and makes it clear that the aiming at effect hitherto thought proper in a poetic style is what he most abhors.[75]

The eighteenth century had of course demanded a style which was natural and sincere, but Wordsworth indicates very clearly that he has something different in view when he points out that the naturalness of his predecessors had been, paradoxically, a conventional naturalness. His strong antipathy to received notions makes him exaggerate his case, but the point is well made:

. . . the taste of men becoming gradually perverted, this language was received as a natural language: and at length by the influence of books upon men, did to a certain degree really become so. Abuses of this kind were imported from one nation to another, and with the progress of refinement this diction became daily more and more corrupt, thrusting out of sight the plain humanities of nature by a motley masquerade of tricks, quaintnesses, hieroglyphics, and enigmas.[76]

Thus, whereas eighteenth-century theorists had agreed that personification, a 'passionate' figure, was always acceptable (within the limits of propriety) as a genuine token of emotion, Wordsworth sees a different motive behind its use:

The Reader will find that personifications of abstract ideas rarely occur in these volumes; and, I hope, are utterly rejected, as an ordinary device to elevate the style, and raise it above prose.[77].

We may now judge to what extent Wordsworth, in spite of his retention of certain elements of Neo-Classical theory, had decided to dispense with the rest of it. In fact we find very little remaining.

The conception, crucial to the theory, of a subject elaborated according to pre-established design, he rejects almost completely. Poetry is spontaneously conceived and written, it is governed not by judgment and invention, but by feeling. For the moment, however, Wordsworth is not prepared altogether to abandon (as he and the other Romantics were later to do) the idea that a given 'subject' is the precondition of a poem.

'Thoughts', in the old sense, are no longer by themselves the materials of poetry. Though there is no hint as yet in the Preface of poetic Imagination, the central concept of later Romantic theory,[78] Wordsworth is moving towards some such idea: he has, at any rate, moved away from the rhetorical view that poetry is discursive in the same way as prose. Poetry expresses thoughts which are associated with feelings, arise out of feelings, and indeed *represent* feelings. 'Sensibility' is its subject-matter. Feeling as 'passion' occupies a subordinate place in the scheme: it is discussed chiefly as a factor in the dramatic portions of a poem.

Above all, no trace remains of the Neo-Classical dogma that language is the 'dress' of thought. The style of poetry must be as natural and spontaneous as its composition.

These ideas are so much, and so consistently, at variance with former theory that they can only be regarded as revolutionary. Moreover, they lead naturally in the direction of Romantic doctrine as it was later to be developed. On the other hand, since the Preface represents in some respects a compromise between the new and the old, and since, for that reason, it does not offer a complete theory of poetry on Romantic lines,[79] it cannot be classed unequivocally as a Romantic document. In its transitional position it is unique. There would be little point in postulating a 'pre-Romantic' movement confined to one work. But there is in fact only one work to which the label can justifiably be applied. For Wordsworth's Preface does not constitute a development of traditional theory: it can only be clearly and correctly understood as an experiment in the direction of a new one.

Part Two: *1800–1820*

10

Romantic Imagination

EIGHTEENTH-CENTURY theorists of poetry held a great many of their ideas in common. The classical-rhetorical premises were still widely accepted, while certain changes in approach and outlook, effected within the tradition, were passed on as part of it. Such positive divergencies as occurred are comparatively easy to observe, define, and 'place'. It has thus been possible to analyse and discuss the last phase of Neo-Classic theory as a whole.

A similar approach to Romantic theory is much less readily justifiable. It goes without saying that there is no established system of Romantic theory to which each individual critic subscribes. Nor does any single critic offer a coherent and complete system of his own. Coleridge's writings, which come nearest to doing this, are yet notoriously diffuse and fragmentary. Of the other critics only Wordsworth approaches Coleridge in the scope and connectedness of his views—and he falls a long way short of Coleridge. Wordsworth, moreover, was given to complaining that he wrote his criticism reluctantly under pressure, and to deprecating the whole idea of his being taken for a critic.[1] The work of both these critics abounds in minor contradictions and inconsistencies. It appears, for the most part—as does the rest of Romantic theory —in scattered prefaces, informal essays or lectures, letters, notes, jottings. There would seem at first sight to be no possible principle on which to collate and classify the mass of disorganized, heterogeneous material.

The lack of system apart, Romantic critics are never to be relied upon for clear definitions of terms, or consistency in the use of them. The idealistic spirit in which they write about poetry encourages enthusiastic effusion rather than analytical clarity, and it is sometimes difficult to extract any but the vaguest evocation of a meaning from their pronouncements.

Moreover, each critic writes from a strongly individual point of view: Shelley's Platonism distinguishes him sharply from Hazlitt, the *soi-disant* empiricist; Coleridge was nothing if not a Kantian, whereas Wordsworth claimed that he had never read Kant,[2] and maintained an obstinate independence of any systematic philosophy. It seems dubious whether, with such widely differing outlooks, these critics could hold any ground in common.

Yet, in spite of the difficulties, generalization to some extent about Romantic theory is possible. From totally different premises these writers arrived at strikingly similar conclusions.[3] As long as no more than the broadest classification of ideas is attempted— certainly no synthesis would be possible on a basis of fine discriminations—a certain community of outlook becomes apparent which is not too vague to be significant. It will, in fact, be the aim of the following chapters to show not only that it is possible to abstract a general theory of composition and style from the work of Romantic critics, but that this general outlook stands in a very definite and striking contrast to the ideas of the preceding age.

Since no more than a broad analysis of Romantic theory will be necessary to the purpose, less space will be devoted to it than to the foregoing analysis of Neo-Classic views. The range of reference will also be more limited. The first important exponents of Romanticism are a small handful: Coleridge, Wordsworth, Hazlitt, Shelley and—on the strength of a few isolated remarks in the Letters—Keats.[4] Inevitably Coleridge will claim the major share of attention: he occupies a position as the original, the influential critic of the period, such as cannot be claimed for any critic of the previous half-century. To say further at this point that he 'represents' Romantic criticism would be begging the question; nevertheless, since he is the most comprehensive and systematic of Romantic theorists, Romantic theory as a whole, as a logical structure of ideas, can best be discussed primarily in Coleridgean terms. His leading ideas offer a convenient frame of reference within or outside of which the views of other critics may be clearly placed.

Central to Coleridge's philosophical scheme is, of course, his theory of Imagination. But before taking up for consideration those aspects of the theory which are relevant here, some attempt must be made to describe certain ideas with which it is closely implicated: ideas about the kind of thought and feeling appropriate to poetry.

It was suggested in the previous chapter that one of the most important and original features of Wordsworth's Preface was his conception of the feeling proper to poetry: a feeling closely involved with thought, an inward feeling, 'emotion recollected in tranquillity'. Nothing in subsequent Romantic criticism comes any nearer a clear explanation of the nature of poetic feeling. ('Feeling' is in fact one of two or three crucial questions about which the Romantics are habitually vague and evasive.) Nevertheless, a great deal is said about the role of feeling in composition, and from what is said it may reasonably be inferred that the Romantics, when they talk of emotion, have something in mind other than the 'passion' or 'enthusiasm' so much in favour with eighteenth-century critics.

Feeling, in the first place, is often spoken of as the motive force of poetry: that which inspires the poet and impels him to write. Wordsworth, in this connexion, speaks of

. . . those primary sensations of the human heart, which are the vital springs of sublime and pathetic composition . . . And as from these primary sensations such composition speaks, so, unless correspondent ones listen promptly and submissively in the inner cells of the mind to whom it is addressed, the voice cannot be heard . . .[5]

Shelley refers to

. . . the pleasure and the enthusiasm arising out of those images and feelings in the vivid presence of which within his own mind consists at once the poet's inspiration and his reward.[6]

Coleridge, in a more philosophical language, says that a man

. . . must always be a poor and unsuccessful cultivator of the Arts if he is not impelled first by a mighty, inward power, a feeling, *quod nequeo monstrare, et sentio tantum;* nor can he make great advances in his Art, if, in the course of his progress, the obscure impulse does not gradually become a bright, and clear, and living Idea![7]

The terminology in each case is different, but this is to be expected not only here but in any possible collocation of Romantic views. Undeniably each of these critics is interpreting the facts in his own way, placing the emphasis on a different aspect of them, but clearly they are all referring to the same facts. Wordsworth's 'primary sensations', echoed in the 'inner cell of the mind', Shelley's 'enthusiasm and pleasure', Coleridge's intimations of an Idea, refer all of them not to extrovert and histrionic passions in the eighteenth-century sense, passions which may be readily labelled 'Love', 'Anger', 'Grief', but to feelings difficult to define, and experienced introspectively.[8]

Passion itself is described by Coleridge in one place as aroused immediately not by an external situation but by reflection upon it. Passion is

. . . a state of emotion, which tho' it may have its pre-disposing cause in the Body, and its occasion in external Incidents or Appearances, is yet not *immediately* produced by the incidents themselves, but by the person's Thoughts and Reflections concerning them. Or more briefly: A Passion is a state of emotion, having its immediate cause not in Things, but in our Thoughts of the Things . . .[9]

It is in fact characteristic of the Romantics to talk of feeling as associated with contemplation: Wordsworth's conception of 'emotion recollected', described in the Preface, is reflected in Coleridge's praise of his 'meditative pathos, a union of deep and subtle thought with sensibility'.[10] Hazlitt elaborates on precisely the same idea of feeling involved with meditation as the source of poetry.[11] Coleridge indeed, in a mood of speculative curiosity rare with the Romantics when they are writing on this topic, contrasts the emotion arising from 'the Life within' with the feeling that displays itself externally, the 'passion' of the rhetoricians. He is commenting on 'the very rare occurrence of strong and deep Feeling in conjunction with free power and vivacity in the expression of it'. 'The most eminent tragedians,' he says,

Garrick for instance, are known to have had their emotions as much at command, and almost as much on the surface, as the muscles of their countenances; and the French, who are all Actors, are proverbially heartless. Is it that it is a false and feverous state for the Centre to live in the Circumference? The vital warmth seldom rises to the surface in the form of sensible Heat, without becoming hectic and inimical to the Life within, the only source of real sensibility. Eloquence itself—I speak of it as habitual and at call—too often is, and is always like to engender, a species of histrionism.[12]

Coleridge recognizes another type of feeling, or, more probably, another manifestation of the same type, in the 'excitement' which accompanies the exercise of the faculties in poetic composition.[13] But though this idea—with what he deduces from it—is an interesting feature of his theory in general (and apparently one of his few really original insights), it seems, unaccountably, to have made no mark on either his contemporaries or successors.

The second important function of feeling which all Romantic theorists acknowledge is its modifying influence upon thought. Feeling, during the eighteenth century, was held to influence the *course* of a poet's thought, his choice of detail or turn of expression: the Romantics consider that feeling modifies not only the form, but the very substance of thought. In view of the fact that feeling for them is contemplative and inward, this follows as a matter of course. Feeling is conceived as the medium of poetic thought, exerting a transmuting and, as it were, cohesive power. Coleridge uses the chemical analogy of a mordaunt, or base, in describing the way in which feeling acts as an 'intermedium of affinity', reconciling the impulse to expression with the impulse to form.[14] His particular view, in this case, is exceptional with its stress on feeling as a determining influence (though at one remove) on the *external* features of poetry, but the conception of feeling generally as a medium, and as a principle of integration is clear. A similar idea is conveyed in different terms by Wordsworth. Having raised in one of his essays upon epitaphs the question of what constitutes perfection in an epitaph, he decides that it consists in a due proportion of feeling ('the common or universal feeling of humanity') with thought ('a distinct and clear conception, conveyed to the reader's mind, of the individual [commemorated]').

The general sympathy ought to be quickened, provoked, and diversified, by particular thoughts, actions, images—circumstances of age, occupation, manner of life . . . and these ought to be bound together and solemnized into one harmony by the general sympathy. The two powers should temper, restrain, and exalt each other.[15]

In its transforming function, feeling is sometimes assimilated with Imagination.[16] Coleridge speaks of 'the blending, *fusing* power of Imagination and Passion'.[17] In a note on *Venus and Adonis* he refers to the imaginative modification of forms by passion, characterized by

the different manner in which inanimate objects, or objects un-
impassioned themselves, are seen by the mind in moments of
strong excitement, and according to the kind of excitement—
whether of jealousy, or rage, or love, in its only appropriate sense
of the word, or of the lower impulses of our nature, or finally, of
the poetic feeling. It is, perhaps, chiefly in the power of producing
or reproducing the latter that the poet stands distinct.[18]

(Here, it will be noticed, is yet further evidence of the Romantic
conception of a poetic feeling that is distinct from passion in the
ordinary sense.) Hazlitt, too, interrelates feeling and Imagination.

Imagination is, more properly, the power of carrying on a given
feeling into other situations, which must be done best according to
the hold which the feeling itself has taken of the mind . . . in
general the strength and consistency of the imagination will be in
proportion to the strength and depth of feeling . . .[19]

Feeling is not only, for the Romantics, the inspiration of the
poet and, as integrated with Imagination, the informing principle
of poetry, it is also as such the very material of poetry: that in which
poetry may be said partly to consist. Coleridge habitually speaks of
a union of feeling and thought as the content of poetry.[20] The
passage in Wordsworth's Preface which describes the connexion of
feeling and thought in the poet's mind has already been commented
on.[21] In another context he emphasizes this necessary fusion of
thought and feeling. 'Your first position', he says in a letter to a
friend,

that every idea which passes through a poet's mind may be made
passionate, and therefore poetical, I am not sure that I understand.
If you mean through a poet's mind when in a poetical mood, the
words are nothing but an identical proposition.[22]

Even more often are images[23] spoken of as 'blended' with
feeling. A typical pronouncement of Coleridge's is reported as
follows:

He had said that images taken from nature and accurately described
did not characterize *the poet*. They must be blended or merged
with other images, the offspring of imagination, and blended,
besides, with the passions or other pleasurable emotions which
contemplation has awakened in the poet himself.[24]

'In a dramatic composition,' says Shelley, 'the imagery and the passion should interpenetrate one another . . .'; and Hazlitt, too, speaks of poetry as blending feeling with 'the most striking forms of nature'.[25]

The evidence clearly shows that when the Romantics talk of feeling in poetry they are not referring to 'passion' in the hitherto-accepted sense. Romantic feeling is closely bound up with thought: it is variously represented as arising from thought, as the medium of thought, as modifying thought, as fused with thought. These different accounts of the function of feeling do not, it is true, contribute much towards a logical definition of the term in its new usage, but they do suggest a fairly clear idea of what is involved. It is not difficult to see that poetic feeling for the Romantics is what, in the absence of a more exact term, we would probably call 'sensibility'. It is a reaction from experience, inward and reflective —as much a matter of thought as of feeling—not a response to experience manifested outwardly, the feeling that is translated immediately into speech and action.

It is not, of course, logical, discursive thought that accompanies sensibility; but thought, again, of a special kind and of which, again, no precise definition can be given. For the first time in the history of criticism, poetic thought is distinguished from the ordinary kind.[26] Coleridge, for example, finds that the poetry of the Augustans was 'characterized not so much by poetic thoughts, as by thoughts translated into the language of poetry'.[27]

Poetic thought, as a product of imagination and feeling, bears no relation whatever to the kind of thinking which analyses, combines and connects. This kind of thought is now regarded as almost irrelevant to poetry. The passage is well known in which Wordsworth condemns

> . . . that false secondary power
> By which we multiply distinctions, then
> Deem that our puny boundaries are things
> That we perceive, and not that we have made.[28]

As Hazlitt says, poetry

does not define the limits of sense, or analyse the distinctions of the understanding, but signifies the excess of the imagination beyond the actual or ordinary impression of any object or feeling.[29]

It is everywhere assumed that the substance of poetry is the uncertain, the unfixed, the intuitive, the ineffable. Each critic makes the assumption in his own way. Coleridge, characteristically concerned with the 'reconciliation of opposites', speaks of

a middle state of mind more strictly appropriate to the imagination than any other, when it is, as it were, hovering between images. As soon as it is fixed on one image, it becomes understanding; but while it is unfixed and wavering between them, attaching itself permanently to none, it is imagination.[30]

In one of his essays upon epitaphs Wordsworth expresses an idea which is often present by implication elsewhere in his writings. 'A distinct conception . . . of the individual lamented' should, he says, be given implicitly rather than explicitly.

The character of a deceased friend or beloved kinsman is not seen, no—nor ought to be seen, otherwise than as tree through a tender haze or a luminous mist, that spiritualizes and beautifies it . . .[31]

Shelley and Hazlitt underline the point, each after his own fashion. 'The province of the imagination', says Hazlitt,

is principally visionary, the unknown and undefined. . . . It is the undefined and uncommon that gives birth and scope to the imagination; we can only fancy what we do not know.[32]

Shelley, in a well-known passage, declares that poetry 'arrests the vanishing apparitions which haunt the interlunations of life', 'redeems from decay the visitations of the divinity in man'.[33] Here is a subject-matter for poetry which is nothing if not indeterminate and a-rational.[34]

A clue to the meaning of these statements in terms of matter of fact is offered by De Quincey, a critic whose work falls outside the period under study, but who can often be relied upon for the succint and clear exposition of Romantic beliefs that one looks for in vain in earlier sources. 'In very many subjective exercises of the mind,' he says,

—as, for instance, in that class of poetry which has been formally designated by this epithet (meditative poetry, we mean, in opposition to the Homeric, which is intensely objective),[35] the problem before the writer is to project his own inner mind; to bring out consciously what yet lurks by involution in many unanalysed feelings; in short, to pass through a prism and radiate into distinct elements what previously had been even to himself but dim and confused ideas intermixed with each other.[36]

This is no philosophic definition of poetic thought, but at least a clear indication in plain English of the factors involved: 'the inner mind', 'unanalysed feelings', 'dim and confused ideas'.[37]

The Romantic account of 'poetic thought' is not confined to general statements of the kind quoted above; and, were a more detailed investigation to be carried out into the subject, striking differences would appear between the views of individual critics. But the purpose of the foregoing has been merely to characterize broadly what was considered the kind of thought proper to poetry, and on these general grounds there is plainly a consensus of opinion. Before leaving the topic it is worth noting that Coleridge almost invariably defines Imagination as a process of 'blending' or 'fusing'. The 'materials' upon which Imagination works must evidently be such as are susceptible to transformation in this way: as Wordsworth calls them, 'the plastic, the pliant and the indefinite'.[38]

In fact it is partly the purpose of Coleridge's and Wordsworth's distinction between Fancy and Imagination to establish that Fancy deals in 'fixities and definites', the images and ideas that are stored in the memory, bounded and clear, whereas the sphere of Imagination is a kind of thought that is diffuse and undefined. And, as regards Imagination it is not only Wordsworth who shares Coleridge's point of view:[39] Shelley and Hazlitt both speak of Imagination as a shaping, synthesizing power, distinct from the discriminating, combining faculty of Understanding.[40]

It would not be to the purpose here to embark on any detailed interpretation of the Romantic theory of Imagination, particularly since the subject has already been very fully discussed. Only one aspect of the theory need be briefly considered: Imagination is, for the Romantics, as it were a first principle of composition, and as such it has nothing in common with eighteenth-century principles of Invention. The latter are principles of association, combination, design and are clearly what Wordsworth and Coleridge intended to subsume under the term Fancy, assigning to them a secondary importance in their scheme. Imagination, all the Romantics agree, is a shaping, unifying power whose function is not to construct according to plan, but to produce (as by a process of natural growth) an integrated whole which is more than simply the sum of its parts. In Coleridge's version of the theory the implications of this view are very obvious, and perhaps in this instance he can, without prejudice to the accuracy of the general picture, be taken to 'represent' Romantic theory. He is the only one of the Romantic critics to examine in any detail the philosophic foundations of ideas about Imagination which all the rest accept; moreover, it will not be so much the precise terms in which he announced his results that count as representative, as the kind of notion he is attempting to define.

It is revealing, in the first place, that for Coleridge poetic or secondary Imagination is an analogue of perception (Primary Imagination).[41] Poetic Imagination, therefore, like perception, is intuitive and immediate, though it 'coexists with the conscious will'. As in perception, there can in poetic Imagination be no distinction between form and substance, or, it follows, between the structure or design of a poem and the 'thoughts' that fill out the design—design and thought are one act and one thing.

In the *Treatise on Method* (and in *The Friend*, which contains another version of this essay) Coleridge further elaborates his views. Imagination mediates between Reason and Sense, that is, it employs the materials of Sense, but it is regulated by Reason. The ideas of Reason—intuitive and unanalysable[42]—are the principles of Method—Method, to which poetry owes 'its whole charm, and all its beauty, and all its power'.[43] But the Ideas are dynamic, creative principles—acting through Imagination, they find embodiment in images of sense. It is as if there were a principle of growth in the seed which, in fulfilling itself, transformed the seed into a plant.

The transcendental vocabulary is perhaps less important here than the process which it describes: a guiding idea, which is intuited, sensed rather than thought, evolves through the instinctive operation of Imagination, and without the mediation of judgment or understanding, into a work of art. It is not only the vocabulary of traditignal theory that has been rejected: invention, disposition, design. Clearly Coleridge is not even talking about the same things. He is describing a way of writing poetry which would probably not have made sense to anyone a generation before.[44]

Conversely, his view of the matter is perfectly compatible with, and something of the sort is distinctly implied by, the convictions in general of his contemporaries.

Necessarily involved in the theory of Imagination as intuitive creation is the belief that poetry is written without calculation or studied forethought. The eighteenth century had acknowledged a considerable element of freedom in the act of composition: the roles of fancy or feeling in invention were, within limits, naturally regarded as unrestricted by rule. But for the Romantics there is no element at all of deliberation or choice in the production of poetry. Conscious design and conscious purpose—with all the inevitable concomitants of 'art'—are no part of Romantic requirements.

This statement must immediately be qualified in the light of Coleridge's theory of metre. Though this seems to be the only occasion on which he explicitly allows an element of deliberation in the writing of poetry, he is, on this one occasion quite un-equivocal and emphatic about it. The poet's state of mind, as he describes it here, is characterized by an involuntary conflict between passion and will ('that spontaneous effort which strives to hold in check the workings of passion'). The conflict is resolved in metre 'by a supervening act of the will and judgment, consciously and for the foreseen purpose of pleasure'. As a result 'the traces of present volition' will be discernible as well in the language of the poem.[45]

It has already been remarked that Coleridge's theory of metre is uniquely his own. It represents, in fact, a subtle variation on the generally accepted view that creation is spontaneous; at the same time it is not strictly compatible with that view. It is worth observing, however, that Coleridge allows the factor of conscious purpose in composition a very limited sphere of influence: metre and diction, the 'externals' of poetry. The role of conscious purpose is limited too by the conditions of its own genesis, as Coleridge conceives it: it is a spontaneous reaction to, and its existence is governed by, the element of 'passion'. So that even as conscious purpose it is the product of an original spontaneous impulse, its only *raison d'être* is to counteract that impulse.

Here or elsewhere, it must be added, there is never any question, with Coleridge, of a formulated plan or even of a specific con-sciously-conceived aim which regulates the writing of poetry. He does state that there are parts of a poem 'of any length' which must

be artificially constructed: a poem need not be all poetry;[46] but
poetry, as he constantly repeats, is spontaneously engendered 'by
the energy without effort of the poet's own mind'.[47]

Wordsworth, too, is to be found saying:

Much is to be done by rule; the great outline is previously to be
conceived in distinctness, but the consummation of the work
must be trusted to resources that are not tangible, though known
to exist.[48]

But elsewhere, and more frequently, he corroborates without
reservation the general Romantic view that 'if Poetry comes not as
naturally as the Leaves to a tree it had better not come at all'.[49]
He claims that his verses 'have all risen up of their own accord'.[50]
And again:

. . . at no period in my life have I been able to write verses that do
not spring up from an inward impulse of some sort or other; so
that they neither seem proposed nor imposed.[51]

Shelley is unequivocally on the side of spontaneity.

Poetry . . . is not subject to the control of the active powers of the
mind, . . . its birth and recurrence have no necessary connexion
with the consciousness or will. It is presumptuous to determine
that these are the necessary conditions of all mental causation,
when mental effects are experienced unsusceptible of being
referred to them.[52]

It is interesting that Jeffrey, hardly a Romantic himself, but not
always unsympathetic to Romantic ideas, tries his hand at analysing
the Romantic method of compostion in the work of one of its
purest exponents. The result is by no means an unfair account of
Romantic principles as revealed in practice. (Jeffrey even attempts,
later in the essay, the kind of philosophic justification of these
principles which the poet in question might have put forward in
his own defence.)

The great distinction . . . between him [Keats] and these divine
authors [Fletcher, Jonson, Milton] is, that imagination in them is
subordinate to reason and judgment, while, with him, it is para-
mount and supreme—that their ornaments and images are
employed to embellish and recommend just sentiments, engaging

incidents, and natural characters, while his are poured out without measure or restraint, and with no apparent design but to unburden the breast of the author, and give vent to the overflowing vein of his fancy. . . . It seems as if the author had ventured every thing that occurred to him in the shape of a glittering image or striking expression . . . and so wandered on, equally forgetful whence he came, and heedless whither he was going, till he had covered his pages with an interminable arabesque of connected and incongruous figures, that multiplied as they extended, and were only harmonized by the brightness of their tints, and the graces of their forms.[53]

As we have seen, the Romantic theory of composition is primarily a theory of Imagination, which in turn involves certain presuppositions about the kind of thought and feeling appropriate to poetry. But the poetic Imagination is autonomous and creates spontaneously. With certain reservations about Coleridge and his theory of metre, it is fair to say that the Romantics are on the whole convinced that poetry is actually written without any preconceived purpose or conscious control from the judgment and will. There would seem little more to be said on the subject of a Romantic theory of composition: poetry is no longer composed, it happens.

However, it is still to the purpose to ask *how* poetry happens, how the unanalysable processes of Imagination can be said to embody themselves in any distinct form, more particularly in language, and it will be the business of the following chapter to examine such attempts as the Romantics made to answer this question.

11

The Romantic View of Composition and Style

THE Romantic critics are, needless to say, not only convinced of the irrelevance of rules, but positively hostile to any conception of poetry as an 'art' which is learnt and practised according to established principles. Their objections to such views are well-known. 'The Genius of Poetry', says Keats,

> must work out its own salvation in a man: It cannot be matured by law and precept, but by sensation & watchfulness itself. That which is creative must create itself . . .[1]

Similar disparagements of law and precept are to be found in Shelley and Hazlitt.[2]

Romantic opinions on composition and style consist, however, in something more than a sweeping rejection of 'art': they have a positive bearing as well, of a kind that Coleridge best indicates.

> Could a rule be given from without [he says] poetry would cease to be poetry, and sink into a mechanical art . . . The rules of Imagination are themselves the very powers of growth and production.[3]

It is about the 'rules of Imagination . . . the powers of growth and production' that the Romantic theorists do find something to say, though they acknowledge no rules in the ordinary sense. Their statements are descriptive, and not prescriptive, but they do at least convey the very positive prescriptive implication that poetry which results from a process other than the one they describe is not poetry, or not worthy of the name.

On the question of composition, as in most other departments of poetic theory, it is Coleridge, of all the Romantics, who is most explicit. He does not of course discuss composition in anything like the thorough and systematic manner of the previous age. But he has enough to say about form and structure, and the way they arise, to constitute a Romantic equivalent in this respect of rhetorical theory.

His definition of a poem, the principal feature of which is a definition of poetic structure, might almost, in fact, be echoing the views of the previous generation. A poem is that species of writing which (among other things) permits

a pleasure from the whole consistent with a consciousness of pleasure from the component parts;—and the perfection of which is, to communicate from each part the greatest immediate pleasure compatible with the largest sum of pleasure on the whole.[4]

This reads like one more formulation of the Neo-Classical ideal of 'propriety', the ideal of a harmonious whole to which each part is delicately adjusted. Coleridge, however, has more than the superficial harmoniousness of 'propriety' in mind, as he makes clear when he repeats the definition in the *Biographia*.

The parts of a poem must each, it is true, yield a 'distinct gratification' which contributes to, and blends with, 'delight from the whole'—so much might be construed as traditional doctrine. On the other hand, no part should be detachable from the whole—and this implies a much more intimate connexion of parts and whole than would have been thought necessary in the previous century. When Coleridge condemns the sort of poem which consists of 'a series of striking lines or distiches, each of which, absorbing the whole attention of the reader to itself, becomes disjoined from its context, and forms a separate whole, instead of a harmonizing part',[5] the principle of unity he considers offended is not merely one which safeguards an external unity of tone and style, as does the principle of 'propriety', but one which demands an inner connexion of the parts with each other and with the whole, so that no one element of a poem can be fully effective when considered by itself.

When we come to examine Coleridge's descriptions of the process of composition, this indication that he regarded unity of structure in a very different light from the Neo-Classical critics—who were satisfied with logic and 'propriety'—is confirmed by everything he says. Poetic creation is analogous to organic growth: the parts of a poem are not 'separately conceived and then by a succeeding act put together'.[6] The whole is not the sum of its parts, an aggregate of discrete, connected elements, but the end-product of a single 'vital' process, in which the parts are merely stages. '*Growth* as in a plant. No ready cut and dried [structure]; and yet everything *prepared* because the preceding involves or was the link of association.'[7]

This part of Coleridge's theory is too well known to need further elucidation here. It will be enough to observe the sharp contrast his view of poetic composition offers to that of the late eighteenth century: Coleridge seeing it as a process of natural growth, resulting in an 'organic' unity, his predecessors as a systematic and piecemeal *construction* resulting in a unity which—the claims of 'propriety' apart—is primarily logical, the consequence of preconceived design.

Coleridge's fellow-Romantics are not nearly as interested as he in questions of form and structure, though his ideas are by no means incompatible with their respective theoretical standpoints, and here and there in their work we do find reflections of, or at least agreement with, his views.[8]

Some further ideas, closely involved with these views, may now be worth examining. The theory of organic form makes no distinction between the subject-matter of a poem and its structure, nor does it admit that a subject may exist *in abstracto* to be elaborated or 'treated' in the process of composition. The poet's method is spontaneous and unanalysable: no theoretical separation is possible between potential subject and actual poem. Subject and poem are one.

Hence references in Romantic writing to 'subjects' for poetry are rare, and, when they do occur, nearly always imply a poet's personal interest in a theme, or its capacity to inspire him, not his objective assessment of its possibilities as a subject.[9] In fact, as scarcely needs pointing out, many of the best Romantic poems have no 'subject' at all in the traditional sense, but originate in slight and trivial occasions—the sight of a landscape, the song of a bird, or the putting down of a book.

If the Romantics show no interest in the sort of subject which may be 'worked up' into a poem, they do not altogether rule out the possibility of a content distinct from its expression—though the word 'content' must here be understood in a sense very different from that suggested by the word 'subject'. For the Romantics, 'content' is the feeling-thought of Imagination; and it is expressed through symbols. The relationship between the two is not a matter of choice—here again the theorist can lay down no rules, he can only describe what happens—nevertheless, to this extent the Romantic poem is discovered to be not simply a natural and direct utterance, but indirect, and dependent, in a sense, upon artifice.

Imagination is a kind of thought, emotional, diffuse, and indistinct, which cannot possibly be directly expressed in the normal categories and structures of language. The indeterminate cannot be determined. But Imagination may find determinate expression in the symbol, which constitutes a clearly-defined focus, as it were, for a complex of undefined thought and feeling. It is this conception of the indefinite expressing itself through the definite that underlies all Coleridge's references to, and descriptions of, imaginative activity, for example his celebrated statement in the *Biographia* that Imagination reveals itself in

the balance or reconcilement of opposite or discordant qualities: of sameness, with difference; of the general, with the concrete; the idea, with the image; the individual, with the representative; the sense of novelty and freshness, with old and familiar objects . . .[10]

In each case the 'reconcilement of . . . discordant qualities' consists in a fusion of the particular with the general, the specific with the undefined.

Elsewhere in his writings Coleridge attempts to explain the function and account for the efficacy of symbols, using the analogy, borrowed from him above, of a focus:

I do not know whether you are opticians enough to understand me when I speak of a Focus formed by converging rays of Light or Warmth in the *Air*. Enough that it is so—that the Focus exercises a power altogether different from that of the rays not converged—and to our sight and feeling acts precisely as if a solid flesh and blood reality were here. Now exactly such focal entities we are all more or less in the habit of creating for ourselves in the world of Thought. For the given point in the Air take any given *word*, fancy-image, or remembered emotion. Thought after Thought, Feeling after Feeling, and at length the sensations of Touch, and the blind Integer of the numberless number of the Infinitesimals that make up our sense of existing, converge in it—

and there ensues a working on our mind so utterly unlike what any
one of the confluents, separately considered, would produce, and
no less disparate from what any mere Generalization of them all,
would present to us, that I do not wonder at the unsatisfactoriness
of every attempt to undeceive the person by an analysis, however
clear. The focal word has acquired a *feeling* of *reality*—it heats
and burns, makes itself be felt. If we do not grasp it, it seems to
grasp us, as with the hand of flesh and blood, and completely
counterfeits an immediate presence, an intuitive knowledge. And
who can reason against an intuition?[11]

The extract has been quoted in full since it is the most detailed,
and the clearest, Romantic explanation of the origin and function
of symbols. We find in Wordsworth, too, however, an extended
account of the way in which an image may acquire symbolic
power. This passage (in a letter to *The Friend*) treats of the efficacy
of symbols in the moral life, rather than in literature, but since the
two are, for Wordsworth, so intimately related, his observations
can reasonably be understood as applying to both.[12]

The Romantic symbol is not, of course, a conventional symbol.
Coleridge is firm on this point:

[A symbol] always partakes of the Reality which it renders intelligible; and while it enunciates the whole, abides itself as a
living part in that Unity, of which it is the representative. The
other [Allegories] are but empty echoes which the fancy arbitrarily
associates with apparitions of matter.[13]

Nor again are Romantic symbols to be understood as images
derived from some ulterior reality, the forms of some visionary
world such as Blake's. *The Fine Arts*, says Coleridge,

belong to the outward world, for they all operate by the images of
sight and sound, and other sensible impressions; and without a
delicate tact for these, no man ever was, or could be, either a
Musician or a Poet . . .[14]

The symbol is an image derived from the material world of
everyday reality. We are given to understand that its symbolic
power is not the result of arbitrary convention, nor of any mystical
virtues inherent in the image itself: it is a feature of ordinary
experience.

Romantic discussions of the *meaning* of symbols, however,

often take us into the realms of metaphysics. The symbol expresses, as we have seen, a concentration of intuitive thought, or feeling, or both. Its content is sometimes described as 'thought' or 'feeling' in a fairly straightforward manner—in terms, in fact, which recall the more recent theory of the 'objective correlative'. Hazlitt describes the method of poetry as 'the perfect coincidence of the image and the words with the feeling we have and of which we cannot get rid in any other way, that gives an instant "satisfaction to the thought"'.[15] Jeffrey, in his attempt at a sympathetic account of Keats's work, finds that he relies largely on 'pure poetry'—in which

a number of bright pictures are presented to the imagination, and a fine feeling expressed of those mysterious relations by which visible external things are assimilated with inward thoughts and emotions, and become the images and exponents of all passions and affections.[16]

But the Romantics are generally bolder in their views on this score. It is one of their stranger beliefs—yet the one which has cast perhaps the most powerful spell of all on succeeding ages—that the exercise of Imagination is also in some way the apprehension of Truth. Hence, the poet in expressing his intuitions by means of symbols is at the same time supplying clues to the enigmas of metaphysics. The symbolic expression of Imagination is a revelation of the reality beyond reality. Symbols are the language of transcendental truth.

This doctrine, conceived in different ways and expressed in different terms, is widely held by the Romantics. In Hazlitt's opinion every object may be to the poet 'a symbol of the affections and a link in the chain of our endless being'. The poet's task is to unravel 'this mysterious web of thought and feeling'.[17] Wordsworth points to the affinity between poetry and religion, religion which deals in the infinite and the ineffable and can only represent its doctrine to human understanding by means of symbols. Poetry is also 'ethereal and transcendent, yet incapable to sustain her existence without sensous incarnation.'[18] Shelley's views are similar:

[Poetry] reproduces the common universe of which we are portions and percipients, and it purges from our inward sight the film of familiarity which obscures from us the wonder of our being.

. . . it strips the veil of familiarity from the world, and lays bare the naked and sleeping beauty, which is the spirit of its forms.[19]

As we might expect, references in Coleridge are innumerable to the transcendental affinities of the symbol, either its power to express 'spirit', i.e. intuitions of truth and beauty,[20] or, which comes to much the same thing, to embody the Ideas of Reason.[21]

Since the symbols of Imagination, being representations of much-in-little (or, in Coleridgean language, of 'multeity in unity') are as much the expression of Beauty as of Truth, we are now on the fringe of aesthetic theory. But our concern is not with aesthetics and we need, before taking leave of this topic, note only one further feature of the Romantic theory of composition—the entire absence from it of any preoccupation with 'effect'.

The Romantics, oddly enough, have nothing to say about the way in which poetry moves a reader: they are content to state that it does. But the appeal of poetry to imagination they conceive of very differently from their predecessors. It appeals, that is, to Imagination in the Romantic sense, and not simply to the image-making faculty which had hitherto gone by that name. 'The poet should paint to the imagination, not to the fancy', says Coleridge, and he quotes a passage from Milton which he calls 'creation rather than painting'. The reader must not be put to the labour of visualizing a picture, image by image: he should receive the 'co-presence of the whole picture flashed at once upon the eye'.[22] The reader's activity is characteristically described in Romantic theory by the words 'energy'[23] or 'power'.[24] He is expected not merely to respond appropriately and sympathetically; he must exercise his own creative faculties in reading.

The Romantic theory of composition could not, by its very nature, receive precise formulation, but we have seen that, unsystematic though it is, it is clearly opposed on every important question to the theory which preceded it. It admits no rules, no possibility of design, no elaboration for effect. Poetic composition is no longer a practical skill; it has become an esoteric activity, insusceptible to analysis, dependent entirely on innate and intuitive talent.

As we might expect, Romantic views on style are equally clearly distinguishable from previous opinion.

Coleridge in the *Biographia*, maintains that a good style is untranslatable: it admits no word or phrase which can be exchanged for another 'without loss of sense of dignity'.[25] By dignity, however, he means only 'the absence of ludicrous and debasing associations'.[26] The implication is clearly that the adventitious dignity conferred by 'amplification' may be dispensed with. Coleridge's position is, in fact, very close to that of Wordsworth in the Preface to *Lyrical Ballads*. The meaning of the words in a good style will be irreducible. This meaning will comprise, of course, not only their sense but the associations they carry by virtue of the 'character, mood and intentions' of the author.[27] But the author's intentions, it goes without saying, will never include a striving after effect. Like Wordsworth, Coleridge puts down rhetorical artifice to 'the desire of exciting wonderment at his powers in the author'.[28]

Coleridge, then—in spite of the fact that he takes issue with Wordsworth about the possibility of a poetry employing the 'real language of men', a phrase of Wordsworth's that he takes too literally[29]—agrees with Wordsworth that the chief criterion of style is naturalness. In other respects his observations on style in the *Biographia* do not diverge very far from Neo-Classical opinion. They may, that is to say, be understood as recommending 'propriety'. It is not until we set them in the context of Coleridge's remarks elsewhere on the same subject that we realize that the 'propriety', if it is such, is not a contrived propriety in relation to the aim or design or emotional tenor of a work, it is integrity, the poet's fidelity to an inner impulse.

For elsewhere in his writings Coleridge maintains that style is as much a spontaneous product of Imagination as the form and the content of poetry: and indeed, given his fundamental assumptions, this is bound to be so.

In the *Treatise on Method* we are told that the man of superior, i.e. 'methodical', mind (and the poet is one representative of the species) may be recognized 'in the unpremeditated and evidently habitual arrangement of his words, flowing spontaneously and necessarily from the clearness of the leading Idea'.[30] Again, of Shakespeare, always his model of the true poet, Coleridge notes:

Even the very diction evidencing a mind that, proceeding from some one great conception, finds its only difficulty in arranging and disciplining the crowd of thoughts which from that matrix rush in to enlist themselves. No looking outward by wit or book-memory.[31]

Other critics agree that the language of poetry springs spontaneously from the Imagination. Shelley, for example:

... poetry ... expresses those arrangements of language, and especially metrical language, which are created by that imperial faculty, whose throne is contained within the invisible nature of man.[32]

A certain deliberation, however, may be required in the process of writing. Wordsworth, replying to a friend who has been discussing the subject with him, asks:

... do you simply mean, that such thoughts as arise in the process of composition should be expressed in the first words that offer themselves, as being likely to be the most energetic and natural? If so, this is not a rule to be followed without cautious exceptions. My first expressions I often find detestable; and it is frequently true of second words as of second thoughts, that they are best.[33]

But revision of this sort is scarcely the careful deliberation that Neo-Classical theory demanded, hedging the writer about as it did with principles he must conscientiously follow. It is simply a rejection of one word or expression for a better, which might, one is to assume, offer itself equally spontaneously. Coleridge, too, in the *Biographia* speaks of poetry 'in which every line, every phrase, may pass the ordeal of deliberation and deliberate choice': it is 'an arduous work'. But it is the negative work of keeping style free from the 'affectations and misappropriations' of current diction, a work which will finally be the 'result and pledge of a watchful good sense, of fine and luminous distinction, and of complete self-possession'[34]—not, one may notice, of ingenious invention or any positive skill in the art of exploiting language.

The idea, it need hardly be added, that language is the 'dress' of thought finds no support from writers so committed to ideals of naturalness and spontaneity. Wordsworth professes not to understand how the poets of former ages could have respected any such principle:

It is unaccountable to me how men could ever proceed as Racine (and Alfieri I believe) used to do, first, writing their Plays in Prose, and then, turning them into Verse. It may answer with so slavish a language and so enslaved a Taste, as the French have, but with us, it is not to be thought of.[35]

His objections to the notion are, characteristically, supported by a moralizing philosophy:

Words are too awful an instrument for good and evil, to be trifled with; they hold above all other external powers a dominion over our thoughts. If words be not . . . an incarnation of the thought, but only a clothing for it, then surely will they prove an ill gift . . . Language, if it do not uphold, and feed, and leave in quiet, like the power of gravitation or the air we breathe, is a counter-spirit, unremittingly and noiselessly at work, to subvert, to lay waste, to vitiate, and to dissolve.[36]

To the idea that language is the *incarnation* of thought, the idea that words are *constituents* of thought is a natural corollary. Wordsworth, in the essay quoted above, and on the same page, speaks of expressions which are a 'constituent part and power or function in thought'; and Coleridge is reported as saying:

. . . could it be supposed that words should be no object of the human mind? If so, why was style cultivated in order to make the movement of words correspond with the thoughts and emotions they were to convey, so that words themselves are a part of the emotion? And in Coleridge's opinion it would be no ill compliment to call [an] author 'a man of words', if the term were used in all the force and sublimity it naturally contained.[37]

This raises the interesting question of how far the 'poetic thought' of the Romantics is thought actually determined *by* language and the associations of words with each other, as distinct from the 'discursive' thought of the Neo-Classics which consists of 'thoughts' that are determined *in* language. Any answer is bound to be highly speculative, but there is one further clue to the Romantic's own view of the matter which will lead us to consider, too, what their opinions were on the relation of style to the symbolic expression of Imagination.

The Romantics, in fact, incline to a conception of words themselves as symbols, not as signs. Coleridge believes that words can arise in the mind as nuclei of feeling, and can serve therefore to represent the feeling.[38] We find several references in Romantic criticism to words as 'coincident' with feeling or state of mind, hence as symbolic representations of much-in-little.[39]

A clear illustration of the Romantic line of thought in this matter is a remark of Coleridge's on the following lines from Gray:

> Wanders the hoary Thames along
> His silver-winding way . . .

Coleridge's reaction perfectly exemplifies the Romantic approach to poetic language, starting as he does from a misreading of Gray's purely illustrative epithet—the use of which is perfectly defensible, in its grammatical boldness, on rhetorical grounds (though perhaps Dr. Johnson would not have approved). For Coleridge, 'silver-winding' is instinct with symbolic power. 'I am not', he says,

so much disposed as I used to be to quarrel with such an epithet as 'silver-winding'; ungrammatical as the hyphen is, it is not wholly *illogical*, for the phrase conveys more than silvery and winding. It gives, namely, the unity of the impression, the co-inherence of the brightness, the motion, and the line of motion.[40]

None of the Romantics attempted an objective analysis of the symbolic function of words, i.e. their power to convey, in concentrated form, a whole context of thought and feeling. The metaphysical explanations they are fond of are no more than descriptions of this function in metaphysical terms. Coleridge, we are told, described words as 'living'—'the products of the living mind and [they] could not be a due medium between the thing and the mind unless they partook of both'.[41] Wordsworth appears to have much the same idea in mind when he says:

In nature everything is distinct, yet nothing defined into absolute independent singleness. In Macpherson's work, it is exactly the reverse; everything (that is not stolen) is in this manner defined, insulated, dislocated, deadened—yet nothing distinct. It will always be so when words are substituted for things.[42]

But such hints at a metaphysical basis for the power of words— they 'partake' of both things and mind, they must not be 'substituted for things'—go nowhere to explain exactly how words function as symbols rather than signs, never 'defining, insulating dislocating', but none the less expressing something 'distinct'.

The only approach to a rational solution of the problem (though, on the whole, the Romantics appear not to have been aware of it as a problem) is to be found in Coleridge's *Aids to Reflection*. Coleridge's argument here is intended to account not for the capacity of words to express 'poetic thought', but for their capacity (despite the fact that, taken singly, they are signs of concepts) to symbolize the non-conceptual intuitions of Reason. The two processes, however, are obviously analogous, and since Coleridge's metaphysics is so closely bound up with his theory of literature, we are probably justified in seeing his argument here as one that he might have offered to explain the symbolic language of poetry.

The argument may be summarized briefly as follows. The Understanding (the faculty by which we 'reflect and generalize') operates with Names (words standing for things, concepts). Reason, however, perceives truths which are not presented to the senses and therefore cannot be conceptualized by the Understanding or expressed by means of Names; yet these truths must be expressed in some form intelligible to Understanding. How?

... [the intuition] can come forth out of the moulds of the Understanding only in the disguise of two contradictory conceptions, each of which is partially true, and the conjunction of both conceptions becomes the representative of *expression* (the *exponent*) of a truth *beyond* conception and inexpressible. Examples: Before Abraham *was*, I *am*.—God is a Circle, the centre of which is everywhere, and circumference nowhere. The soul is all in every part.[43]

This explanation may in some measure account for the way in which words may operate as poetic symbols, as nuclei of thought and feeling. A clash of meaning and association is produced by juxtaposing mutually irreconcilable words or images—irreconcilable, that is, from a logical point of view. The combination cannot be understood conceptually: to understand it at all, we are forced to accept its elements as symbols, not as signs. Hence we receive a meaning from the whole which is more than, and different from, the meaning of the parts, a sort of meaning moreover which language, in its normal use, cannot possibly express.

It is, at all events, this kind of clash which is always present—or discovered to be present—in examples chosen by the Romantics to illustrate the expression of Imagination. We have seen that

Coleridge (having been disposed initially to quarrel with the epithet) found *more* than 'silvery' and 'winding' in Gray's 'silver-winding way'.[44] Similarly, examples of the imaginative 'fusion' of entire images (such as the stone, the sea-beast and the leech-gatherer cited by Wordsworth in the 1815 Preface[45]) are clearly instances of images which cannot be understood as logically connected, which acquire, for the very reason that their normal associations conflict, a symbolic value.

The Romantics evince no interest whatever in the functions traditionally attributed to figurative language: understandably, since they dismiss the conception of the 'dress of thought' and everything that that implies. They retain only the belief that figurative language is the expression of feeling.[46] Characteristically, however, and consistently with the rest of their outlook, their interest is not in the expressive value of tropes and figures as such, but in images and the interplay of images.[47]

The Romantics, as we have seen, rejected the rhetorical tradition almost *in toto* and developed a conception of the methods of poetry almost completely at variance with the one their predecessors had subscribed to. For the traditional idea of design, elaboration, presentation, they substitute a belief in spontaneity: necessarily, since they no longer consider the materials of poetry as 'thought-dressed-in-language', but as a specifically poetic thought which cannot be separated from the language which expresses it. Language is 'living', its function no longer to present ideas, but to *be* those ideas.

One consequence of this is that, whereas the Neo-Classicists had found it impossible to discover any radical difference between the style of poetry and that of discursive prose, a mode of expression can now be distinguished which belongs to the poet alone. Paradoxically, however, poetry may now be written in prose, since its external characteristics of versification and metre are no longer primary and essential. Defined by its content of 'poetic thought', it is properly opposed not to prose, but to the prosaic—to any form, even a versified form, of rational or matter-of-fact discourse.

Another corollary is that the poetry most favoured by critical theory no longer consists in the vividly pictorial or lyrico-dramatic. That sort of poetry depends too excusively on artifices of structure, style and tone, on the objective 'presentation' of a subject or the writer's attitudes, or both. The Romantic ideal is a poetry of impassioned meditation, expressing 'inward' feeling and deep thought, a blend of sensibility with philosophy:

> Then a wish,
> My last and favourite aspiration, mounts
> With yearning toward some philosophic song
> Of Truth that cherishes our daily life;
> With meditations passionate from deep
> Recesses in man's heart, immortal verse
> Thoughtfully fitted to the Orphean lyre; . . . [48]

Neo-Classical ideas did not, with the advent of the Romantics, immediately lose their hold on critical minds. We find, for example in the reviews of Gifford and Jeffrey, and most notably in the critical comments of Byron in his letters a great deal of evidence that Neo-Classicism was still a live force in the early nineteenth century. But even these critics make their concessions to Romantic ideas, sometimes with little regard for consistency. [49]

Conversely, the Romantics themselves are prone on occasion to repeat traditional views which do not quite square with the ideas they are at pains to emphasize elsewhere. [50] But these are minor inconsistencies or individual eccentricities. They have no bearing, in the long run, on the historical facts which it has been the object of this and preceding chapters to establish, namely, that the theory we call 'Romantic' made its first appearance in Wordsworth's Preface of 1800, and that by 1820 it had been elaborated into a fairly complete and consistent body of ideas which stands in sharp contrast to the critical thought of the preceding age.

The theoretical views of Blake do not fit into this historical pattern, and it is perhaps worth inquiring into the difficulties of 'placing' him. Although chronologically his critical observations (most notably his annotations to Reynolds's *Discourses*) belong to the period *post* 1800, he cannot readily be classed as a Romantic. Still less does he belong with the surviving Neo-Classicists, the 'postscript of the Augustans', to borrow Byron's phrase.

In some respects he does, it is true, stand very close to the Romantics. He believes that art owes nothing to reason; it is the product solely of imagination and feeling. But his ideas in this connexion are at once more definite and uncompromising than those of any Romantic, and much less intelligible. For, to Blake, the poetic imagination has no communication with nature. In a

note on Wordsworth's title, 'The Influence of Natural Objects . . .',
he says:

Natural objects always did and do now weaken, deaden & obliterate
Imagination in Me. Wordsworth must know that what he Writes
Valuable is Not to be found in Nature.[51]

Imagination is the 'Divine Vision' and supplies the poet with
'Forms':

All Forms are Perfect in the Poet's Mind, but these are not
Abstracted nor compounded from Nature, but are from Imagination.[52]

The poet, in other words, is the delineator of a world of Ideas.
He is a visionary, or nothing. 'The Man who never in his Mind
and Thoughts travel'd to Heaven Is No Artist'.[53]

Hence, when Blake emphasizes inspiration, enthusiasm, the
irrelevance to art of reason and rule, he is doing so for reasons
which the Romantics, who were never so unmitigatedly other-
wordly, would not have appreciated. He is probably at one with
them on the question of organic form,[54] but, this apart, can only be
said to share their views in the general sense that he rejects Neo-
Classicism on very similar though not the same, grounds.

In his conception of 'execution' Blake takes leave of Romantic
theory altogether. It is true that he refuses to consider 'execution'
as distinct from 'invention',[55] and thus far the Romantic theorist
would agree. On the other hand, one of Blake's most forcefully-
asserted opinions is that the Forms of Imagination are absolutely
clear and precise. The Artist, who merely 'copies' them, necessarily produces 'definite and determinate' images.[56] Hence, he is able
to say: 'Real Effect is Making out the Parts, & it is Nothing Else
but That . . . To Generalize is to be an Idiot. To Particularize is the
Alone Distinction of Merit.'[57]

In principle Blake agrees with the Romantics, since he sees
composition as the delineation of symbolic forms, but his conception of the process is very different from theirs. The stress on
precision and clarity is almost Neo-Classical, but Blake's closest
affinity here (from a technical point of view, and setting aside his
metaphysical concerns) is perhaps with Romantic theory in one of
its latest manifestations: the imagism of, for example, Hulme.

Blake's views certainly have no clearly perceptible relation to the rhetorical tradition; indeed he is violently hostile to one of its most distinguished representatives, Sir Joshua Reynolds. On the other hand, he is at best a highly eccentric Romantic, if he can be called one at all. His critical thought, like his poetry, resists the historian's effort to categorize. However, in the case of his theoretical views at least, this circumstance need not be too discouraging. Blake's theories are too private—both in the sense that they were never, in his lifetime, made public and in the sense that he alone could have fully understood them—to count as a factor in the development of critical thought.

The crucial step in that development at this period was taken, as we have seen, when a certain conception of the practical purposes and methods of poetry was abandoned for a new one. The Romantic revolution was primarily a revolution in ideas about *how* poetry functions and *how* it is written.

We have noticed that one consequence of this revolution was to upset the established hierarchy of genres: the lyrico-philosophical poem came to take precedence over all other species. But the effects of the revolution were infinitely more far-reaching, even in this one respect, than could have been suggested in the course of the preceding analysis. The next, and concluding, chapter sets out accordingly to examine some, at least, of the wider implications of the Romantic change of mind, and to consider a few of the more interesting issues it raises for the contemporary theorist and historian.

12

Conclusion

WE have seen that, with respect to poetic composition and
style, two widely differing, and indeed mutually incompatible, systems of thought prevail, one before, and one after, the
turn of the eighteenth century. The year 1800 marks the first
appearance of the new theory, though it is not fully developed
until later: the old one continues to flourish, though sometimes in
modified form, and it no longer has the allegiance of the more
enterprising and influential minds.

Hence it is correct to speak of a Romantic 'revolution' in poetic
theory. Apart from the more obvious facts that the Romantics
ignored large tracts of their predecessors' thought, and devised a
few doctrines of their own which clearly owed nothing to previous
theory, they ascribed new meanings to all the essential key-terms
of the theoretical vocabulary, words such as 'imagination',
'thought', 'feeling', 'expression'. They adopted, in other words, an
entirely different set of philosophical presuppositions, so that even
where their opinions are most apparently in concord with the views
of the preceding age, they have in fact a different bearing.

The difference is naturally not a feature only of their views on
composition and style. The new ideas about poetic technique had
necessarily an intimate relation with more general notions about
the nature, function and value of poetry. It has not been the business of this study to investigate this relation, but it may at least have
suggested in what ways the new conception of composition and
style, like the old, was bound up with a complete philosophy of
poetry. It may have indicated, too, how a larger contrast between
the two systems of thought may profitably be derived from the
smaller one. Coleridge's theory of imitation, for instance, patently
differs from Johnson's, yet we cannot accurately gauge the nature
and extent of the difference except in the light of their respective
views on composition. So with regard to their opinions on the way

poetry fulfils a moral function, on the role assumed by the poet *vis-à-vis* his public, or on the criteria to be applied in judging his work.

It is fairly obvious why and how principles of style and composition are connected with these more general views. The present chapter is devoted accordingly to considering three further questions which, though they arise with equal immediacy from what has gone before, are of a kind less readily supplied with answers.

The first, unfortunately, cannot be considered at length. For any attempt at an adequate answer would necessarily entail an investigation far outside the limits of the present study. The question, however, does immediately present itself—and demands some notice—whether the Romantic 'revolution' occurred merely on the theoretical plane, or whether a directly related, and equally definite, change took place in literature itself. Common sense and observation suggest, of course, that few poets obey implicitly the prescriptions of contemporary doctrine, but that there is usually some perceptible relation at any given time between theory and practice and that, as seems to be the case during the Neo-Classical epoch, the relation is sometimes a close one. Analysis, on the other hand, would surely reveal that the earlier Romantics never entirely rid themselves in fact of preconceptions which they had discarded in idea, and no doubt even the Romantics of the second generation would be found less thoroughgoing in their application of Romantic principles than, at first sight, they might seem to be. Nevertheless, there would obviously be striking evidence of change. So much is apparent enough in a general way, but how could any detailed investigation of the facts proceed? It could scarcely confine itself to a recording of 'impressions'.

The difficulties would be great, but a review which follows later in this chapter of the experimental validity of the two theories (i.e. the correspondence of their leading-ideas with observable facts), may at least indicate that the task is a feasible one.

To the second question we may attempt a fuller, if by no means a complete, answer. The Romantic 'revolution', as it has been described above, occurred with some suddenness. What can have brought about so rapid and radical a transformation of the critical scene?

Probably in this particular form the question is unanswerable. Certainly any excursus into social or cultural history to look for 'causative' factors would be doomed to vagueness, if not confusion. But if we cannot discover reasons for the sweeping change in critical thought we can at least postulate a condition: the Romantic revolution in poetic theory could not have occurred with the same rapidity and decisiveness were it not for Kant's 'Copernican revolution' in philosophy.

The key-concept of Romantic theory, the all-important definition of Imagination in contra-distinction to Fancy, originated, though it is through the intermediacy of other writers that it may have found its way to England, with Kant.[1] It is not only that Kant's psychology distinguishes between two types of imagination, one of which is associative and 'subject entirely to empirical laws' (the 'reproductive' imagination = Fancy) while the other is spontaneous and 'determinative . . . not, like sense, merely determinable' (the 'productive' imagination = Imagination);[2] Kant's aesthetic theory, too, is the source of many of the more important Romantic ideas about the function of Imagination. This is not to imply that Kant's theory was a Romantic one: at many points it rests upon a substructure of traditional views. Since, in addition, the understanding of art it implies is so much deeper and more comprehensive than any evinced by the English Romantics, a full-scale comparison would probably reveal more differences than similarities. Nevertheless, Kant undoubtedly had ideas to offer the Romantics which they could not have received from any other source. A few examples follow.

Art is the language of Imagination, and Imagination is non-conceptual.[3] While Kant by no means dismisses 'art' in the sense of 'skill'—he admits the Neo-Classical aims of pleasure and instruction, and accepts that empirical rules apply to the fulfilment of these aims[4]—it is in the creation of beauty that he sees the ultimate goal of the artist, and in the possession of genius his only assurance of attaining it. The activity of genius is spontaneous and self-directing: no rules can be imposed upon it from without.[5] The unity of a work of art is intuitively produced; the language of Imagination is symbolic; poetry is sharply distinguished from rhetoric, which, as an art, is judged inferior to it.[6]

These very brief indications of the Romantics' debt to Kant require more elaboration than they can be given here: it remains to be demonstrated, moreover, how Kant's ideas could have affected those Romantic critics who, unlike Coleridge, seem not to have had direct access to them.[7] In fact there is an interesting study still to be made of the importance of German Idealism to the Romantic revolution in England, on the other hand of the relations between English empirical philosophy and the Neo-Classical tradition.[8] It should be sufficiently obvious none the less that ideas of the kind noted above were not available to the Neo-Classical writers: Kant was not known in England until the later 1790s, and then very little known. Coleridge, on the other hand, was already familiar with his philosophy no later than 1801.[9]

It would be going too far, of course, to suggest that Kant was the original architect of English Romanticism: nevertheless, there seems little doubt that it was he who made possible a major diversion in the current of English critical thought, if only because of his revolutionary innovations in psychology. It was he who initiated a conception of the human mind which is indispensable to Romantic theory. We may not incorrectly see his philosophical revolution as a necessary condition of the literary one in England.

There is, however, one objection to this view: Wordsworth, as we have seen, had departed very far from traditional theory in the Preface to Lyrical Ballads; he had approached very close to what was ultimately to be the Romantic position, and he had done so with no other philosophical support than the associationism of Hartley and his school. May not Wordsworth—and Coleridge, too, for that matter, if we adopt the generally accepted view that the Preface expresses jointly-developed opinions—have arrived at a complete and coherent Romantic theory without the smallest obligation to Kant?

It is usually idle to speculate about what might have been, but in this case an answer can be attempted without wholly gratuitous conjectures. Wordsworth had adopted the 'emotions of Taste' of the eighteenth-century aestheticians as the subject-matter of poetry: that is to over-simplify a little, but we have seen that the two conceptions of 'sensibility' were closely similar. Poetry had thus become, at a stroke, a subjective and spontaneous activity, directed by feeling; it was no longer primarily an 'art'. So much association theory could perfectly adequately explain and justify; it might also have served to vindicate other Romantic requirements: the use of symbols to express sensibility, the non-logical unification of a poem, even (allowing it a single leap into the dark of metaphysics) the poetic apprehension and expression of Truth.[10]

Something very close to a comprehensive Romantic theory may easily have been developed along these lines, but it must have revealed a fatal flaw. An associationist theory of composition which excludes the possibility of intention, deliberation and choice must inevitably reduce the writer to complete passivity, following 'blindly and mechanically', in Wordsworth's revealing words, the dictates of his emotions. All writing necessarily becomes automatic writing, for an empiricist psychology can supply no substitute for 'art', that is for the exercise of judgment and volition. Such a theory must necessarily have fallen short of completeness, unless its function were merely to justify expressionistic aberrations.

It was only because Coleridge supplied the defect with his principle of the synthesizing Imagination, a faculty which 'co-exists with the conscious will' that Romantic theory was able to achieve full stature; but then *ipso facto* it was entirely refashioned on a new philosophical basis.

A final question now invites consideration, and it is perhaps the one most relevant to the purposes of this study. The Romantics rejected ancient and over-familiar ways of thinking about poetry: but was their transformation of critical theory necessarily a change for the better?

From the standpoint of a twentieth-century rationalism, and judging the two theories on their own merits, the answer must be unequivocally that it was, on the contrary, a change for the worse.

Neo-Classical theory is far from secure against a strictly positivist criticism. Much of its psychological speculation is dubious, in so far as it aims to explain processes which are not wholly amenable to observation. Some of its vaguer concepts, too, (e.g., 'vivacity', 'propriety') are handled with far more confidence than their limited correspondence with observable facts can warrant. Above all, Neo-Classical theory makes an unrealistically clear distinction between 'language' and 'thought', and this dubious antithesis runs like a dangerous crack through its foundations.

Those foundations, nevertheless, are fairly secure. Though Neo-Classical assumptions about the psychology of language are often doubtful, if not false,[11] the theory as a whole is firmly based on a correct acceptance of the conventional nature of words and their uses. For this reason, its rhetorical approach to literary questions is undoubtedly a valid one. For, if the 'meanings' of words are, by convention, more or less fixed, if our responses to the basic elements of language, in other words, run more or less to type, then there is every reason to think that our reactions to more complex conventions—the larger elements of style and structure—are equally consistent, though never, of course rigidly so. Since dictionaries and grammars are able to define a consensus of opinion about the meanings of separate words and of grammatical structures and inflections, rhetoric (and literary theory of the rhetorical type) is justified in adopting the same approach to the more complex features of literary language. Indeed it seems there can be no other valid approach to the analysis of literary techniques and, by extension, of literary values. For our response to literature is not governed by permanent and unchanging principles, notwithstanding a natural and very widely prevalent tendency to believe that it is: it is wholly determined, like our response to language, by artificial, though often spontaneously developed and unconsciously assimilated rules—some of them, like the conventions of language itself, more durable than others, but all of them subject to change.

This method of analysing literary effects and their causes, a continual defining of what is proper and acceptable according to current conventions, may, of course, exert an undesirable influence in standardizing literary procedure: the effect of grammars and dictionaries is, after all, towards a stabilization of language. But we are, for the moment, discussing the merits of the rhetorical theory as a true, rather than as a good one. The rhetorical method was not, in the later eighteenth century, always discreetly, nor was it ever very exactly, applied. A severe critic would now want to know a great deal more about the rule of propriety, the mechanism of amplification, or the precise difference between a 'lively' image and one which is not, before accepting eighteenth-century dicta on these subjects as beyond cavil. But, if our criticism is not too exacting, we can still see a large part of Neo-Classical theory as valid: it defines accurately enough observable features of composition and style and the means to attaining them. Its results, crude though they may be, might still be acceptable as a basis for further elaboration, or as a model for a new theory, explaining another kind of literature.

The chief defects of the theory, as we have noticed already, are its tendency to over-elaborate speculation in psychological matters;[12] more especially, its insufficient psychology of language. Romantic theory, however, leaves far more to be desired in both these respects.

Its entire structure rests on the kind of philosophical speculation which is totally beyond argument or verification. Only introspection can tell us whether there is any truth in Coleridge's theory of the Imagination, and introspection we are bound to consider an altogether unreliable test in such matters. Romantic theory, however, says little than can be checked in any other way: we have to take it on trust, or not at all. Wordsworth's phrase 'a spontaneous overflow of powerful feelings' may vividly express a state of mind and its effects, and our subjective experience will supply us with a lively, if logically not very precise, sense of what it means. But as a theoretical definition of poetry the phrase is useless, for its meaning cannot be explained in terms of any given poem. How is spontaneous overflow to be recognized? Similarly, anyone who wants to believe, with Coleridge, that metre in poetry is the result of an 'interpenetration of passion and will' would be hard put to it to explain, with his finger on a text, where, and by what signs, he discovers the interpenetration occurring.

Nearly all Romantic definitions and explanations are of this kind: they impel us to introspection, and the hints they often contain of the esoteric and profound encourage us to believe that when we have arrived at an 'intuitive' understanding of what they mean we have also discovered a truth. Their objective validity, however, is nil. In this respect, and assuming that literary theory is more to be trusted the closer it approaches to science, the Romantic revolution must be considered a disaster. We are still suffering the consequences of that full-scale retreat into subjectivism and metaphysics: we are very little nearer an understanding of the why's and how's of poetry than were the literary scholars of the late eighteenth century. This, curiously, despite the fact that linguistics—a science which must necessarily form the basis of any reliable theory of literature—has of recent years taken rapid strides forward in the devising of methods, discovery of principles and accumulation of data.

Theories of poetry, however, have more than one function to serve and from the purely literary point of view it is probably inappropriate to discuss and compare them in this literal-minded way. No theory of poetry need stand the test of rational scrutiny if we consider it primarily as an expression of ideals and values: the criterion then to judge it by is not its accuracy as explanation, but its efficacy as inspiration.

We have already encountered the difficult question whether poetry is ever directly influenced by theory. Without going much further into the matter, it will perhaps be accepted that though the relationship may be a highly indirect one, some relationship there must be. The beliefs and attitudes which have been codified in a widely-known theory must inevitably make their mark on poetry as well, though not necessarily by way of the theory: a poet need not study the theoretical documents of his time in order to embody in his poetry ideas which are 'in the air', though it is in the documents that they may have been originally defined. Few writers, it seems, have insulated themselves completely from every contemporary 'current of ideas'.

Judging the Romantic revolution from this point of view, we must come to the opposite conclusion that it was a triumph. Not that Romantic values were intrinsically superior to those of their predecessors. Sensibility and spontaneity produce one kind of art, judgment and rule another, and it is only prejudice which can set them in contrast to each other as 'living' and 'mechanical'. Neo-Classical theory, as we have seen, was neither simple-minded, nor obtuse, nor oppressively strict. It must be agreed, none the less, that the Romantics expressed and publicized, explained and justified, a body of beliefs and ideals very much more remarkable in its practical consequences than that of the half-century immediately preceding.

This conclusion scarcely needs arguing here, though it will in due course require some qualification. First, however, some attention must be given a question which, it may seem, is about to be conveniently begged. It has been maintained that Romantic theory is philosophically unsound, and for that reason largely meaningless, yet that it served an important practical purpose in defining and making known a new outlook on poetry. How could it possibly achieve such a purpose were its content not meaningfully related to fresh observations and discoveries of fact?

It was so related, of course, but we must be careful to bear in mind here a distinction between, on the one hand, descriptions of experiences and facts and, on the other, assertions about their origins or their relations. The Neo-Classical and Romantic theories

have been taken equally seriously in the above chapters, and discussed without demur in their own respective languages, on the
assumption that, as accounts of how poetry is written, they are at
least descriptively meaningful. Their definitions and deductions
may be false or illusory, but the facts they notice and emphasize
are quite real. The difference between the theories may indeed be
seen largely as a difference of focus: the Romantics discovered new
areas of fact to be interested in. However, a brief review of their
main features seems to be necessary at this point in case there
should be any suspicion that the preceding chapters have been
devoted to drawing superfluous distinctions between chimerical
concepts.

First, as to 'thought'. Neo-Classical 'thought' has been called
'conceptual' or 'discursive': we may regard it as expressed in statements of wholly objective reference, statements, that is, which can
ultimately be explained—however abstract they may be—by pointing to features of sensible experience. The statements of Romantic
'poetic thought' cannot be so explained: they bear a certain subjective meaning, a meaning derived from the emotional value of
words which cannot be demonstrated to anyone in a practical way.

The elements in an objective statement, moreover, are logically
related; the pattern, that is, reflects, at one or more removes, a
pattern we can find in objective reality. Their reference necessarily
limited by these clear relations, the elements appear separate and
distinct. In a Romantic statement the connexions are liable at any
moment to become a-logical. In the absence of a clear syntax,
distinctions dissolve: the juxtaposed elements appear to blend and
merge.

The difference becomes clearer when we examine the attitudes
of the two theories to the non-denotative function of words. Neo-
Classical theory evinces little interest in the subjective reference of
words. Its view of the connotations of language (as exploited in
'amplification') may be understood as an appreciation of the conventional association of words with different degrees of social
approval ('warrior' is more dignified than 'soldier'), or aesthetic
approval ('Phoebus' is more pleasing than 'sun'). It recognizes only
those connotations derived from public opinion or taste, and such
connotations make no difference to the explainable meaning,
though they may add to the force, of the idea expressed.

The Romantic conception, on the other hand, of feeling-merged-with-thought appears to be primarily a conception of meaning as *defined* by connotation, a meaning, that is, which cannot be objectively explained, but can only be 'sensed'. The connotations in question are not of the public, conventional kind, but those which words derive from their connexion with personal feeling or sensory experience.

An example may make this clear. An eighteenth-century metaphor defines by its denotation: even an unusually bold one such as Gray's 'drowsy tinklings' illustrates the process (it is really a case of wholesale ellipsis: 'tinklings as from the bells of drowsy sheep'). The effect is of two words interacting but retaining distinct, because clearly-related, meanings. A typical Romantic metaphor such as 'scarlet pain' is amenable to no such simple explanation. Here the two words are brought together on no clearly-definable ground of connexion. We do, however, make a connexion, or rather, it seems, a great many tenuous and indirect connexions: we attend to 'connotations'. The words, understood only in terms of this multiplex and indistinct relationship, lose their identities: they appear to 'fuse'. And the final effect is of a 'thought' which seems as much to warrant the description 'feeling'.

The Romantics necessarily regarded language as the 'incarnation' of thought. There is an indissoluble link between particular words and the emotional value they carry: there can be no synonyms or substitutes in the Romantic vocabulary. Furthermore, the exploitation of subjective values to define sensation or intuitive feeling seems incapable of being effected by conscious intention or skill. Neo-Classical theory, on the other hand, with its exclusive interest in objective denotation and the conventional associations of language regarded words as instruments with established functions. It was thus readily able to regard writing as a matter of discrimination and ingenuity in fulfilling a given intention, hence to look upon style as the 'dress of thought'.

Romantic 'sensibility' we may consider as the feeling expressed in statements which exploit the subjective references of language. Neo-Classical 'passion' is that class of feelings for which we have a nomenclature because they are easily recognized in their sensible effects—no less in the choice and arrangement of words than in gesture, expression and tone.

The results of 'design' and 'Imagination' may be distinguished as different structures of ideas, the one consisting of a progression of 'discursive' statements forming a logically analysable whole; the other a series of statements between which, or within which, the connexions are frequently a-logical, the whole cohering, if at all, by means of a network of indirect associations which could never be exhaustively analysed and defined. The unity of the latter may be observed in a singleness of theme, or in a non-logical pattern of some sort, but the 'organic' integration of elements alleged to occur in a good Romantic poem cannot possibly be confirmed or denied. The only available criterion (a non-logical interconnexion of parts) is worthless because it will always, applied with a little ingenuity, produce a positive result. To look at it from the other point of view—there may be ways of establishing the irrelevant or disproportionate; there is none of discovering the non-organic.

The creative processes manifested in these two types of composition must (as the two theories describe them) be considered as plausible fictions: on the other hand they can certainly be understood in terms of the effects of which they are the supposed origin, and they may also be broadly distinguished as rationalizations of two types of activity, two methods of writing—one which is determined by conscious intention, which therefore involves preparation, deliberation and choice, the details only being left to chance inspiration and the stimulus of the purpose in hand; the other which is spontaneous and immediate, characterized, we may infer, by *singleness* of intention, a sense of 'having something to say', but not by any 'distinct purpose formally conceived'.

The leading-ideas of the two theories may thus be given fairly objective definition. With some such definitions as criteria, moreover, it should certainly be possible, as was suggested above, to study the reflections in poetry itself of the revolutionary developments in critical thought.

But to return to our assessment of those developments: the remarkable achievement of the Romantic poets, the distinction of which may certainly in some part be put down to the freedom, the release from constraint which the new theory both proclaimed and justified, may from one point of view be regarded as triumphantly vindicating the theory. But neither the brilliance of the immediate results, nor the strength and impressiveness of the Romantic tradition for a century thereafter, should blind us to certain disadvantages inherent in Romanticism, which, as the splendour of the tradition has waned and its theoretical basis becomes ever more sophisticated and etiolated, have come to assume an ever more depressing consequence.

The Romantics admired only one kind of poetry: the lyrical and meditative, preferably with philosophic overtones or implications. The resources of this kind of poetry are limited: it relies heavily, sometimes exclusively, on metaphor and symbol, on the use of evocative imagery. It may depend for some of its effect upon the sensuous 'music' of language, but to no different purpose. Its aim is always the expression of a particular sort of thought and feeling, intuitive and personal.

The Romantics, because they approved most of this kind of poetry, wrote it well, and persuaded their successors that no other kind was worthy of the name, brought about a virtual extinction of all the traditional genres: the dramatic, the epic, the didactic, the satirical, and so on.[13] These kinds of poetry express a very different sort of feeling, or none at all; to them is not necessary what the Romantics called 'poetic thought'. With the renunciation of classical genres, a vast battery of technical resources, too, was lost to poetry: the tropes and figures of rhetoric, with a few exceptions, fell into disuse; 'amplification' was abjured; classical qualities of perspicuity and propriety ceased to be cultivated for their own sake. The principle of structure-by-argument, an inexhaustible source of aesthetic effect, and one on which the novel still to a large extent relies, was abandoned. Most regrettably of all, this relinquishment of logical progression and point was accompanied by a loss of that intellectual strength which will both justify and sustain any mode of emotional expression from the most passionate grandiloquence to the dryest irony and wit. It would scarcely be just to accuse the Romantic poets of monotony but their range in this respect is inevitably narrow. The typical Romantic, brooding upon the world as he finds it reflected in his feelings, is rarely safe outside the vein of impassioned meditation. When he 'speaks out' he runs the risk of falsity or loss of equilibrium. Indeed one might say that the Romantic poem, given that it lacks an intellectual structure (and is therefore typical of its kind), tends to exaggeration and hysteria in direct proportion as its tone becomes more emphatic. That there are undoubtedly exceptions only proves the rule that the impressions and intuitions of sensibility normally require very discreet utterance. The natural romantic voice is the one which is— to borrow J. S. Mill's terms—*over*heard rather than heard. Capable of the utmost poignancy and intensity, it is yet ruminative and intimate. This, in effect, has been the sort of tone most cultivated by English poets for the last century and a half.

Thus one effect of the Romantic revolution was to exclude a very great deal from the art of poetry. Yet there was no immediate impoverishment, since the Romantics replaced what they had discarded with much that was new. Their achievement, however, and that of their successors throughout the nineteenth century, a very substantial and impressive one, would seem to have exhausted the potentialities of the new ideas and methods. These innovations set narrow limits to any possibility of development, and the limits were soon all but reached. By the second decade of this century Romanticism in its pure form was obviously a played-out force, and something like a new revolution occurred.

Unfortunately it was in no sense a true revolution: the ideology of Romanticism was never challenged. It still exerts virtually uncontested sway over poets and critics alike. Late events—in both poetry and poetic theory—have amounted to no more than a refinement, a subtilization of Romanticism: not a change to new ideas and methods, but a re-distillation, as it were, of the old ones. We may see an example of this in the poetic theory of T. S. Eliot— in every way a theory which demands respect, but still a Romantic theory, and one which is even more exclusive than Coleridge's: it restricts poetry within even narrower bounds.[14] One might perhaps —without the least suggestion of a sneer—call it a 'sub-Romantic' theory.

'Sub-Romantic', too, is a good deal of the poetry which has been written since 1920 or thereabouts. It is still Romantic in inspiration, the expression of Romantic imagination and sensibility, but Romantic intensity, richness, sweep have been foregone in favour of a greater subtlety, complexity and, at the same time, concision: poets, in other words, now set themselves smaller but more intricate tasks.

Such developments have been, perhaps, inevitable. Given that Romanticism established itself with brilliant *éclat*, that its exponents from the beginning included some of the most splendid talents in the history of literature, that these great names—nearer to us in time than any others—still loom very large, even if unregarded, in the background of our consciousness, it is not surprising that the Romantic view of literature has continued to dominate our own, long after it has become impossible to write, or to expect to find written, a fully Romantic poetry. An alternative has been sought, necessarily, in refinements and subtleties.

But this is unfortunate, for it means that poetry has entered a sort of Alexandrian age. It is no longer much read except by those with a taste for the 'difficult' and *recherché*. Poets are no longer 'men speaking to men'. For once the Philistine objections to 'modernism' seem in order, since the poets of our day are not aiming at something new, reaching beyond the frontiers of their art while momentarily leaving their contemporaries behind them— they are exploring ever remoter and darker corners within the old frontiers, where few are interested in following them. The subjective personal content of the Romantic poem has become private, esoteric, at times an almost impenetrable secret; the Romantic interest in image and symbol has become an obsession: poems have been written in what can only be called code; Romantic 'sensibility' is now expressed in its purest possible form, free from all the distortions of conventional communication: the vestigial rhetoric the Romantics allowed themselves has finally been dispensed with: not even the laws of grammar and syntax need now apply; it follows that even the small gamut of Romantic tones has been reduced to barely one: in most of the poetry we read now, where we can recognize a voice at all, we hear only an inhibited stammer. Poetry seems not to be developing, but disintegrating. The brilliant exceptions only prove the rule, for, however things may look upon the surface, their real strength is derived from the past: they are bold enough to revert in the important respects, and good enough in those respects to challenge the past once more upon its own ground.

Critics are content to tolerate and encourage this state of affairs, for they, too, are under the Romantic spell. Poetry is of one sort only, and if that sort has now become inordinately devious and complicated that makes it—arguing from their own first principles —more, and not less, interesting. Theorists, significantly, have been rare over the past half-century: Eliot, the most distinguished, has modified accepted views but without fundamentally changing them. Such writers as Collingwood or Richards would not, one imagines, impress Coleridge as particularly strange.[15]

If these strictures have any substance, then we must see the Romantic revolution as a mixed historical blessing. Its initial triumphs we cannot wish away, and no one could want to: but it looks very much as if those triumphs, and the extreme one-sidedness of the outlook they embody, have exerted, in the long run, a stultifying influence.

It would be absurd, however, to pretend to propaganda in a study of this kind: it is the makers of literature who change the course of literary history. The above remarks have been intended only to emphasize what the findings of this study most immediately suggest: that no historical evaluation of the Romantic achievement need start from the assumption that it was climactic, final and definitive. For when the Romantic creed is compared with that of the previous age we find no evidence that the one represents a culmination or completion of the other. The comparison undertaken here will have achieved its purpose if it has established that Romantic theory, whether or not it was a better theory than its Neo-Classical counterpart, was not, being a radically different theory, of necessity a better one.

Notes

NOTES TO INTRODUCTION

[1] G. Saintsbury: *A History of English Criticism* (Edinburgh, 1911); J. W. H. Atkins: *English Literary Criticism: 17th and 18th centuries* (London, 1951); René Wellek: *A History of Modern Criticism*, Vols. I and II (London, 1955); W. K. Wimsatt and Cleanth Brooks: *Literary Criticism: A Short History* (New York, 1957).

[2] M. Abrams: *The Mirror and the Lamp* (London, 1960); W. J. Bate: *From Classic to Romantic: Premises of Taste in Eighteenth-century England* (Cambridge, Mass., 1946); S. H. Monk: *The Sublime: A Study of Critical Theories in 18th-century England* (New York, 1935); *et al.*

[3] The most illuminating account of the relationship appears in Abrams's *The Mirror and the Lamp*—by far the best available book in this field. It has provided not only a starting-point for this study, but much incidental assistance and stimulus.

[4] René Wellek states in his *History of Modern Criticism* (I, 105) that it is 'now the fashion to deny the existence of preromanticism'. There seems little evidence of the fashion: certainly no major work of English critical history over the past quarter-century could offer support for such a generalization. A short review of eighteenth-century theory by R. S. Crane ('English Neoclassical Criticism: An Outline Sketch', in *Critics and Criticism*, ed. R. S. Crane: Chicago, 1952) does indeed, as cogently as is possible in a brief summary, argue the view that Neo-Classical theory was characterized by 'a single dominant conception of [poetry], in relation to which even the more seemingly revolutionary changes in the latter part of the period can be interpreted as so many shifts of emphasis within the framework of a common conceptual scheme' (p. 374). Nevertheless, even Crane is disposed to acknowledge at least one 'pre-Romantic' tendency during the period (cf. ibid., p. 388).

[5] See Wordsworth: Preface to *Lyrical Ballads*, in *Lyrical Ballads* (ed. R. L. Brett and A. R. Jones, London, 1963), p. 249; Hazlitt: 'On the Living Poets', in *Lectures on the English Poets: The Complete Works of William Hazlitt* (ed. P. P. Howe, London, 1930), V, 161-2; Shelley: Preface to *Prometheus Unbound*, in *Complete Poetical Works* (ed. Thomas Hutchinson: Oxford Standard Authors, 1943), p. 206; Byron: *Letters and Journals* (ed. R. E. Prothero, London, 1900), III, 76; IV, 169, 196-7, etc.; Leigh Hunt: Preface to *Foliage*, in *Leigh Hunt's Literary Criticism* (ed. L. H. and C. W. Houtchens, New York, 1956), pp. 129-30;

T. L. Peacock: *The Four Ages of Poetry*, in *Works* (ed. Henry Cole; London, 1875), III, 333–4. Coleridge's disclaimer of 'a new school of poetry' (*Biographia Literaria*, ed. George Watson, Everyman's Library, 1960: Chap. IV, p. 41) is clearly sophistical: the rest of the chapter emphasizes not only the originality of Wordsworth's poetry, but of the theory Coleridge devised (as he says) to explain it. Coleridge, however, saw the new developments not as a revolution but as a revival, hence his anxiety to eradicate any impression of them as novel and perverse.

⁶ Hume's *Inquiry Concerning Human Understanding* appeared in 1748, Hartley's *Observations on Man* in 1749. Hume's earlier version of the Inquiry (*A Treatise on Human Nature:* 1739-40) had, in his own words, fallen 'dead-born from the press'.

NOTES TO CHAPTER ONE

¹ Though it is true that an anti-Romantic minority continued, until late in the nineteenth century, to insist, sometimes very forcibly, on the importance of this question, e.g. in the *Quarterly Review* from the time of Gifford onwards.

² Such works as I. A. Richards's *Philosophy of Rhetoric*, Kenneth Burke's *Philosophy of Literary Form* or Northop Frye's *Anatomy of Criticism* share the aims of rhetoric properly so-called only in so far as they are concerned with analysing language or style or structure. They aim to some extent at establishing criteria, but criteria chiefly for the *critic's* use. The traditional rhetorical treatise which laid down rules for good *writing* now exists only at a non-literary level: handbooks on composition and style for the student or the technical expert, guides to short-story writing for the 'commercial' market, etc.

³ See D. L. Clark: *Rhetoric and Poetry in the Renaissance* (New York, 1922) Part I, Ch. 8; R. Tuve: *Elizabethan and Metaphysical Imagery* (Chicago, 1947), Ch. 11.

⁴ *The Art of Poetry on a New Plan*, published, and possibly written, by John Newbery (London, 1762).

⁵ *Poetics*, Ch. 19, in *Works*, Vol. XI (Oxford, 1946).

⁶ See C. S. Baldwin: *Renaissance Literary Theory and Practice* (New York, 1939).

⁷ *Aesthetic*, trans. Douglas Ainslie (London, 1953), pp. 422 ff.

⁸ Isolated topics and/or periods have been studied, as for example in Tuve, op. cit.; in W. S. Howell: *Logic and Rhetoric in England, 1500-1700* (Princeton, 1956), etc., but a general historical investigation tracing the modifications and changes of emphasis within rhetorical theory, hence the variations in its rapport with literature, would be of great interest and value.

⁹ Quintilian: *Institutio Oratoria*, trans. H. E. Butler (Loeb Classics. London, 1921), I, 301-15.

¹⁰ See W. G. Crane: *Wit and Rhetoric in the Renaissance* (New York, 1937), pp. 4-5.

¹¹ In so far as he redistributed the traditional 'parts' of rhetoric, retaining only Elocutio and Pronuntiatio as the sphere of rhetoric proper, assigning the remaining three to logic.

¹² George Campbell: *The Philosophy of Rhetoric* (London, 1776), I, 25; Hugh Blair: *Lectures on Rhetoric and Belles Lettres* (London, 1783). Cf. also Richard Sharp: *On the Nature and Utility of Eloquence* (*Memoirs of the Literary and Philosophical Society of Manchester.* Vol. III. Warrington, 1790), p. 325.

¹³ John Ward: *A System of Oratory* (London, 1759), I, 19.

¹⁴ 'For tho rhetoric is said to be the art of speaking well, and grammar the art of speaking correctly; yet since the rules for speaking and writing are the same, under speaking we are to include writing, and each art is to be considered as treating of both.'—Ward, ibid., I, 23.

¹⁵ (John Newbery) *Circle of the Sciences*, Vol. VI: *The Art of Rhetorick* (London, 1746); John Lawson: *Lectures concerning Oratory* (London, 1769); Ward, op. cit.

¹⁶ Here, for example, is an explanation of the effect of grandeur, traditionally connected with 'the sublime': 'The mind, as was observed before, conforming and adapting itself to the object to which its attention is engaged, must, as it were, enlarge itself, to conceive a great object. This requires a considerable *effort of the imagination*, which is also attended with a pleasing, though perhaps not a distinct and explicit consciousness of the strength and extent of our own powers.'—Joseph Priestley: *A Course of Lectures in Oratory and Criticism*, in *The Theological and Miscellaneous Works of Joseph Priestley* (London, 1824), XXIII, 368. Priestley sets out to confirm a traditional dogma by adducing 'facts' of experience in support of it. The argument squares neatly with his general thesis that a certain class of literary properties gives pleasure by exercising our mental faculties; but, judged on its own merits, it is scarcely persuasive.

¹⁷ See Henry Home, Lord Kames: *The Elements of Criticism*, 6th ed. (London, 1785), I, 6-7; Campbell: *Philosophy*, I, 12-13.

¹⁸ *The Mirror and the Lamp*, p. 157.

¹⁹ Consider such vacuous statements as the following:
'Two emotions are said to be similar when they tend each of them to produce the same tone of mind ...' *Elements*, I, 126.
'... a man never finds himself more at ease, than when his perceptions succeed each other with a certain degree, not only of velocity, but also of variety.'—Ibid., I, 315.
The Elements of Criticism ran, notwithstanding, into eight editions.

An abridged version was published as late as 1823. Even Johnson allowed it merit, though not enough to atone for the author's nationality: 'BOSWELL. "But, Sir, we have Lord Kames". JOHNSON. "You *have* Lord Kames. Keep him; ha, ha, ha." '—Boswell, *Life* (Oxford Standard Authors, 1952) p. 392, but cf. pp. 279, 414.

[20] There are remarkable anticipations of Wordsworth and Coleridge in, e.g. Priestley. Compare his sketch of an associationist theory of aesthetics (Lectures, in *Works*, XXIII, 352 ff.) with Wordsworth's statement of aims in the early pages of the Preface to *Lyrical Ballads*; also his remarks on proportioning the density of a poem's texture to its length (ibid, p. 361) with Coleridge's definition of a poem in the *Biographia Literaria*.

[21] The difficulty is, of course, to find a sound basis in psychology—the psychology of reading—for research of this kind. Current beliefs in the matter, i.e., that there is a simple cause-and-effect relationship between language and reader's response leave the investigator helpless before an infinite variety of phenomena, extremely difficult to analyse and impossible to classify. A recent and brilliant work, however, on what might be called the psychology of rhetoric in painting, E. H. Gombrich's *Art and Illusion* (London, 1960) suggests a hypothesis which literary researchers might well find fruitful, viz. that even the simplest response to painting (seeing a picture as a picture *of* something) is not a natural but an acquired response, the result of practise in interpreting a highly conventional language which varies in make-up from age to age. The effect of art has thus not one but two determining causes—not only the language itself, but the reader's deliberate (though perhaps unconscious) attempt to make sense of it according to one or another set of regulations. If it can be assumed for literature, too, as surely it must, that the reader's response is not simply stimulated by the words on the page, but is a purposeful interpretation of them according to familiar conventions—artistic conventions, that is, not merely grammatical ones—then the analyst's task might begin to look possible.

[22] '. . . however interested the 18th-century may have been in rhetoric, it had nothing new to offer on the subject . . . With this static rhetoric we are in no way concerned.'—S. H. Monk: *The Sublime*, p. 12. W. K. Wimsatt and C. Brooks (*Literary Criticism: A Short History*) take Croce's view of Neo-Classic rhetoric as primarily a theory of ornament and agree on the whole with his opinion that the theory reached the peak of its development in the early seventeenth century and thereafter fossilized or decayed. 'The large part of a century that follows the effort of Pope, before the rise of romantic theory, produces, as we have already suggested, only a more or less dismal continuation of the ornamentalist view concerning metaphor and related figures.'—op. cit., p. 245.

[23] Gerard, e.g. says: 'No two arts are more analogous than poetry

and eloquence . . .'—*An Essay on Genius* (London, 1774), p. 314; and Lawson: '. . . the Connexion between Poesy and Eloquence is so close, that in most Cases, Examples from the one extend equally to the other.' —*Lectures*, p. 22.

24 Life of Milton, in *Lives of the Poets: The Works of Samuel Johnson* (London, 1787) II, 154.

25 Robert Lowth: *Lectures on the Sacred Poetry of the Hebrews*, trans. G. Gregory (London, 1787), 1, 7; I, 367.

26 William Belsham: *Essays, Philosophical, Historical, and Literary* (London, 1789), II, 275-6.

27 James Beattie: *On Memory and Imagination*, in *Dissertations, Moral and Critical* (London, 1783), p. 167. Cf.: 'To instruct, is an end common to all good writing . . . but the poet must do a great deal for the sake of pleasure only; and if he fail to please . . . as a poet he has done nothing.'—Beattie: *On Poetry and Music as they affect the Mind*, in *Essays* (Edinburgh, 1776), p. 10.

28 *System of Oratory*, II, 299. Campbell, Priestley, Blair similarly regard pleasing, moving and conviction as essential means to the orator's ultimate end of persuasion.

29 *Philosophy*, I, 14.

30 Thomas Sheridan: *British Education: or, the Source of the Disorders of Great Britain* (London, 1756), p. 414.

31 Oliver Goldsmith: *Essays*, in *The Works of Oliver Goldsmith*, ed. J. W. M. Gibbs (London, 1884), I, 341. The essays cited here and elsewhere in this study as Goldsmith's form part of a series which appeared anonymously in the *British Magazine* (July 1761–January 1763). They were first republished in 1798 in a volume entitled *Essays and Criticisms by Dr. Goldsmith*. Gibbs considers that they are partly at least Goldsmith's work, but Caroline F. Tupper ('Essays Erroneously Attributed to Goldsmith': *PMLA*, XXXIX, 1924) argues that they are more likely to have been written by Smollett. Miss Tupper's case for the inauthenticity of the essays, though not her suggestion of Smollett's authorship, has been accepted both by N. S. Crane (*New Essays by Oliver Goldsmith*, Chicago, 1927, p. xix) and by Goldsmith's latest editor A. Friedmann (*Complete Works of Oliver Goldsmith*, Oxford, 1966, III, 88). However, since the essays are most readily available in Gibbs, and since his remains both the fullest account of the bibliographical data and the fairest résumé of arguments for and against the attribution to Goldsmith (I, 323 n. and 406-8), there will be some advantage here in referring to his edition.

32 Blair: *Lectures*, II, 312.

33 *On Genius*, p. 314.

34 Chapter 8.

35 Chapter 9.

NOTES TO CHAPTER TWO

[1] 'The same medium language is made use of, the same general rules of composition, in narration, description, argumentation, are observed; and the same tropes and figures, either for beautifying or for invigorating the diction, are employed by both [arts]'—Campbell, *Philosophy*, I, 15. Cf. James Burnett, Lord Monboddo: *Of the Origin and Progress of Language* (2nd ed. London, 1786) III, 12-13. Monboddo, having classified the 'materials' of style, concludes: 'Of these materials all style is made . . . the didactic and the historic . . . the rhetorical and the poetic . . .'

[2] *The Art of Poetry on a New Plan*, I, 18. 'Prose' is here understood as the normal province of rhetoric. The equivalence: rhetoric = prose (with its corollary: poetry = verse) is often assumed.

[3] Chapter 8.

[4] Sir Joshua Reynolds: *Discourses on Art*, ed. Robert R. Wark (Huntington Library, 1959), p. 64. See also Campbell, *Philosophy*, I, 339: 'It is the intention of eloquence, to convey our sentiments into the minds of others, in order to produce a certain effect upon them. Language is the only vehicle by which this conveyance can be made.'

[5] Campbell, ibid., II, 2.

[6] Kames: *Elements*, II, 263.

[7] Blair: *Lectures*, I, 184. The same views are, of course, expressed with reference to composition as a whole: see e.g., Beattie; *Dissertations*, p. 184.

[8] *The Art of Poetry on a New Plan*, I, 46.

[9] William Duff: *An Essay on Original Genius* (London, 1767), p. 146 (my italics).

[10] *Essays*. I, 216-18.

[11] Ibid., I, 218.

[12] Blair: *Lectures*, I, 34, 37; cf. Campbell: *Philosophy*, I, 17-18; Reynolds: *Discourses*, pp. 131-2; Hume: Of the Standard of Taste', in *Essays, Literary, Moral, and Political* (1753-4. Reprinted in one vol., London, 1870), pp. 134 ff.

[13] '. . . Kames and Priestley were carrying on the analysis of the aesthetic experience and were broadening its significance by a closer adherence to psychology. The old critical and objective method of discussing art was destined to lose out as such speculation became general . . . the objective criteria of the rules were gradually invalidated and the perceptions of individuals, together with their personal emotions and their independent imaginative interpretation of experience could usurp the place of the older truth to nature.'—Monk: *The Sublime*, p. 236. E. N. Hooker ('The Discussion of Taste, from 1750 to 1770, and The New Trends in Literary Criticism': *PMLA*, XLIX, 1934) assumes

that since aesthetics could find no ultimate support in *reason* for its principles the entire Neo-Classical system had inevitably to founder.

[14] The term is A. O. Lovejoy's: see *Essays in the History of Ideas* (Baltimore, 1948), V: 'The Parallel of Deism and Classicism.'

[15] *Lectures*, in *Works*, XXIII, 357. In this he is repeating David Hartley (*Observations on Man:* London, 1749, p. 254). See also *The Light of Nature Pursued* by Edward Search Esq. [Abraham Tucker], London, 1768: Vol. I, Part II, pp. 102-3.

[16] *Lectures*, I, 30.

[17] It was general practice among rhetoricians to recommend, along with the study of theory, the analysis and imitation of (especially classical) models. Cf. Quintilian: *Institutio*, IV, 75.

[18] *Origin and Progress*, III, 43-44; cf. Priestley: *Lectures*, in *Works*, XXIII, 260-1; Campbell: *Philosophy*, I, 1-2; Blair: *Lectures*, I, 4-6; Lawson, *Lectures*, pp. 10-14.

[19] '. . . a genius, which . . . must be nursed, and educated, or it will come to naught.'—*Conjectures on Original Composition*, ed. E. J. Morley (Manchester, 1918), p. 15. Young's *Conjectures* will be considered in detail below (Chapter 9).

[20] See Blair: *Lectures*, I, 37; also—if this near-hysterical attack on Warton's 'Pope' can be taken seriously—Percival Stockdale's *An Inquiry into the Nature, and Genuine Laws of Poetry* (London, 1778). Pp. 167-8 assert the superiority of the poet to 'cold, formal rules, and systems': the poet acquires a knowledge of his art from higher sources. On pp. 5-7, however, characteristics of this art have been detailed ('sagacity and accuracy . . . deliberation and choice . . . propriety, order, embellishment') which in no way distinguish it from the 'art' postulated by literary theorists.

[21] See Priestley: *Lectures*, in *Works*, XXIII, 260; *The Art of Poetry on a New Plan*, I, 8; Monboddo: *Origin and Progress*, III, 9; Ward: *System of Oratory*, I, 19; etc.

[22] *On Genius*, pp. 389-90.

[23] Ibid., p. 390.

[24] Cf. Priestley: *Lectures*, in *Works*, XXIII, 320; Blair: *Lectures*, II, 323; Joseph Warton: *An Essay on the Genius and Writings of Pope* (5th ed. London, 1806) I, 198-9.

[25] *On Genius*, pp. 378-81 and pp. 391 ff. (discussion of 'taste' as a faculty of judgment). The other writers who deplore excessive 'correctness' concur in admitting the validity up to a point of rules. Even Joseph Warton, often cited as one of the important 'pre-Romantics', is full of praise for Boileau's *Art of Poetry* (*Essay on Pope*, I, 189), and—it should be remembered—assigns Pope a place only just below Milton partly on the very grounds of his 'correctness' (ibid., II, 404).

[26] *Discourses*, p, 17.

²⁷ Ibid., p. 97.
²⁸ *Conjectures*, p. 14; cf. Blair: *Lectures*, I, 6; Belsham: *Essays*, I, 211-12.
²⁹ Lawson: *Lectures*, pp. 101-2.
³⁰ See Beattie: *On Poetry and Music*, in *Essays*, pp. 3-4; Reynolds: *Discourses*, pp. 141-2.

NOTES TO CHAPTER THREE

¹ The fourth and fifth divisions (*Memoria* and *Pronuntiatio*) of classical rhetoric are not, of course, relevant to composition as such.
² *System of Oratory*, I, 39.
³ Ibid., I, 43 ff.
⁴ *Lectures*, in *Works*, XXIII, 266 ff, 286 ff and 308 ff. Priestley favours the geometer's method of laying out an argument.
⁵ *Philosophy*, I, 233 n.
⁶ Book One treats of general rhetorical principles and includes an analysis of types of evidence; Book Two of 'The Foundation and Essential Properties of Elocution'.
⁷ See Kames on the necessity of design and orderly arrangement (*Elements*, I, 27); Blair on the essential properties of a good speech: 'Solid argument, clear method . . . joined with . . . graces of style . . .' *Lectures*, II, 3).
⁸ But see Tuve: *Elizabethan and Metaphysical Imagery*, pp. 309-30, for an interesting detection of the use of 'topics' in Renaissance poetry.
⁹ John Ogilvie: *Philosophical and Critical Observations on the Nature, Characters, and Various Species of Composition* (London, 1774), I, 11.
¹⁰ Ibid., I, 111, 121, 143.
¹¹ See below, Chapter 4.
¹² *Observations*, I, 45.
¹³ *Observations*, I, 11. A faculty of 'Taste' is also postulated by certain theorists. But both 'discernment' and 'taste' are types of intuitive judgment and play a similar role to that of judgment proper. See Chapter 7 for a fuller discussion of the role of Taste in composition.
¹⁴ Ibid., I, 44. My italics.
¹⁵ Ibid., I, 29.
¹⁶ *On Genius*, p. 42.
¹⁷ Ibid., pp. 95-96, 98.
¹⁸ Ibid., pp. 37, 38.
¹⁹ Ibid., p. 44.
²⁰ Ibid., p 64. Gerard, like Campbell (quoted above), will distinguish between invention and disposition only in theory.
²¹ Ibid., p. 85.
²² Ibid., p. 84.

23 Ibid., p. 416.

24 Gerard means skill, e.g., in versification, and knowledge, e.g., of grammar and syntax.

25 Ibid., p. 422.

26 *Essay on Original Genius*. Duff adopts Taste as a faculty of intuitive judgment, with wider, vaguer, and more purely aesthetic powers than Ogilvie's 'discernment'.

27 *Dissertations*, p. 72.

28 Ibid., p. 147.

29 The most striking example is Lowth, the extent of whose disagreement with conventional views will be discussed below (Chapters 4 and 9). Another notable case in point is Thomas Warton, who, because he finds in Spenser's poetry 'the careless exuberance of a warm imagination and a strong sensibility', considers the *Faerie Queene* none the worse for being 'destitute of that arrangement and oeconomy which epic severity requires'. (*Observations on the Fairy Queen of Spenser:* London, 1762, I, 15-16.) Warton's position, however, is equivocal: he is anxious to excuse Spenser's 'faults' without condoning them (cf. ibid., II, 268). It is worth remarking that another admirer of Spenser, Richard Hurd, acquits him of the same faults on the grounds that they are more apparent than real. Spenser's method may not be classically correct, but it 'arose out of the order of his subject. And would you desire a better reason for his choice?' (*Letters on Chivalry and Romance:* London, 1762, p. 64). His poem displays 'a unity of *design*, and not of action' (ibid., p. 67).

30 I.e., that part of the theory concerned with feeling and fancy (see Chapter 7).

31 Duff, previously mentioned, is a spokesman for enthusiasm.

32 E.g. Monboddo (*Origin and Progress*, III, 2).

33 One meaning of Imagination in the eighteenth century is that of a power of forming clear and vivid mental images, usually visual. See Beattie (*Dissertations*, p. 74) who recognizes this as one function of Imagination, the other corresponding to Johnson's Invention.

34 Life of Pope, in *Works*, IV, 135.

35 He does, however, defend or excuse Pope's 'arrangement', e.g. in *Windsor Forest* and *The Rape of the Lock*. (ibid., IV, 111, 123-4).

36 Sometimes indeed carried to extremes: cf. *The Art of Poetry on a New Plan* (I, 7), which recommends the composition of a preliminary plan for even the shortest poem; and Joseph Warton (*Essay on Pope*, I, 106-7), who speaks with approval of the practice of Racine and Pope in writing the first drafts of their work in prose.

37 See A. W. Schlegel, quoted by R. Wellek in *A History of Modern Criticism*, II, 48. Schlegel is echoed by Coleridge. (*Coleridge's Shakespearean Criticism*, ed. T. M. Raysor. Everyman's Library, 1960), I, 4-5,

198. Strictly speaking, it was the resulting poetic *form* which they called 'mechanical', i.e. matter determined by design, and not design by matter.

[38] Chapter 12.

[39] *Philosophy*, I, 431.

NOTES TO CHAPTER FOUR

[1] E.g. the *Rhetorica ad Herennium*, Quintilian's *Institutio*, etc.

[2] '—we ought in fairness to fight our case with no help beyond the bare facts.' *Rhetoric:* 1404a, 5. (*The Works of Aristotle*, Vol. XI: Oxford.)

[3] *Rhetoric, or, A View of its Principal Tropes and Figures, in their Origin and Powers* (London, 1767), p. 122; cf. Lawson, *Lectures*, p. 179; see also Campbell, who postulates a hierarchy of faculties to which rhetoric may address itself, one giving access to the next in the scale: understanding, imagination, emotion, will. The appeal to understanding is of course *sine qua non*. (*Philosophy*, I, 26 ff.)

[4] Priestley: *Lectures*, in *Works*, XXIII, 263.

[5] See Tuve: *Elizabethan and Metaphysical Imagery*, Chs. XI, XII.

[6] '—though LOGIC may indeed subsist without RHETORIC or POETRY, yet so necessary to these last is a sound and correct LOGIC, that without it, they are no better than warbling Trifles.' (James Harris: *Hermes, or a Philosophical Inquiry concerning Universal Grammar*. 3rd ed. London, 1771, p. 6).

[7] *Critical Essays on some of the Poems of several English Poets* (London, 1785), p. 11.

[8] *Essays Moral and Literary* (London, 1778), p. 39.

[9] Ibid., p. 95.

[10] See, e.g., his remarks on the wit of the Metaphysicals, Life of Cowley, in *Works*, II, 23; his objections to Gray's Odes, Life of Gray, in *Works*, IV, 303-4.

[11] *Lectures*, I, 80.

[12] Ibid., I, 308.

[13] Ibid., I, 31.

[14] Ogilvie: *Observations*, I, 39-40; Beattie: *Dissertations*, p. 167; cf. Lawson's discussion of method in poetry, *Lectures*, pp. 284-9.

[15] Kames: *Elements*, I, 27; Burke: *A Philosophical Enquiry into the Origin of our Ideas of the Sublime and Beautiful* (1757. ed. J. T. Boulton, London, 1958) p. 171.

[16] Gerard (*On Genius*, pp. 147 ff.) offers an elaborate explanation of this phenomenon.

[17] Gerard: ibid., p. 147.

[18] Cf. Gerard: *On Genius*, passim; Kames's discussion of association

(*Elements*, I, 17 ff.) See Chapter 7 for fuller exposition of eighteenth-century ideas about the role of feeling in composition.

[19] Gerard: *On Genius*, p. 27.

[20] Ibid., p. 37.

[21] Ibid., pp. 77-78.

[22] Ibid., p. 319.

[23] *Dissertations*, p. 166. There is some terminological confusion here, but it will be seen that Beattie, for the moment, assimilates clearness of conception with vividness of imagination, i.e. image-forming. Clear comprehension is his leading idea.

[24] *Lectures*, I, 93; II, 371-2.

[25] *Elements*, II, 329; *Lectures*, I, 117-18. Lowth declares that ideas derived from sense, especially sight, are clearer than those 'explored by reason and argument', hence are more appropriate to poetry.

[26] Kames: *Elements:* II, 19; Blair: *Lectures*, I, 185; *Art of Poetry on a New Plan*, I, 52; etc.

[27] *Lectures*, in *Works*, XXIII, 363.

[28] E.g. by Campbell (*Philosophy*, II, 268) among others; but Blair (*Lectures*, II, 356) will not acknowledge that obscurity is ever necessary, and William Belsham ridicules the idea. He is here referring to a passage in Ossian: 'Of this strange jargon, may it not be said, in the stile and language peculiar to this Poet—Thy thoughts are dark, O Fingal! thy thoughts are dark and troubled. They are a a dim meteor, that hovers round the marshy lake. Comest thou, O son of night, in the darkness of thy pride, as a spirit speaking through a cloud of night? Thou art enveloped in obscurity, Chief of Morna!' (*Essays*, II, 203.)

[29] *Philosophical Enquiry*, pp. 58 ff.

[30] Chapter 9.

[31] Ward: *System of Oratory*, II, 113; Blair: *A Critical Dissertation on the Poems of Ossian, the Son of Fingal* (London, 1763) pp. 44-45; etc. Cf. Warton, who says 'The "man of rhymes" may be easily found; but the genuine poet of a lively plastic imagination . . . is a prodigy.' (*Essay on Pope*, I, 108).

[32] Campbell: *Philosophy*, II, 159; Priestley: *Lectures*, in *Works*, XXIII, 317; Kames: *Elements*, II, 352; and many others.

[33] Blair: *Lectures*, I, 4; and cf. Johnson, *Life of Milton*, in *Works*, II, 155.

[34] Stockdale: *Inquiry*, p. 107.

[35] Beattie: *Essays*, p. 37; cf., too, Gerard: *On Genius*, I, 31-32.

[36] Cf. Chapter 5, note 34.

[37] As we find, moreover, stated in *The Art of Poetry on a New Plan* (I, 40), 'there are other thoughts to be introduced into every work which neither strike us with their grandeur, beauty, delicacy, or pointed wit, but which are fraught with good sense and solidity; that carry weight in

their meaning, and sink deep in the understanding: these, therefore, and common thoughts, are to be considered as the basis and superstructure, and the other as the ornamental parts of the work . . .'

[38] Sentiment, as invariably in eighteenth-century usage = thought, idea.

[39] Ogilvie: *Observations*, I, 136–41.

[40] Coleridge's objection to Augustan poetry rests on a distinction which would have been meaningless in the previous century: '. . . the matter and diction seemed to me characterized not so much by poetic thoughts, as by thoughts translated into the language of poetry'. (*Biographia*, p. 9)

[41] It has sometimes been assumed that when associationists such as Hartley, Priestley and Tucker speak of the 'coalescence' or 'blending' of elementary sensations into compound ideas, they have in mind a kind of thought distinct from the logical and discursive. W. J. Bate, for instance, (*From Classic to Romantic*, pp. 118 ff.), claims that Abraham Tucker forestalls the Romantics by postulating a form of a rational synthesis as one fundamental activity of the mind. Tucker, it is true, details circumstances in which a congeries of simple ideas may be fused into a whole which is different from the mere sum of its parts (*The Light of Nature Pursued*, Vol. I, Part I, p. 221). But he is defining at this point a mode of perception, not a mode of purposive thought: it does not occur to him, as it did not to any contemporary psychologist, that there may be a sort of 'creative' thinking which is, as Coleridge maintained, *analogous* to pereception.

NOTES TO CHAPTER FIVE

[1] Cicero (*De Oratore*, II, 121-3) explains the function of figurative language by analogy with the function of clothes; Quintilian, too, compares language to apparel (*Institutio*, III, 189).

[2] See Tuve: *Elizabethan and Metaphysical Imagery*, Ch. 4.

[3] Kames: *Elements*, II, 5.

[4] Scott of Amwell (in *Critical Essays*, p. 272) quotes a couplet from *The Deserted Village*, the 'expression' of which he finds inferior to the 'sentiment'.

[5] *Rambler*, 168, (*Works*, VII, 164); cf. Ogilvie: *Observations*, II, 19.

[6] Ward: *System of Oratory*, II, 155; cf. Monboddo: *Origin and Progress*, III, 2; Isaac D'Israeli: *Miscellanies; or Literary Recreations* (London, 1796), pp. 46-47; Lawson: *Lectures*, p. 226. Lawson claims, however, that there is, 'generally speaking', one perfect expression of a given thought. Reynolds (*Discourses*, pp. 196–7) draws an analogy between painting and literature in their ability to give the same 'thought' a variety of expressions.

7 *Origin and Progress*, III, 138 ff.

8 *Philological Inquiries* (London, 1781), I, 184-5.

9 *Art of Poetry on a New Plan*, I, 18.

10 Campbell: *Philosophy*, I, 96.

11 See Quintilian: *Institutio*, III, 351.

12 E.g. Blair: '[Style] is different from mere Language or words . . . [It] has always some reference to the author's manner of thinking. It is a picture of the ideas which rise in his mind, and of the manner in which they rise there . . .' (*Lectures*, I, 183.)

13 *Lectures*, I, 32.

14 *Rhetoric*, p. 19; see also Johnson: *Rambler*, 168, in *Works*, VII, 164.

15 Priestley: *Lectures*, in *Works*, XXIII, 308; Blair: *Lectures*, I, 184. Warton says that in the *Essay on Man* Pope 'has relied chiefly on the poetry of his style for interesting his readers . . . He has many metaphors and images, artfully interspersed in the driest passages, which stood most in need of such ornaments.' (*Pope*, 11, 55.)

16 The rule of decorum was always considered to apply, as Rosemond Tuve rightly argues (*Elizabethan and Metaphysical Imagery*, p. 65). Nevertheless, the passage she quotes from Puttenham (the poet applies his ornament 'as the embroderer doth his stone and perle, or passements of gold upon the stuffe of a Princely garment') is couched in the very terms that Blair—quoted below—deplores.

17 *Lectures*, I, 364-5.

18 *Art of Poetry on a New Plan*, I, 41.; see also Ogilvie on simplicity as an ideal of style. Simplicity is achieved by naturalness and absence of strain, by allowing 'the language to rise with the thought'. (*Observations*, II, 78-79.)

19 There is classical precedent for this too. Quintilian had recommended that study of 'art' which makes 'art' unnecessary. (*Institutio*, III, 193.)

20 *Lectures*, I, 276.

21 Thus simplicity, for Ogilvie, requires a mind 'in which the understanding exerts considerable influence'. A writer must thoroughly comprehend his subject and be attentive to the kind of expression it requires (*Observations*, II, 78-79). *The Art of Poetry on a New Plan* requires writers to think clearly, to be 'masters of the language', and to have 'obtained for the memory a good stock of expressions, by a constant perusal of the best and most elegant authors'. (I, 41.) The prior acquisition of skill is clearly understood as necessary to spontaneity.

22 *Lectures*, I, 190; see also Beattie: *Essays*, p. 211; and Ogilvie; *Observations*, II, 40, where the term preferred is 'simplicity'.

23 *Observations*, II, 40.

24 *Philosophy*, II, 262.

25 Ibid., II, 331 ff.

[26] Ibid., II, 346-7; Kames: *Elements*, II, 76; and cf. Blair: *Lectures*, I, 225; Ogilvie: *Observations*, II, 199.

[27] See Campbell: *Philosophy*, I, 367 ff; Blair: *Lectures*, I, 187; Ward: *System of Oratory*, I, 308 ff. Johnson's remarks concerning purity of style in the Preface to Shakespeare (*Works*, IX, 251-2) are famous. He takes up the subject again in the *Life of Dryden* (*Works*, II, 386).

[28] Ogilvie: *Observations*, II, 136; Beattie: *Essays*, p. 211.

[29] *Philosophy*, II, 4. It is possible, since Campbell deals in the last section of his work with two only of the five 'simple and original qualities of style' he has distinguished, that the *Philosophy of Rhetoric* was left unfinished.

[30] Blair: *Lectures*, I, 247 ff; Ward: *System of Oratory*, I, 337; Beattie: *Essays*, pp. 293-4.

[31] Ward: *System of Oratory*, I, 367 ff; Beattie: *Essays*, pp. 294 ff.

[32] Beattie: *Essays*, pp. 302 ff; Blair: *Lectures*, I, 248.

[33] *Philosophy*, II, 235; cf. Priestley: *Lectures*, in *Works*, XXIII, 467.

[34] Since, however, Neo-Classical aesthetics will receive little further discussion in the following pages, some account should in justification be given at this point of its relation in general to the theory of composition and style.

The categories of the aestheticians (beauty, sublimity, elegance and the rest) are relevant to (a) the objects represented in poetry and (b) qualities of structure and style. In the first case, since no difference in kind is assumed between the aesthetic effect of real objects and that of their representations in literature, aesthetic theory has no more to offer the writer than a system of criteria to apply to the subjects he proposes to represent. It is assumed that he will choose beautiful, or elegant etc., objects to describe, and describe them accurately; alternatively, that he will express the kind of ideas which in real situations would arouse aesthetic feeling: 'elevated' thought, e.g., which concerns great objects or contains noble sentiments (cf. 'The poet, or the orator, is then possessed of this excellence [sublimity], when the sentiments he utters, or the subjects he professedly describes, contain in themselves the sublime, either of nature, or of the passions and character: and the grander the originals are, the greater is the sublimity of the imitation . . .'—Alexander Gerard: *An Essay on Taste*, 2nd edition, with corrections and additions. Edinburgh, 1764, p. 23).

To structure and style the views of the aestheticians are more directly relevant. Since they show how the simpler qualities of variety, contrast, novelty, etc., account, in various combinations, for the effect of the more complex ones (beauty or grace or wit), certain fairly definite principles concerning the combination and arrangement of ideas (the use of contrast, proportion, surprise, etc., to achieve more complex effects) could be, and often are, deduced from their arguments. Such principles, however, since they no more than supplement the basic laws of the 'art' of poetry, are of marginal interest here.

It remains to be added that the 'emotion' or 'sense' of Taste is conceived of by the aestheticians as a *reaction* to aesthetic qualities in real objects or in art: it does not enter into the process of composition. Taste, in the writer, is a *faculty*, the fruit of his aesthetic experience, which guides him in the selection and disposition of his materials (see Chapter 7 for a fuller discussion of this point).

35 The term is not now used in literary theory with the meaning 'good breeding', although decorum in this sense is still a requirement: see discussions of euphemism and periphrasis, figures which are used to avoid arousing disgust or giving offence. (Campbell: *Philosophy*, II, 217 ff; Kames: *Elements*, II, 302; Gibbons: *Rhetoric*, p. 231; Beattie: *Essays*, p. 255; etc.)

36 Blair: *Lectures*, I, 187.

37 Monboddo: *Origin and Progress*, III, 414; cf. Kames: *Elements*, II, 23–24.

38 *Essays*, p. 215.

39 See Kames: *Elements*, I, 339; Richard Polwhele: *The Art of Eloquence, a didactic poem* (London, 1785), p. 30; and cf. Belsham who praises Shakespeare for a highly figurative style which yet is rarely improper. (*Essays*, I, 25.)

40 *Art of Poetry on a New Plan*, I, 20; cf. Polwhele: *Art of Eloquence*, pp. 21–22.

41 Ward: *System of Oratory*, I, 303; Burke: *Philosophical Inquiry*, p. 166—see Chapter 9 for a discussion of Burke's views on style; Beattie: *Dissertations*, p. 184.

42 *Elements*, I, 97; Blair sees vivacity as the chief quality of good poetry (*Ossian*, pp. 44–45); and it is one of Campbell's major preoccupations (*Philosophy*, II, 158 ff.); cf. also Ogilvie: *Observations*, II, 115–16.

43 Classical rhetoric considered vivid description a figure of thought. Quintilian (*Institutio*, III, 396) following Cicero (*De Oratore*, Book III: Loeb Classical Library: II, 160) calls it *sub oculos subiectio*.

44 Campbell: *Philosophy*, I, 37; Ward: *System of Oratory*, II, 92–93; Priestley: *Lectures*, in *Works*, XXIII, 330; Kames: *Elements*, II, 334; etc. It is by this means, of course, that the 'typical' is expressed through the 'individual'. (See Reynolds: *Discourses*, pp. 192–3.) The apparently conflicting demands of Neo-Classical literary theory for both 'generality' and 'particularity' have puzzled some commentators, but see Abrams: *The Mirror and the Lamp*, p. 39.

45 Campbell: *Philosophy*, II, 159; Kames: *Elements*, II, 352. Campbell also mentions sound and rhythm, brevity, and certain syntactical

devices (e.g. asyndeton) as factors contributing to vivacity. (*Philosophy*, II, 229 ff.)

[46] *Art of Poetry on a New Plan*, I, 42: '. . . these short allegories and images . . . have a fine effect in poetry, that delights in imitation, and endeavours to give to almost everything, life, motion, and sound; . . . In short, poetry is a sort of painting in words.'

[47] Ogilvie: *Observations*, II, 112; Blair: *Lectures*, I, 186; Ward: *System of Oratory*, I, 303, 307.

[48] Campbell: *Philosophy*, I, 190; *Art of Poetry on a New Plan*, I, 46 (in 'descriptions'); Gibbons: *Rhetoric*, p. 384 (in personifications).

[49] Campbell: *Philosophy*, I, 191; Priestley: *Lectures*, in *Works*, XXIII, 321; Kames: *Elements*, I, 100.

[50] Campbell: *Philosophy*, I, 37; Priestley: *Lectures*, in *Works*, XXIII, 315; Kames: *Elements*, I, 97; Ogilvie: *Observations*, II, 115–16; etc. It was the function of the rhetorical figure 'hypotyposis' (vivid description) to arouse feeling: this figure and its function are still recognized, see Ward: *System of Oratory*, II, 90; Monboddo: *Origin and Progress*, III, 117; Gibbons: *Rhetoric*, p. 318.

[51] Campbell: *Philosophy*, I, 208; Kames: *Elements*, I, 92.

[52] Ward: *System of Oratory*, II, 144.

[53] Blair: *Lectures*, I, 379–80.

[54] Ibid., I, 382–3.

[55] Ward: *System of Oratory*, II, 155. The sublime style is less relevant to the point here: it consists of lofty thoughts expressed in a bold and elevated language, though it is consistent with perfect simplicity. See Monboddo: *Origin and Progress*, III, 289–91; *Art of Poetry on a New Plan*, I, 48; Ward: *System of Oratory*, II, 163 ff. Blair recognizes only 'great things in few and plain words' as characteristic of the sublime style (*Lectures*, I, 77). He rejects the florid style as bombast (Ibid., I, 76, 384).

NOTES TO CHAPTER SIX

[1] Blair: *Lectures*, I, 274; cf. Priestley: *Lectures*, in *Works*, XXIII, 486; Polwhele: *The Art of Eloquence*, p. 26; Ward: *System of Oratory*, II, 156.

[2] See Cicero: *De Oratore*, Book III, Vol. II, 119, 123; Quintilian: *Institutio*, III, 303, 305.

[3] Ward: *System of Oratory*, I, 384; Monboddo: *Origin and Progress*, III, 32–33; Gibbons: *Rhetoric*, p. 3.

[4] E.g. Priestley: *Lectures*, in *Works*, XXIII, 388–9.

[5] *Elements*, II, 299.

[6] Blair: *Lectures*, I, 285; Beattie: *Essays*, p. 252; Lowth: *Lectures*, I, 106 (translator's note); Ward: *System of Oratory*, I, 387–8.

⁷ Campbell: *Philosophy*, II, 183 ff.; Blair: *Ossian*, p. 2; etc.

⁸ Campbell: *Philosophy*, II, 177. Campbell believes that as language develops, and a nation's taste with it, people become 'more averse to the admission of new metaphors . . . Hence it is that in modern times the privilege of coining these tropes, is almost confined to poets and orators; and as to the latter, they can hardly even be said to have this indulgence, unless where they are wrought up to a kind of enthusiasm by their subject.' (Ibid., II, 187); cf. Kames (*Elements*, II, 184) who thinks only 'correct' metaphors and similes admissible.

⁹ Priestley: *Lectures*, in *Works*, XXIII, 379; Kames: *Elements*, II, 183; Blair: *Ossian*, p. 52.

¹⁰ Metaphors: Priestley: *Lectures*, in *Works*, XXIII, 389; Blair: *Lectures*, I, 297; Ward: *System of Oratory*, I, 389; etc. Personifications: Priestley: ibid., XXIII, 440; Kames: *Elements*, II, 236; Campbell: *Philosophy*, II, 204.

¹¹ *Philosophy*, II, 190 ff.

¹² *Lectures*, in *Works*, XXIII, 389.

¹³ For the function of metaphor and comparison in amplification see Blair: *Lectures*, I, 288 and *Ossian*, p. 52; Hartley: *Observations on Man*, p. 254; Ward: *System of Oratory*, II, 184; Lowth: *Lectures*, I, 115. Kames gives his own rather far-fetched explanation of the way in which comparisons amplify. (*Elements*, I, 288 ff.)

¹⁴ Priestley: *Lectures*, in *Works*, XXIII, 486; Ward: *System of Oratory*, I, 390; Beattie: *Essays*, p. 285.

¹⁵ Kames: *Elements*, II, 183; Duff: *On Original Genius*, p. 146; Blair: *Ossian*, p. 52; etc. According to Hartley the perception of resemblance is heightened by a previous perception of dissimilarity. (*Observations*, p. 253.)

¹⁶ See Quintilian: *Institutio*, III, 351; Cicero: *De Oratore*, Book III, Vol. II, 123 ff. (tropes), pp. 161 ff. (figures).

¹⁷ See Quintilian: *Institutio*, III, 359: '. . . there is no more effective method of exciting the emotions than an apt use of figures.'

¹⁸ E.g. Monboddo: *Origin and Progress*, III, 12–13, 66 ff. ('figures of construction'); 107 ff. ('figures of sense'); Gibbons: *Rhetoric*, pp. 3, 122–3.

¹⁹ Ward: *System of Oratory*, II, 35–36.

²⁰ Blair: *Lectures*, I, 275-6; Beattie: *Essays*, pp. 264-5; *Art of Poetry on a New Plan*, I, ii; etc.

²¹ See Gibbons: *Rhetoric*, pp. 124–5; or cf. Blair: *Lectures*, I, 275 and I, 288.

²² E.g. by Blair (*Lectures*, I, 360): 'Let nature and passion always speak their own language, and they will suggest figures in abundance.'; cf. Goldsmith: *Works*, I, 363; Beattie: *Essays*, p. 267. Many others state or imply the same thing.

[23] Blair (*Lectures*, I, 364) says: '. . . we should never interrupt the course of thought to cast about for Figures. If they be sought after coolly, and fastened on as designed ornaments, they will have a miserable effect.' Lowth (*Lectures*, I, 309) sniffs at rhetoricians for 'attributing that [figurative language] to art, which above all things is due to nature alone . . .' Cf. Gibbons: *Rhetoric*, p. 125.

[24] Lowth: *Lectures*, I, 120–1; Campbell: *Philosophy*, II, 116; Duff: *On Original Genius*, p. 147. The caution applies as well to figures (see Lawson: *Lectures*, pp. 257–8; Kames: *Elements*, II, 324), and sometimes to 'ornament' generally (see Hume: *Essays*, p. 114).

[25] Lawson: *Lectures*, p. 260; Kames: *Elements*, II, 321; Campbell: *Philosophy*, II, 225–6. Campbell particularly deplores the use of synaesthetic metaphor.

[26] Kames: *Elements*, II, 295; Blair: *Lectures*, I, 346; Goldsmith: *Works*, I, 363; *Art of Poetry on a New Plan*, I, 39–40; Lowth's translator would allow metaphors, but not comparisons (*Lectures*, I, 108 n.).

[27] Priestley: *Lectures*, in *Works*, XXIII, 313; Blair: *Lectures*, I, 360.

NOTES TO CHAPTER SEVEN

[1] See the list in Quintilian: *Institutio*, III, 377 ff.

[2] See Blair: *Lectures*, I, 355 ff.; Ward: *System of Oratory*, II, 65 ff.; Monboddo: *Origin and Progress*, II, 66 ff.

[3] Blair: *Lectures*, I, 318 ff.; Beattie: *Essays*, p. 265.

[4] *Philosophy*, II, 275; I, 242; cf. Blair: *Lectures*, II, 7; Ward: *System of Oratory*, II, 38–39; Lawson: *Lectures*, p. 171.

[5] *Lectures*, I, 367–8; cf. Gerard: *On Genius*, p. 357: passion is expressed partly by 'those effects, *imitable* in the particular art, by which each passion naturally shows itself'. (My italics.)

[6] *Philosophical Enquiry*, p. 173.

[7] *Lectures*, I, 309; Beattie says that tropes and figures are necessary to imitating the *language* of passion. (*Essays*, p. 264.)

[8] Priestley: *Lectures*, in *Works*, XXIII, 313; cf. Burke: *Philosophical Enquiry*, p. 175. Lowth finds that style (and here he particularly mentions figures) expresses feeling in the same way as tone of voice or gesture. It is for this reason that music and the dance were originally associated with poetry. And Lawson says (*Lectures*, p. 251): 'Inward Emotion displayeth itself as readily in the Language as in the Features . . .'.

[9] Beattie: *Essays*, pp. 55–56.

[10] Campbell: *Philosophy*, I, 32; Lowth: *Lectures*, I, 309.

[11] Gerard: *On Genius*, p. 357; Beattie: *Dissertations*, p. 181.

[12] Gibbons: *Rhetoric*, p. 122; Blair: *Lectures*, II, 315; Monboddo: *Origin and Progress*, III, 115; Lawson: *Lectures*, p. 252.

[13] Kames: *Elements*, I, 36, 40, 43; Lawson: *Lectures*, p. 156.

[14] *On Genius*, p. 147.

[15] Coleridge speaks of passion as one of the objects of poetic contemplation. (*Shakespearean Criticism*, ed. Raysor, I, 147–8). For further discussion of the Romantic association of feeling with meditation see Chapter 10.

[16] Thomas Twining: *Dissertation on Poetry considered as an Imitative Art* (prefaced to translation of Aristotle's *Treatise on Poetry*): London, 1789, pp. 16–17.

[17] *Art of Poetry on a New Plan*, I, 39–40.

[18] Beattie: *Dissertations*, p. 167.

[19] Lowth: *Lectures*, I, 38; cf. also Kames: *Elements*, I, 503; Lawson: *Lectures*, p. 250.

[20] *On Genius*, p. 152.

[21] Ibid., p. 170.

[22] Ibid., p. 357; cf. Beattie: *Essays*, p. 52.

[23] This does not, of course, preclude the possibility of a writer's feeling determining his *choice* of a subject.

[24] *Lectures*, I, 309; cf. Goldsmith: *Works*, I, 378, and Campbell (*Lectures*, II, 268–9) who discusses the effect of feeling on style in the writing of odes.

[25] *Elements*, II, 204; cf. Priestley: *Lectures*, in *Works*, XXIII, 393.

[26] *Lectures*, II, 315; cf. Ward: *System of Oratory*, II, 36 and, for an explanation along the same lines of the origin of prosopopoeia, Gibbons: *Rhetoric*, pp. 392–3.

[27] E.g. Lawson (*Lectures*, pp. 252–3) and Kames (*Elements*, II, 259) who as much as say that hyperbole is effective as a *sign* of feeling.

[28] See Lowth: *Lectures*, I, 111 (figurative language may 'exhibit objects . . . in a sublimer or more forcible manner'); Priestley: *Lectures*, in *Works*, XXIII, 393 (metaphor is used to convey strong ideas of objects). Kames explains that amplification causes the reader to re-appraise the object described: it works its effect primarily because the object 'is judged to be more strange or beautiful than it is in reality' (*Elements*, I, 288 ff., 292).

[29] Kames: *Elements*, I, 93; Campbell: *Philosophy*, I, 295; Priestley: *Lectures*, in *Works*, XXIII, 317.

[30] There is no relation, of course, between this principle and that of either the Romantic symbolic image or the 'objective correlative' of a later date. The latter are direct and immediate vehicles of feeling, of which the sole function is to convey that feeling.

[31] Goldsmith: *Works*, I, 378; Hartley: *Observations*, p. 254.

[32] Scott of Amwell: *Critical Essays*, p. 189.

[33] A description will give aesthetic pleasure primarily in so far as it depicts a pleasing object. Figurative language contributes to the effect

simply as an embellishment or enlivening of the representation (see e.g., Beattie, *Essays*, p. 285). The question of how and why 'embellishment' occurs is rarely gone into, though we find attempts at an explanation in the work of the associationists, e.g. Priestley and Alison. For them it is *abstract qualities* which are associated with pleasure; these are transferred from object to object, and the emotions of taste with them, when a metaphorical substitution of names occurs. Thus, for Priestley, metaphor carries with it the *ideas* of beauty or dignity attached to the object it names (*Lectures*, in *Works*, XXIII, 389), or gives pleasure (not by virtue of its meaning, but by virtue of its mode of operation) by suggesting *ideas* of uniformity and variety (ibid., p. 379). Alison elaborates this principle much further; his views will be discussed in Chapter 9.

34 *Lectures*, pp. 17–18, 20.

35 See Duff: *On Original Genius*, p. 11; Gerard: *On Taste*, pp. 171–2, and *On Genius*, p. 299; Blair: *Lectures*, I, 41.

36 Many incidental remarks show unmistakably that this assumption is made, e.g.: 'A writer of genius', says Blair, 'conceives his subject strongly . . . He puts on no emotion which his subject does not raise in him . . .' (*Lectures*, I, 365). Beattie states that, when agitated, the mind does not 'run out into' such tropes and figures as 'tend to withdraw the fancy from the object of the passion' (*Essays*, p. 264). Cf. Also Lowth, (*Lectures*, I, 309): 'The mind, with whatever passion it be agitated, remains fixed upon the object that excited it . . .'

37 Campbell: *Philosophy*, I, 242; Blair: *Lectures*, II, 7; and many others, though the reference to Horace is not always explicit.

38 *On Genius*, p. 257; cf. Lowth: *Lectures*, I, 366.

39 *Elements*, I, 454. Evidently the word 'sensibility' in both these passages means no more than 'susceptibility' (cf. Johnson's Dictionary which defines the principal meaning of 'sensibility' as 'quickness of sensation'). Otherwise the resemblance to certain of Wordsworth's views, expressed in the Preface to *Lyrical Ballads*, is very striking. See, however, Chapter 9 for a discussion of the differences which are also to be noticed.

40 *Lectures*, pp. 255–6.

41 These remarks apply to 'enlivening' and 'amplifying' as well.

NOTES TO CHAPTER EIGHT

1 See Beattie's essay 'On Poetry and Music as they Affect the Mind': 'In a prose work, we may have the fable, the arrangement, and a great deal of the pathos, and language, of poetry; and such a work is certainly a poem, though perhaps not a perfect one.' For perfection, verse is necessary. (*Essays*, pp. 294, 296.) See below for 'fiction', 'pathos', 'language', as invalid defining characteristics of poetry.

² This opinion is usually supported by the assumption that poetry originated amongst primitive peoples as an ebullition of passion or enthusiasm. See Lowth: *Lectures*, I, 37–38; Blair: Ossian, p. 3; *Art of Poetry on a New Plan*, I, ii; etc.

³ Blair: *Lectures*, II, 312.

⁴ Beattie: *Essays*, p. 288.

⁵ See Chapter 7. Blair is of course also a believer in 'vivacity'. He says that the true poet makes us see what he describes. 'This happy talent is chiefly owing to a strong imagination, which first receives a lively impression of the object; and then . . . transmits that impression in its full force to the imagination of others.' (*Lectures*, II, 372.)

⁶ See Joseph Warton: *Essay on Pope*, I, 108, 317; Goldsmith: *Works*, I, 354–5; Duff: *On Original Genius*, pp. 171–2; Lowth: *Lectures*, I, 37–38, 81–82, 367–8; *Art of Poetry on a New Plan*, I, iii–iv; etc.

⁷ See Ward: *System of Oratory*, I, 338, 407; Scott of Amwell: *Critical Essays*, p. 248. Thomas Twining (*Dissertation* prefaced to Aristotle's *Treatise*) distinguishes between descriptive imitation (producing 'illusive perception') and fictive imitation (producing 'illusive belief') as characteristic procedures of poetry (p. 19).

⁸ Goldsmith: *Works*, I, 352–3.

⁹ Ibid., I, 355.

¹⁰ Ibid., I, 354.

¹¹ Lowth: *Lectures*, I, 75.

¹² 'Composition' = *compositio*, arrangement of words; not in the wider sense. Ibid., I, 308; cf. D'Israeli: *Miscellanies*, p. 208.

¹³ Beattie: *Essays*, p. 247.

¹⁴ Kames, *Elements*, II, 100–1.

¹⁵ *Lectures*, II, 313.

¹⁶ Belsham: *Essays*, I, 221; I, 223.

¹⁷ Campbell: *Philosophy*, I, 14–15.

¹⁸ *Memoirs of the Literary and Philosophical Society of Manchester*, Vol. I (Warrington, 1785).

¹⁹ Op cit., p. 55; cf. Twining, who argues that not all poetry is imitation, nor all imitation poetry. (*Dissertation* prefaced to Aristotle's *Treatise*, p. 24.)

²⁰ Op cit., p. 57. 'Elevation' comprises the idea of passion. Barnes, in presenting this particular account of poetry, includes the usual argument brought up to support it. Poetry originated with primitive peoples. 'Their lives were full of danger and variety . . . Hence their *feelings* were amazingly intense. And hence their *language* was bold, and poetically sublime . . .' (p. 58).

²¹ Ibid., p. 61.

²² Ibid., pp. 61–62.

²³ Ibid., p. 63.

[24] Blair: *Lectures*, II, 313.

[25] Campbell, e.g., classifies the kinds according to the faculties they are designed to address (passion, fancy, will), the means adopted (conformation, insinuation, persuasion), and the role assumed in each case by the poet (representer, narrator, reasoner). (*Philosophy*, I, 71–72.)

[26] Scott's *Critical Essays* are concerned entirely with long descriptive poems. Cf. Kames: 'Writers of genius, sensible that the eye is the best avenue to the heart, represent every thing as passing in our sight . . .' (*Elements*, II, 351); and Blair: 'A poet of original genius is always distinguished by his talent for description.' (*Ossian*, p. 44).

[27] Alison, in *Essays on the Nature and Principles of Taste* (1790. 5th, ed. Edinburgh, 1817), assumes that poetry appeals to Taste because it is imitative in the sense 'descriptive'. Cf. Twining's *Dissertation* prefaced to Aristotle's *Treatise:* '. . . of all the extended or analogical applications of the word [imitation], this [i.e. description] is perhaps the most obvious and natural. There needs no other proof of this than the very language in which we are naturally led to express our admiration of this kind of poetry, and which we perpetually borrow from the arts of strict imitation. We say the poet has *painted* his object; we talk of his *imagery*, of the lively *colours* of his description, and the masterly touches of his *pencil.*' (Pp. 9–10.)

[28] *N.B.* the admiring tone of such works as Lowth's *Lectures on the Sacred Poetry of the Hebrews*, Blair's *Critical Dissertation on the Poems of Ossian*. A not uncharacteristic tribute to the Ode is found in the *Art of Poetry on a New Plan:* 'The ode . . . is very ancient, and was probably the first species of poetry. It had its source, we may suppose, from the heart, and was employed to express, with becoming fervour and dignity, the grateful sense man entertained of the blessings which daily flowed from God the fountain of all goodness . . .' (II, 39).

NOTES TO CHAPTER NINE

[1] Abrams, since he traces one important element in 'expressive' (i.e. Romantic) theory back to Longinus, implies a 'pre-Romantic' trend which begins in England with John Dennis. (*The Mirror and the Lamp*, pp. 72 ff.)

[2] The controversy over this issue has been very well summed up by René Wellek ('The Concept of "Romanticism" in Literary History': *Comparative Literature*, Vol. I, 1949). Wellek can see no objection to the idea of 'pre-Romanticism'. He acknowledges that writers termed 'pre-Romantic' can readily be shown to have adhered in the main to traditionalist views. Their 'Romantic' ideas, however—even when wrenched out of context—are a legitimate topic of interest, he thinks, and impor-

tant to the historian. 'The fact that a later age could fasten on certain passages in Young or Hurd or Warton is relevant—not the intentions of Young, Hurd, or Warton.' It is submitted here that no historian can understand Young, Hurd and Warton unless he considers their intentions relevant, nor can he understand Romantic theory if he considers that it originated in the work of these writers.

If 'pre-Romantic' implied simply 'supplying stimulus and suggestion to the Romantics' no one could quarrel with the term. But Wellek himself demonstrates that a wider meaning is inevitably attached to it. He points to the 'problem of the preparation of the new age'. There *must* have been 'preparations, anticipations, and undercurrents' in the eighteenth century: Wordsworth and Coleridge did not 'fall from Heaven'. But revolutions occur precisely because new ideas do 'fall from heaven': in this case they may not all have occurred in the first instance to Wordsworth or Coleridge (cf. Chapter 12), but as certainly were they not thought up by Young, Hurd or Warton. The work of the latter may be regarded as 'preparation' in that it may have afforded an impetus to new ways of thinking, but it contains no idea that was not transformed out of all recognition by the radically different approach of the Romantics.

Wellek finally argues that unless we postulate pre-Romantic trends in eighteenth-century critical thought, we make the unwarrantable assumption that 'the neo-Classical age was unperturbedly solid, unified, and coherent in a way no age has ever been before or since'. This does not, of course, follow: are we driven into the same absurd position if we deny to eighteenth-century culture a pre-Hegelian logic, a pre-Marxist social theory, or a pre-Freudian psychology?

³ Cf. Quintilian: *Institutio*, IV, 75 ff.

⁴ *Conjectures*, p. 11,

⁵ Ibid., p. 6.

⁶ Ibid., p. 8; pp. 6–7.

⁷ Ibid., p. 13 ff.

⁸ Ibid., p. 13.

⁹ Ibid., pp. 13, 14.

¹⁰ Ibid., p. 15.

¹¹ Ibid., p. 7.

¹² Ibid., p. 16.

¹³ Ibid., p. 12.

¹⁴ Ibid., pp. 15, 14.

¹⁵ Ibid., p. 27.

¹⁶ Ibid., p. 24.

¹⁷ Ibid., p. 32.

¹⁸ Ibid., pp. 4 (wit), 8 (thoughts), 11, 15 (sense), 17 (knowledge), 6 (imitation), 36 (pathos).

¹⁹ Ibid., p. 24.

[20] See pp. 14–15, 34–35 (Shakespeare); pp. 29–30 (Pope).

[21] Many of Young's ideas stem from Longinus, or at least the Longinian tradition, e.g. the notion that the faults of genius must be overlooked (*On the Sublime:* Chs. XXIII–XXIV); that genius goes beyond 'art' (ibid., Chs. II; XXXV–XXXVI); that imitation should be emulation rather than copying (ibid., Chs. XIII–XIV); that the important elements in poetry depend on native gifts, not on 'art' (Ch. VIII), etc.

[22] See Abrams: *The Mirror and the Lamp*, pp. 201–2.

[23] See M. W. Steinke: *Edward Young's 'Conjectures on Original Composition' in England and Germany* (New York, 1917), pp. 14–15; and cf. Chapter 2.

[24] *Enquiry*, p. 62.

[25] Ibid., p. 163.

[26] Ibid., p. 165.

[27] Ibid., pp. 166–7.

[28] Cf. ibid., p. 166: '. . . when words commonly sacred to *great* occasions are used, we are affected by them even without the occasions'; and p. 171: '. . . if poetry gives us a *noble* assemblage of words, corresponding to many *noble* ideas . . . [it can achieve its end]'—(my italics).

[29] Ibid., p. 59.

[30] Ibid., p. 171 (design: 'the picturesque connection' is not demanded, but Burke clearly regards logical pattern as necessary); p. 166 (propriety); p. 175 (the impassioned style).

[31] See *Coleridge's Miscellaneous Criticism* (ed. T. M. Raysor), London, 1936, p. 403.

[32] *Enquiry*, p. lxxxii (editor's introduction).

[33] *Lectures*, p. 79.

[34] Ibid., pp. 106 ff. (fig. language), 116–17 (vivacity), 120 ff. (perspicuity), 31–32 (the dress of thought).

[35] See Chapter 7.

[36] Abrams's emphasis on the 'expressive' features of Lowth's theory (*The Mirror and the Lamp*, pp. 76–78) makes him sound more extraordinary than he is. A later reference to Lowth (p. 84) acknowledges that in his 'formal and systematic discussion of poetry and its kinds' he 'reverted to the traditional pattern of analysis', but Abrams does not show that Lowth's 'expressive' doctrines were in themselves rhetorical ones.

[37] E.g. Blair, Gerard, Beattie, Kames, Priestley, Reynolds, etc. W. J. Bate (*From Classic to Romantic:* New York, 1961, see esp. Ch. 4) sees the associationist aestheticians as supplying 'the main foundation for many of the familiar tenets of English romantic poets and critics'. (p. 102); cf. E. N. Hooker: 'The Discussion of Taste'.

[38] See Chapter 2. The aestheticians of the earlier part of the century,

even the so-called Platonists among them who are sometimes described as the original 'pre-Romantics', come still less close to a subjective view of art. Shaftesbury, for example, insists on the importance of authoritative critical principles and of fixed rules applying to literary composition (see *Characteristics*, ed. J. M. Robertson, London, 1900: I, 127 and 151 ff.)

39 See Chapter 7.

40 *Essays on Taste*, II, 417.

41 Ibid., II, 434.

42 E.g. '. . . the Poet . . . in the selection of the objects of his *description*, and in the decision of their expression . . . [has unbounded freedom]'; '. . . by the preservation of Unity of character or expression . . . the excellence of poetical *description* is determined . . .' (ibid., I, 133—my italics).

43 Ibid., I, 118.

44 '. . . what distinguishes *pure* poetry from other writing, is its aptitude . . . to please the fancy, and move the passions, by a lively imitation of nature'. (Beattie *Essays*, p. 288.)

45 *Essays on Taste*, II, 418–19.

46 Ibid., pp. 178–9, 183.

47 Ibid., I, 132.

48 Cf. 'How much the effect of descriptions of natural scenery arises from that personification which is founded upon such associations [i.e. of objects with human qualities], I believe there is no man of common taste who must not often have been sensible.' (Ibid., I, 184.) The poet has 'the mighty spell of mind at his command, with which he can raise every object that he touches into life and sentiment . . .' (ibid., I, 134).

49 Ibid., I, 132.

50 See also the passage quoted in note 42 above: 'the *selection* of the objects . . . the *decision* of their expression . . .'.

51 Ibid., I, 4.

52 Ibid., I, 58.

53 Ibid., I, 76.

54 Ibid., I, 120.

55 There is one further respect in which Alison might seem to deserve the title of 'pre-Romantic'. Though he considers that objects become signs of 'mental qualities' through the normal processes of association, he also believes that there is a metaphysical power at work in Nature which makes its phenomena signs to us of 'higher qualities, by which our moral sensibilities are called forth'. A passage towards the end of his book (II, 436 ff.) which proclaims this faith in the moral value of aesthetic reactions to Nature, very strikingly anticipates some of Wordsworth's pronouncements in the Preface to *Lyrical Ballads* and in the

earlier philosophical poems. But we are here on the metaphysical verge of poetic theory; besides, it is not this particular part of Wordsworth's earlier views which can be called distinctively Romantic (see further below). Romantic theory, in which associationism plays no part, conceives the ethical value of the aesthetic response in a different way (Imagination is a means to *Knowledge:* Beauty is Truth) and explains the relevant psychological process in totally different terms.

[56] Preface to *Lyrical Ballads*, in *Lyrical Ballads* (ed. R. L. Brett and A. R. Jones, London, 1963), p. 256 (1800); cf. pp. 240, 261 (1800). (Since it is a point of some interest that most of the important ideas in the Preface first appeared in the 1800 version, the date of its original publication is noted against each passage cited.)

[57] Ibid., p. 249 (1802); p. 308 (Appendix, 1802).

[58] Ibid., p. 254 (1802).

[59] Ibid., p. 255 (1802).

[60] Cf. Chapter 8.

[61] Op. cit. pp. 256 ff. (1800). Cf. Priestley's views on the aesthetic function of metre and rhyme (*Lectures*, in *Works*, XXIII, 450 ff.)

[62] Preface, p. 249 (1802).

[63] Ibid., pp. 239, 241 (1800).

[64] Preface, pp. 240–1 (1800).

[65] Ibid., p. 248 n. (1800 and 1802). It is impossible to agree with Abrams (*The Mirror and the Lamp*, pp. 96–97) that Wordsworth derives many of his ideas from the essay by William Enfield in the *Monthly Magazine* (July 1796) entitled 'Is Verse Essential to Poetry?' Enfield shares not only his 'primitivistic' doctrines with other writers of the time, but also his thesis that, except for metre, poetry possesses no special features to distinguish it from prose (cf. Chapter 8). His opposition of poetry, not to prose, but to *philosophy* implies something very different from Wordsworth's opposition of poetry to *science*. Enfield is mainly concerned to point out that the poet (who speaks 'the language of fancy, passion, and sentiment') should properly aim at pleasing, while the philosopher (speaking 'the language of reason') should aim to instruct. This may be, as Abrams suggests, to distinguish between 'rational and emotive language', but it is not to distinguish between a discursive and an imaginative subject-matter as the Romantics, and Wordsworth to begin with, set out to do. Enfield is quite ready to accept discursive thought as the basis of poetry: 'the stores of knowledge and sentiment are equally open to the man of sense and information, or to the man of feeling and fancy . . .' (op. cit. p. 454); both poetry and prose exhibit 'exact and lively pictures of men and things. . . . The same objects [in either case] lie before the eye, or imagination of the writer . . . he has equal scope for the exercise of judgment and taste in the arrangement of his materials.' (Ibid., p. 455.)

66 Preface, p. 251 (1802).
67 Ibid., pp. 253–4 (1802).
68 Ibid., p. 240 (1800).
69 Ibid., p. 242 (1800).
70 Ibid., p. 260 (1800).
71 Ibid., pp. 249–50 (1802).
72 See Chapter 7, esp. n. 39.
73 Preface, p. 250 (1802). Wordsworth of course makes a great deal of the poet's sensibility and its relation by means of 'the grand elementary principle of pleasure' with the intuitive understanding of Nature (Ibid., pp. 252–3: 1802). 'Sensibility' in this passage is nearer than ever to the 'emotions of Taste' of, e.g., Alison.
74 My italics. Preface, pp. 309, 308 (App. 1802).
75 Ibid., pp. 238, 244 (1802); p. 308 (App. 1802).
76 Ibid., pp. 309–10 (1802).
77 Ibid., p. 244 (1802); cf. the original version of this passage:
'. . . I propose to myself to imitate, and, as far as possible, to adopt the very language of men, and I do not find that such personifications make any regular or natural part of that language.' (Ibid., p. 244.)
78 Wordsworth's opposition (Preface, p. 248 n.: 1800) of Poetry to Science is indeed the same opposition that Coleridge was to insist on. But there is little suggestion in the Preface of the kind of argument that Coleridge devised to support the distinction.
79 Wordsworth is, in any case, limited in the Preface by his dependence on associationist psychology. Romantic theory could not reach its fullest development, i.e. its clearest definition, until it had freed itself completely from the empiricism which supported traditional beliefs about literature (see Chapter 12 for a fuller discussion of this point).

NOTES TO CHAPTER TEN

1 'I am not a critic—and set little value upon the art. The preface which I wrote long ago to my own Poems I was put upon to write by the urgent entreaties of a friend . . .'
'. . . I never cared a straw about the "theory" and the "preface" was written at the request of Mr. Coleridge, out of sheer good nature.'
Both remarks occur in letters and are quoted in Markham L. Peacock: *The Critical Opinions of William Wordsworth* (Baltimore, 1950), pp. 33, 453.
2 See René Wellek: *Immanuel Kant in England 1793–1838* (Princeton, 1931), p. 160.
3 'Because of their hospitality to ideas from many sources, romantic critics in fact exhibit greater diversity in philosophical presuppositions,

descriptive vocabulary, dialectical motifs, and critical judgments than the writers of any earlier period . . . however, we may notice that there are a limited number of assertions about poetry which turn up so persistently although in very different theoretical frames, that they may perhaps be called *the* romantic complex of ideas about poetry.' (Abrams: *The Mirror and the Lamp*, p. 100.) Albert Gérard, whose book, *L'Idée romantique de la poésie en Angleterre* (Paris, 1955), analyses romanticism as a poetical philosophy, comes to the same conclusion. The inquiries of both writers are of wider scope than the one attempted here. But their remarks apply with the same, if not added, force: there is nothing about which the Romantics are, at bottom, more agreed (or more at variance with their predecessors) than the philosophy of poetic composition.

[4] Byron was self-confessedly a Neo-Classic by conviction, though a Romantic in practice, and theorized, in any case, very little about poetry. Blake's unique position will be discussed in the next chapter, as will that of certain minor figures who constitute for criticism what Byron called 'the postscript of the Augustans'.

[5] *Upon Epitaphs II* (*Wordsworth's Literary Criticism*, ed. Nowell Smith; London, 1905), p. 108.

[6] Preface to *The Revolt of Islam*, in *The Complete Poetical Works*, ed. Thomas Hutchinson (Oxford Standard Authors, 1943), p. 33.

[7] *Treatise on Method*, ed. Alice D. Snyder (London, 1934), p. 62.

[8] Cf. also Hazlitt ('On Poetry in General'). 'The poetical expression of any object is that uneasy, exquisite sense of beauty or power that cannot be contained within itself. . . .' (*Lectures on the English Poets*, in *The Complete Works of William Hazlitt*, ed. P. P. Howe; London, 1930; V, 3.)

[9] MS. Quoted in *Inquiring Spirit*, ed. Kathleen Coburn. (London, 1951) p. 66. Compare the passage in *Biographia Literaria* (p. 17) where the mind of genius is characterized as 'affected by thoughts, rather than things'.

[10] *Biographia*, p. 270.

[11] 'On Poetry in General'. 'Wherever any object takes such a hold of the mind as to make us dwell upon it, and brood over it, melting the heart in tenderness, or kindling it to a sentiment of enthusiasm . . . this is poetry.' (*English Poets*, in *Works*, V, 12.)

[12] T. Allsop: *Letters, Conversations and Recollections of S. T. Coleridge*, II, 85 (quoted in *Inquiring Spirit*, p. 33).

[13] See his theory of metre (*Biographia*, p. 211) and an early version of his definition of a poem (*Shakespearean Criticism*, ed. T. M. Raysor, I, 147–8).

[14] *Biographia*, p. 211.

[15] *Upon Epitaphs I* (*Literary Criticism*, ed. Smith), p. 91.

[16] No clear distinction is preserved by the Romantics between feeling,

thought, imagination: they are concerned rather to emphasize the unity of the creative process. The distinction made here has a purely pragmatic basis: discussion would be needlessly complicated by avoiding it.

[17] *Biographia*, p. 270; and cf. p. 177 where he speaks of images 'modified' by passion; *Shakespearean Criticism*, I, 148, where feeling is again identified with Imagination as a modifying power.

[18] *Shakespearean Criticism*, I, 193.

[19] 'On Genius and Common Sense'. (*Table Talk*, in *Works*, VIII, 42.)

[20] *Biographia*, pp. 48, 180, 270; and cf. p. 17—in the mind of the genius feeling blends 'more easily and intimately' with thought.

[21] Chapter 9.

[22] Letter to Gillies. 22.12.1814. (Quoted in Peacock: *Critical Opinions*, p. 21.)

[23] It is not easy to judge how far an 'image' was still, for the early Romantics, a 'picture'. Most of the evidence (the lack of interest in definition and clarity; the references to 'blending' with feelings, and with other images; the fact that language is considered inseparable from thought) strongly suggests that the term 'imagery' had already lost its pictorial implications and had acquired its present more imprecise meaning of 'figurative (esp. metaphorical) language which expresses a poetic form of thought'. (See the following chapter for a discussion of Romantic views on the relation between thought and language.)

[24] *Shakespearean Criticism*, II, 64.

[25] Shelley: Preface to *The Cenci* (*Poetical Works*, p. 277); Hazlitt: 'On Poetry in General' (*English Poets*, in *Works*, V, 5).

[26] Thought is here being distinguished as the *content* of poetry from Imagination as the poetical faculty—purely, however, in the interests of a clear argument at this point.

[27] *Biographia*, p. 9.

[28] *The Prelude*. Book II. (*Poetical Works*, ed. Thomas Hutchinson: Oxford Standard Authors, 1953: p. 505.)

[29] 'On Poetry in General'. (*English Poets*, in *Works*, V, 3.)

[30] *Shakespearean Criticism*, II, 103.

[31] *Upon Epitaphs I* (*Literary Criticism*, ed. Smith, p. 92).

[32] 'On Poetry in General'. (*English Poets*, in *Works*, V, 9.)

[33] *A Defence of Poetry* (*Shelley's Literary and Philosophical Criticism*, ed. John Shawcross; London, 1909; p. 155).

[34] Perhaps Keats's idea of Negative Capability, which he considered 'Shakespeare possessed so enormously', is also not without relevance here. It is a state of 'uncertainties, mysteries, doubts, without any irritable reaching after fact and reason . . .' (*The Letters of John Keats*, ed. Buxton Forman; Oxford, 1947, p. 72).

[35] The distinction, borrowed from the Germans (Goethe, Schiller, Schlegel), between subjective or Romantic and objective or Classical

poetry had by now become a critical commonplace. See Abrams: *The Mirror and the Lamp*, p. 242.

[36] *Style* (*The Collected Writings of Thomas De Quincey*, ed. David Masson. Edinburgh, 1890. Vol. X), p. 226.

[37] Cf. a note of Coleridge's: 'By deep feeling we make our *ideas dim*, and this is what we mean by our life, ourselves.' (*Anima Poetae*, ed. E. H. Coleridge; London, 1895, p. 15).

[38] Preface to *Poems of 1815*. (*Poetical Works*, p. 755). See also in this connexion Wordsworth's letter to Lady Beaumont (*Literary Criticism*, ed. Smith, pp. 51–53) in which he gives an account of the composition of a sonnet. This is interesting as an analytic description of the non-conceptual character and the a-logical movement of Romantic poetic thought.

[39] It is difficult to disagree with Miss A. E. Powell who says: 'Wordsworth's definition of imagination is substantially the same as that of Coleridge. We know that the poets were so closely associated in working it out that it was impossible to say with whom the conception arose.' The differences are more apparent than real. 'Coleridge's chief interest lay in tracing imagination to its "seminal principle", whereas the interest of Wordsworth was in its manifestations.' (*The Romantic Theory of Poetry*. London, 1926, pp. 145, 146).

[40] Shelley: opening para. of the *Defence of Poetry* (*Literary and Philosophical Criticism*, p. 120); and Hazlitt: '. . . the imagination is that faculty which represents objects not as they are in themselves, but as they are moulded by other thoughts and feelings, into an infinite variety of shapes and combinations of power. . . . The province of the imagination is principally visionary, the unknown and undefined: the understanding restores things to their natural boundaries, and strips them of their fanciful pretensions.' ('On Poetry in General', *English Poets*, in *Works*, V, 4, 9.) It is only, however, Wordsworth and Coleridge, of the earlier Romantics, who distinguish Fancy from Imagination as a secondary, and inferior, inventive faculty, though their distinction was to be taken up by a later generation of critics (see Alba H. Warren, Jr.: *English Poetic Theory 1825-1865;* Princeton, 1950, p. 19).

[41] *Biographia*, p. 167.

[42] *Treatise on Method*, p. 6: 'The Idea may exist in a clear, distinct, definite form, as that of a circle in the Mind of an accurate Geometrician; or it may be a mere *instinct*, a vague appetency towards something which the Mind incessantly hunts for, but cannot find, like a name which has escaped our recollection, or the impulse which fills the young Poet's eyes with tears, he knows not why.'

[43] Ibid, p. 36.

[44] Even the most convinced Platonist could not, without a smattering of transcendental philosophy, have understood the function of Imagina-

tion in expressing Ideas. All eighteenth-century theorists were limited by their psychological presuppositions to the traditional theory of invention (cf. Ch. 12).

⁴⁵ *Biographia*, p. 206.

⁴⁶ Ibid., p. 173.

⁴⁷ *Shakespearean Criticism*, I, 150. Coleridge's attitude to the question of 'purpose' is best summed up in a MS. fragment (quoted *Treatise on Method:* Appendix, p. 85): '. . . every work of Genius, containing the End in the Means, is a *poesis*, as distinguished from a mere *syntaxis*, or collocation for an external and conventional end.' There is yet another function attributed to the will by both Wordsworth and Coleridge. They both evidently believe that although the act of creation is spontaneous in itself, yet the necessary conditions for poetic activity, the emotions involved, are at the poet's command. Shakespeare's feelings, says Coleridge, 'were under the command of *his own will*'. (*Shakespearean Criticism*, I, 187.) Compare the account in Wordsworth's Preface of the characteristics of the poet, which include 'an ability of conjuring up in himself passions, which etc.' (*Lyrical Ballads*, p. 250).

⁴⁸ Letter to Pasley, 28.3.1811. (*Critical Opinions*, p. 21.)

⁴⁹ Keats: *Letters*, p. 108.

⁵⁰ Two letters of 1816. (*Critical Opinions*, p. 22.)

⁵¹ Letter to Montgomery, 21.1.1824. (*Critical Opinions*, p. 22.)

⁵² *A Defence of Poetry* (*Literary and Philosophical Criticism*, p. 157; cf. p. 153). See also Hazlitt: 'On Poetry in General' (*English Poets*, in *Works*, V, 1), and a criticism of Dryden's lack of spontaneity in a paraphrase of Chaucer: ('On Manner', *Miscellaneous Writings*, in *Works*, XX, 54–55.)

⁵³ *Contributions to the Edinburgh Review* (London, 1853), pp. 526–7. Jeffrey acknowledges that there can be in this kind of composition, where the traditional recomendations of poetry are wanting, 'a fine feeling expressed of those mysterious relations by which visible external things are assimilated with inward thoughts and emotions, and become the images and exponents of all passions and affections'. (P. 527.)

NOTES TO CHAPTER ELEVEN

¹ *Letters*, p. 222–3.

² Shelley: Preface to *The Revolt of Islam* (*Poetical Works*, pp. 35–36); Hazlitt: 'The Indian Jugglers,' *Table Talk*, in *Works*, VIII, 82.

³ *Biographia*, p. 218.

⁴ *Shakespearean Criticism*, I, 148; cf. *Biographia*, p. 172.

⁵ *Biographia*, p. 172.

⁶ *Shakespearean Criticism*, I, 4.

⁷ Ibid., I, 206. Coleridge explains this part of his theory most fully

in the *Treatise on Method*, where he aims to show that all methodical mental operations are analogues of organic growth: they are burgeonings, as it were, of a seed which is the creative Idea. (An Idea is an intuition of the relations between things in any given sphere.)

8 Wordsworth appears to be echoing Coleridge in his *Essay Upon Epitaphs II* (*Literary Criticism*, ed. Smith, p. 136); cf. also Hazlitt (*Lectures on the English Comic Writers*, in *Works*, VI, 109), who remarks on the 'involuntary unity of purpose' in Cervantes and his 'instinct of Imagination' which 'works unconsciously, like nature'.

9 See the Introduction to *The Prelude*, and the Preface to *The Cenci*. It is the story *per se* of the Cenci which appeals to Shelley, and not any objective perception of its artistic possibilities. He notes 'the overwhelming interest which it seems to have the magic of exciting in the human heart', and it is this, he says, which suggested to him its 'fitness for a dramatic purpose'. It only remained 'to clothe it to the apprehensions of my countrymen in such language and action as would bring it home to their hearts'. (*Poetical Works*, p. 276.) Nothing could be more typical of the Romantic approach to a 'subject' than these statements, unless it be the play itself which betrays a minimum of care for dramatic structure and an extravagant emphasis on 'the poetry which exists in . . . tempestuous sufferings and crimes'.

10 *Biographia*, p. 174.

11 *Inquiring Spirit*, p. 101; cf. Coleridge's definition of the symbol, ibid., p. 104.

12 *Literary Criticism*, ed. Smith, pp. 68–70 (Letter to *The Friend*).

13 *Inquiring Spirit*, p. 104.

14 *Treatise on Method*, p. 62

15 'On Poetry in General', *English Poets*, in *Works*, V, 7.

16 *Contributions*, p. 527.

17 'The Indian Jugglers', *Table Talk*, in *Works*, VIII, 83.

18 Essay Supplementary to the Preface of 1815, *Poetical Works*, p. 744.

19 *Defence*, in *Literary and Philosophical Criticism*, pp. 156, 155.

20 *The Philosophical Lectures of Samuel Taylor Coleridge*, ed. Kathleen Coburn (London, 1949), p. 193; 'On the Principles of Genial Criticism' (in *Biographia Literaria*, ed. J. Shawcross. Oxford, 1907), II, 239.

21 ('Reason' in the Kantian sense). See *Miscellaneous Criticism*, p. 396; and *Treatise on Method*, p. 27, where Shakespeare's characters are said to be embodiments of the Idea of the human race.

22 *Biographia*, p. 252.

23 *Shakespearean Criticism*, II, 135.

24 Wordsworth: Essay Supp. 1815, in *Poetical Works*, p. 750; cf. Jeffrey: *Contributions*, pp. 439–40 and Shelley: *Defence*, in *Literary and Philosophical Criticism*, p. 131: 'A man, to be greatly good, must imagine intensely and comprehensively . . . Poetry strengthens the faculty which

is the organ of the moral nature of man, in the same manner as exercise strengthens a limb.'

25 *Biographia*, pp. 12, 263; cf. p. 4.

26 See a note which appears only in the 2nd ed. of *Biographia Literaria* (ed. H. N. Coleridge, 2 vols., London, 1847: I, 7 n.). Watson (*Biographia*, Everyman ed.: note on the text, p. xxiii) states that this edition has no authority: the note, however, has an authentically Coleridgean ring.

27 *Biographia*, p. 263.

28 Ibid., p. 12.

29 He is, of course, able to show that to reproduce exactly the language of rustic life in poetry is neither possible nor, if it were, desirable (*Biographia*, Chs. XVII and XVIII). But, though a certain vagueness in Wordsworth's argument lays him open to this sort of attack, it is doubtful whether he was proposing anything so extreme as the aim of his own poetry, much less as an aim proper to all poetry. Coleridge's disagreement with Wordsworth about the effects of metre on poetic style is of course a real one.

30 *Treatise on Method*, p. 14.

31 *Shakespearean Criticism*, I, 201.

32 *Defence*, in *Literary and Philosophical Crit.*, p. 125; cf. also Preface to *The Revolt of Islam, Poetical Works*, p. 34, though Shelley's statement here, implying as it does that imagination involves empathy with Nature, has a Wordsworthian rather than Coleridgean flavour. De Quincey, too, is convinced that the best style is spontaneous and artless, and he offers this belief as a basis for a new rhetoric which will not presume to lay down positive rules for good writing, but will prescribe cautionary negative ones only (*Collected Writings*, X, 193).

33 Letter to Gillies, 22.12.1814. (*Critical Opinions*, p. 22). Hazlitt says much the same thing, though he is not here discussing poetry alone: '. . . Mr. Cobbett is hardly right in saying that the first word that occurs is always the best. It may be a very good one; and yet a better may present itself on reflection from time to time.' He adds none the less: 'It should be suggested naturally, however, and spontaneously, from a fresh and lively conception of the subject.' ('On Familiar Style', *Table Talk*, in *Works*, VIII, 244–5.)

34 *Biographia*, pp. 263–4. De Quincey speaks from a very similar point of view when he says that the 'mechanism' of style (the deliberate, and analysable, process for which an 'art' of rhetoric can legislate) applies to 'no meritorious qualities of style, but to its faults, and, above all to its awkwardness; in fact, to all that now constitutes the *friction* of style, the needless joltings and retardations of our fluent motion'. (*Collected Writings*, X, 193.)

35 Letter to Gillies, 14.2.1815. (*Critical Opinions*, p. 22.) The hated Pope was, of course, equally guilty of this practice.

184 *Notes to pages 129–132*

36 *Upon Epitaphs II, Literary Criticism*, ed. Smith, pp. 129–30. De Quincey acknowledges that there are two kinds of style, two methods of writing, appropriate respectively to an objective and a subjective subject-matter. 'Ponderable facts and external realities are intelligible in almost any language. But, the more closely any exercise of the mind is connected with what is internal and individual in the sensibilities . . . precisely in that degree . . . does the style . . . cease to be a mere separable ornament, and in fact the more does the manner . . . become confluent with the matter.' (*Collected Writings*, X, 229.) He quotes Wordsworth approvingly, however, on language as the 'incarnation' of thought: 'never in one word was so profound a truth conveyed . . . if language were merely a dress, then you could separate the two; you could lay the thoughts on the left hand, the language on the right. But, generally speaking, you can no more deal thus with poetic thoughts than you can with soul and body. (Ibid., X, 230.)

37 Lectures on Shakespeare and Milton V, *Shakespearean Criticism*, II, 74; cf. Hazlitt: 'On Writing and Speaking', *The Plain Speaker*, in *Works*, XII, 277–8. De Quincey believes that language and thought co-exist 'not merely *with* the other, but each *in* and *through* the other. An image, for instance, a single word, often enters into a thought as a constituent part.' (*Collected Writings*, X, 230.)

38 *Inquiring Spirit*, p. 101.

39 See Hazlitt: 'On Poetry in General', *English Poets*, in *Works*, V, 7; Coleridge: *Biographia*, p. 248, and *Anima Poetae*, p. 155: 'the instinctive passion in the mind for a *one word* to express *one act* of feeling—one that is, in which, however complex in reality, the mind is *conscious* of no discursion and synthesis *a posteriori*.'

40 *Miscellaenous Criticism*, p. 307.

41 *Shakespearean Criticism*, II, 74; cf. I, 185.

42 Essay Supp. 1815, in *Poetical Works*, pp. 748–9.

43 *Aids to Reflection* (London, 1913), p. 154 n.

44 Cf. Wordsworth's series of quotations in the 1815 Preface, each illustrating the imaginative use of one word which transforms a whole context (*Poetical Works*, p. 754). None of these metaphors has (or is assumed by Wordsworth to have) a specific rhetorical function to serve: introduced into a context with which they 'clash', they generate overtones of idea and feeling which are suffused, as it were, throughout the entire passage. There can be no neat, logical assimilation of a given part of their meaning into the meaning of the whole, as would be the case if they could be read as metaphors of the ordinary rhetorical kind. Coleridge's example (*Biographia*, p. 178) of two lines of verse converted, by a suitable use of the pathetic fallacy, into imaginative poetry illustrates, though less clearly, the same phenomenon. It is not stretching a point too far to cite the above passages as illustrating the Romantic conception of *symbols*.

Though it is entire images, and not isolated verbs and epithets, which we normally describe by that name, the Romantic definition of a symbol required it only to operate as a vehicle of Imaginative thought and feeling. Single words and complete images will serve that function to a different degree perhaps, but, it is suggested here, will do so in the same way and for the same reasons.

45 *Poetical Works*, p. 754.

46 See Wordsworth: Preface to *Lyrical Ballads;* Coleridge: *Biographia* pp. 163–4.

47 E.g. in the *Biographia* and 1815 Preface, *passim.*

48 *The Prelude*, I, 227–33 (*Poetical Works*, p. 497). Coleridge, his enthusiasm for the idea conveyed in the use of capitals, thought Wordsworth capable of the 'FIRST GENUINE PHILOSOPHICAL POEM' (*Biographia*, p. 275). Wordsworth is, of course, regarded as the chief exemplar of the new kind of poetry (cf., e.g., Hazlitt: 'On Genius and Common Sense', *Table Talk*, in *Works*, VIII, 44–45), though in fact all the early Romantics wrote their most ambitious pieces in this vein. Jeffrey, protesting against the trend in the name of common sense (apropos of Byron in this instance), strikes a note which now sounds almost comically ineffectual: 'Philosophy and Poetry are both very good things in their way; but, in our opinion, they do not go very well together. It is but a poor and pedantic sort of poetry that seeks chiefly to embody metaphysical subtleties and abstract deductions of reason—and a very suspicious philosophy that aims at establishing its doctrines by appeals to the passions and the fancy...' (*Contributions*, p. 412).

49 Cf. Byron's remark on poetry as the 'lava of the imagination' (*Letters and Journals*, ed. R. E. Prothero; London, 1900), III, 405. Jeffrey seems to have much modified his initial anti-Romantic prejudices: compare the article on Crabbe (1808) in which he refers to 'the Wordsworths, and the Southeys, and the Coleridges and all that ambitious fraternity, that, with good intentions and extraordinary talents, are labouring to bring back our poetry to the fantastical oddity, and puling childishness of Withers, Quarles, or Marvel' (*Contributions*, p. 483); with his account of literary history in the article on Swift (1816), which is far more sympathetic to the Romantics (*Contributions*, pp. 73 ff. esp. p. 77). Jeffrey's later ideas draw progressively nearer the new theory; see the articles on Keats (1820) and Felicia Hemans (1829).

50 See especially some of Wordsworth's statements at a later period e.g. in a letter to Hamilton (1827): '... I am certain ... that you will be brought to acknowledge that the logical faculty has infinitely more to do with poetry than the young and inexperienced ... ever dreams of ... the application of it requires an adroitness which can proceed from nothing but practice; a discernment, which emotion is so far from bestowing that at first it is even in the way of it' (*Critical Opinions*, p. 120); and, in

another letter to a friend (1831), a passage beginning '. . . Again and again I must repeat, that the composition of verse is infinitely more of an *art* than men are prepared to believe . . .' (*Literary Criticism*, ed. Smith, p. 243).

[51] *Poetry and Prose of William Blake* (ed. Geoffrey Keynes; London, 1956), pp. 821–2.

[52] Ibid., p. 787.

[53] Ibid., p. 786.

[54] 'Grecian is Mathematic Form: Gothic is Living Form. Mathematic Form is Eternal in the Reasoning Memory: Living Form is Eternal Existence.' (Ibid., p. 583.) In view of Blake's often-expressed hostility to reason, one may infer that he does not admire both types equally.

[55] Ibid., p. 772.

[56] Ibid., p. 785.

[57] Ibid., pp. 776, 777.

NOTES TO CHAPTER TWELVE

[1] Schelling, of course, is the predominant influence in Coleridge's *Biographia:* but Schelling's *System of Transcendental Idealism* has been called 'Kant's system not written by Kant'.

[2] See Kant: *Critique of Pure Reason* (trans. J. M. D. Meiklejohn, Everyman's Library), pp. 104–5; cf. *Critique of Judgment* (trans. J. C. Meredith; Oxford, 1952), p. 86. It seems unlikely that the Romantic conception of Fancy represents, as Gérard suggests (*L'Idée romantique*, p. 185), an independent borrowing from eighteenth-century association-ism.

[3] This is a simplification, though not necessarily a falsification, of one of Kant's key-ideas in the *Critique of Aesthetic Judgment*, cf. esp. pp. 175–6.

[4] Ibid., pp. 171–2.

[5] Ibid., pp. 166–71.

[6] Ibid., pp. 182, 177–80, 184–5, 191–2.

[7] The case of Hazlitt is particularly interesting, since although he set up for an empiricist, his psychology—and a large part of his poetic theory which depends upon it—is paradoxically a product of idealist beliefs. (See for a brief account of his general position, *Prospectus of a History of English Philosophy* in *Works*, II, 113 ff.)

[8] 'Influences' have been studied in individual cases, and a few general matters of fact, such as the basis in association theory of the work of certain eighteenth-century critics, are too obvious to have escaped notice. But there has been, as far as I know, no detailed com-

parative study of the parallel trends in philosophy and literary theory in either part of the period.

9 See Wellek: *Immanuel Kant in England*, Ch. I; on Coleridge's familiarity with Kant, see pp. 70–71.

10 The arguments could have been found in the work of Alison, whose aesthetic theory might have been suitably adapted, see Chapter 9.

11 Except in the case of Burke, who did perceive that no one-to-one correspondence necessarily obtains between words and 'ideas', but that words derive their force from the purposes for which, and the contexts in which, they are habitually used. (Cf. Chapter 9.)

12 The trend in favour of psychology, however, cannot but have had its beneficial effects. The psychology of the time, defective though it undoubtedly was, aimed at least to offer an account of the mind which tallied as far as possible with perceptible fact (the principles of association, e.g., may certainly be observed in operation). Their interest in psychology is bound to have focused the attention of critics upon the more palpable properties of literature and their effects, to have drawn them away from arbitrary guess-work about imponderables, and dissatisfied them with over-elaborate and ineffective conventions.

13 Epics and poetic dramas flowed, of course, in plenty from the pens of Romantic and post-Romantic poets; but these are generally strange and unsatisfactory hybrids, Romantic poems in an uncomfortable rhetorical dress which is thrown off at every available opportunity.

14 The doctrine of the 'objective correlative', for example, literally restricts the expressive resources of poetry to images and symbols (or to characters and incidents considered as images and symbols). Eliot's concern for 'art' in the early essays wears a classical air, yet here again he is propounding no more than a narrower version of Coleridge's theory of imagination. He envisages the same process of ideas and emotions fusing into a new unity, but with a difference which must rarefy and attenuate the result, since the emotions need not be 'real' emotions, and the fusion is no part of the experience expressed but takes place in the 'crucible of talent'. The purpose is still Romantic expression, but it is achieved by highly indirect means, through a sort of impersonal simulation, in fact, of the process Coleridge described (see 'Tradition and the Individual Talent', in *Selected Essays;* London, 1932). Eliot in his later essays returns to a more conventional Romanticism (cf. esp. 'The Music of Poetry' and 'The Three Voices of Poetry', in *On Poetry and Poets;* London, 1957), but here, too, one may find evidence of 'sub-Romantic' ideas. His views, e.g., that the poet's function is to express the sensibility of an age on its behalf may be seen simply as a retrenchment on Romantic claims for the poet as prophet and seer (ibid., 'The Social Function of Poetry').

15 The situation is much the same in America, where theorists are

more numerous, and perhaps more adventurous, but no less Romantic in their basic assumptions. A curious development there, represented in the work of the 'Chicago critics' reveals the irresistible strength of Romantic prejudice. The 'Chicago critics', with all their reverence for Aristotle, feel quite able, and indeed desire, to reconcile their 'classicism' with non-classical approaches to literary theory. Their very interpretation of Aristotle's views may on occasion reveal a Romantic bias (cf. the remarks on 'beauty' in Elder Olson: *An Outline of Poetic Theory*, in *Critics and Criticism;* Chicago, 1952, pp. 556–7—which sound very like a Coleridgean improvement on Aristotle). Yvor Winters, who, more than any other critic of recent years, has freed himself from Romantic preconceptions, is by no means always unequivocally anti-Romantic. He can still speak, e.g., of the poet's function as the 'discovery of values' through the exercise of his sensibilities in an 'act of perception'— Romantic language this, or something very close to it ('The Morality of Poetry', in *In Defense of Reason;* London, 1937, p. 17).

Bibliography

(The following is intended only as a reference—list of works cited in the text.)

I CLASSICAL:

ARISTOTLE: *Poetics* and *Rhetoric*, in *The Works of Aristotle* (Oxford, 1946), Vol. XI.
CICERO: *De Oratore*, (trans. E. W. Sutton and H. Rackham, Loeb Classical Library, 1948).
LONGINUS: *On the Sublime*, (trans. W. H. Frye, Loeb Classical Library, 1927).
QUINTILIAN: *Institutio Oratoria* (trans. H. E. Butler, Loeb Classical Library, 1921).

II EIGHTEENTH CENTURY:

ALISON, ARCHIBALD: *Essays on the Nature and Principles of Taste* (1790; 5th ed. Edinburgh, 1817).
Art of Poetry on a New Plan, The (pub. John Newbery; London, 1762).
Art of Rhetorick, The: The Circle of the Sciences. Vol. VI (pub. John Newbery; London, 1746).
BARNES, THOMAS: 'On the Nature and essential Characters of Poetry, as distinguished from Prose' (*Memoirs of the Literary and Philosophical Society of Manchester*, Vol. I. Warrington, 1785).
BEATTIE, JAMES: *Dissertations, Moral and Critical* (London, 1783); *Essays* (Edinburgh, 1776).
BELSHAM, WILLIAM: *Essays, Philosophical, Historical, and Literary* (London, 1789).
BLAIR, HUGH: *A Critical Dissertation on the Poems of Ossian, the Son of Fingal* (London, 1763); *Lectures on Rhetoric and Belles Lettres* (London, 1783).
BOSWELL, JAMES: *Life of Johnson* (Oxford Standard Authors, 1952).
BURKE, EDMUND: *A Philosophical Enquiry into the Origin of our Ideas of the Sublime and Beautiful* (1757. Ed. J. T. Boulton; London, 1958).
CAMPBELL, GEORGE: *The Philosophy of Rhetoric* (London, 1776).
D'ISRAELI, ISAAC: *Miscellanies; or Literary Recreations* (London, 1796).
DUFF, WILLIAM: *An Essay on Original Genius* (London, 1767).
ENFIELD, WILLIAM: 'Is Verse Essential to Poetry?' (*Monthly Magazine*, July 1796).

GERARD, ALEXANDER: *An Essay on Genius* (London, 1774); *An Essay on Taste* (2nd ed., with corrections and additions; Edinburgh, 1764).

GIBBONS, THOMAS: *Rhetoric, or, a View of its Principal Tropes and Figures, in their Origin and Powers* (London, 1767).

GOLDSMITH, OLIVER: *The Works of Oliver Goldsmith* (ed. J. W. M. Gibbs; London, 1884); *New Essays* (ed. R. S. Crane; Chicago, 1927); *Complete Works* (ed. A. Friedmann; Oxford, 1966).

HARRIS, JAMES: *Hermes, or a Philosophical Inquiry concerning Universal Grammar* (3rd ed., revised and corrected; London, 1771); *Philological Inquiries* (London, 1781).

HARTLEY, DAVID: *Observations on Man* (London, 1749).

HUME, DAVID: *Essays, Literary, Moral and Political* (1753-4. Reprinted in one vol.; London, 1870).

HURD, RICHARD: *Letters on Chivalry and Romance* (London, 1762).

JOHNSON, SAMUEL: *The Works of Samuel Johnson* (London, 1787).

KAMES, HENRY HOME, LORD: *The Elements of Criticism* (6th ed., with the author's last corrections and additions; London, 1785).

KANT, IMMANUEL: *Critique of Judgment* (trans. J. C. Meredith; Oxford, 1952); *Critique of Pure Reason* (trans. J. M. D. Meiklejohn, Everyman's Library, 1942).

KNOX, VICESIMUS: *Essays Moral and Literary* (London, 1778).

LAWSON, JOHN: *Lectures concerning Oratory* (London, 1759).

LOWTH, ROBERT: *Lectures on the Sacred Poetry of the Hebrews* (pub. orig. as *De sacra poesi Habraeorum*; Oxford, 1753. Trans. G. Gregory; London, 1787).

MONBODDO, JAMES BURNETT, LORD: *Of the Origin and Progress of Language* (1773–6. 2nd ed.; London, 1786).

OGILVIE, JOHN: *Philosophical and Critical Observations on the Nature, Characters, and Various Species of Composition* (London, 1774).

POLWHELE, RICHARD: *The Art of Eloquence, a didactic poem* (London, 1785).

PRIESTLEY, JOSEPH: *A Course of Lectures on Oratory and Criticism* (1777), in *The Theological and Miscellaneous Works of Joseph Priestley* (London, 1824), Vol. XXIII.

REYNOLDS, SIR JOSHUA: *Discourses on Art* (1769–91. Ed. Robert R. Wark, Huntington Library, 1959).

SCOTT OF AMWELL, JOHN: *Critical Essays on some of the Poems of several English Poets* (London, 1785).

SHAFTESBURY, ANTHONY ASHLEY COOPER, 3RD EARL OF: *Characteristics* (ed. J. M. Robertson; London, 1900).

SHARP, RICHARD: 'On the Nature and Utility of Eloquence' (*Memoirs of the Literary and Philosophical Society of Manchester*, Vol. III. Warrington, 1790).

SHERIDAN, THOMAS: *British Education: or, the Source of the Disorders of Great Britain* (London, 1756).

STOCKDALE, PERCIVAL: *An Inquiry into the Nature, and Genuine Laws of Poetry* (London, 1778).

TUCKER, ABRAHAM: *The Light of Nature Pursued, by Edward Search Esq.* (London, 1768).

TWINING, THOMAS: *Dissertation on Poetry considered as an Imitative Art* (prefaced to a translation of Aristotle's *Treatise on Poetry;* London, 1789).

WARD, JOHN: *A System of Oratory* (London, 1759).

WARTON, JOSEPH: *An Essay on the Genius and Writings of Pope* (1756, 1782. 5th ed., corrected, London, 1806).

WARTON, THOMAS: *Observations on the Fairy Queen of Spenser* (London, 1762).

YOUNG, EDWARD: *Conjectures on Original Composition* (1759. Ed. Edith J. Morley; Manchester, 1918).

III NINETEENTH CENTURY:

BLAKE, WILLIAM: *Poetry and Prose of William Blake* (ed. Geoffrey Keynes; London, 1956).

BYRON, GEORGE GORDON, LORD: *Letters and Journals* (ed. R. E Prothero; London, 1900).

COLERIDGE, SAMUEL TAYLOR: *Aids to Reflection* (London, 1913); *Anima Poetae* (ed. E. H. Coleridge; London, 1895); *Biographia Literaria* (ed. George Watson; Everyman's Library, 1960); *Biographia Literaria* (ed. H. N. Coleridge; London, 1847); *Inquiring Spirit* (ed. Kathleen Coburn; London, 1951); *Coleridge's Miscellaneous Criticism* (ed. T. M. Raysor; London, 1936); *The Philosophical Lectures of Samuel Taylor Coleridge* (ed. Kathleen Coburn; London, 1949); 'On the Principles of Genial Criticism', in *Biographia Literaria* (ed. J. Shawcross; Oxford, 1907); *Coleridge's Shakespearean Criticism* (ed. T. M. Raysor; Everyman's Library, 1960); *Treatise on Method* (ed. Alice D. Snyder; London, 1934).

DE QUINCEY, THOMAS: *The Collected Writings of Thomas De Quincey* (ed. David Masson; Edinburgh, 1890).

HAZLITT, WILLIAM: *The Complete Works of William Hazlitt* (ed. P. P. Howe; London, 1930).

HUNT, LEIGH: *Leigh Hunt's Literary Criticism* (ed. L. H. and C. W. Houtchens; New York, 1956).

JEFFREY, FRANCIS: *Contributions to the Edinburgh Review* (London, 1853).

KEATS, JOHN: *The Letters of John Keats* (ed. Buxton Forman; Oxford, 1947).

Bibliography

PEACOCK, THOMAS LOVE: 'The Four Ages of Poetry', in *Works* (ed. Henry Cole; London, 1875), Vol. III.

SHELLEY, PERCY BYSSHE: *Shelley's Literary and Philosophical Criticism* (ed. John Shawcross; London, 1909); Prefaces, in *Complete Poetical Works* (ed. Thomas Hutchinson; Oxford Standard Authors, 1943).

WORDSWORTH, WILLIAM: *The Critical Opinions of William Wordsworth* (ed. Markham L. Peacock: Baltimore, 1950); *Wordsworth's Literary Criticism* (ed. Nowell C. Smith; London, 1905); Preface to *Lyrical Ballads*, in *Lyrical Ballads* (ed. R. L. Brett and A. R. Jones; London, 1963); Preface to *Poems of 1815* and Essay Supplementary to the Preface, in *Poetical Works* (ed. Thomas Hutchinson; Oxford Standard Authors, 1953).

IV TWENTIETH CENTURY:

ABRAMS, M.: *The Mirror and the Lamp* (London, 1960).

ATKINS, J. W. H.: *English Literary Criticism: 17th and 18th centuries* (London, 1951).

BATE, W. J.: *From Classic to Romantic: Premises of Taste in Eighteenth-century England* (Cambridge, Mass., 1946).

CLARK, D. L.: *Rhetoric and Poetry in the Renaissance* (New York, 1922).

CRANE, W. G.: *Wit and Rhetoric in the Rennaissance* (New York, 1937).

CRANE, R. S. (ed.): *Critics and Criticism* (Chicago, 1952).

CROCE, BENEDETTO: *Aesthetic* (trans, Douglas Ainslie; London, 1953).

ELIOT, T. S.: *Selected Essays* (London, 1932); *On Poetry and Poets* (London, 1957).

GÉRARD, ALBERT: *L'Idée romantique de la poésie en Angleterre* (Paris, 1955).

GOMBRICH, E. H.: *Art and Illusion* (London, 1960).

HOOKER, E. N.: 'The Discussion of Taste, from 1750 to 1770, and the new trends in Literary Criticism' (*PMLA*, XLIX, 1934).

HOWELL, W. S.: *Logic and Rhetoric in England 1500–1700* (Princeton, 1956).

LOVEJOY, A. O.: *Essays in the History of Ideas* (Baltimore, 1948).

MONK, S. H.: *The Sublime: A Study of Critical Theories in 18th-century England* (New York, 1935).

POWELL, A. E.: *The Romantic Theory of Poetry* (London, 1926).

SAINTSBURY, G.: *A History of English Criticism* (Edinburgh, 1911).

STEINKE, M. W.: *Edward Young's 'Conjectures on Original Composition' in England and Germany* (New York, 1917).

TUPPER, CAROLINE F.: 'Essays Erroneously Attributed to Goldsmith' (*PMLA*, XXXIX, 1924).

TUVE, ROSEMOND: *Elizabethan and Metaphysical Imagery* (Chicago, 1947).

WARREN, ALBA H.: *English Poetic Theory 1825-1865* (Princeton, 1950).

WELLEK, RENÉ: 'The Concept of "Romanticism" in Literary History' (*Comparative Literature*, Vol. I, 1949); *A History of Modern Criticism* (London, 1955); *Immanuel Kant in England 1793–1838* (Princeton, 1931).

WIMSATT, W. K. and CLEANTH BROOKS: *Literary Criticism: A Short History* (New York, 1957).

WINTERS, YVOR: *In Defense of Reason* (London, 1937).

Index

Abrams, M., 14, 151 n.2, n.3, 165 n.44, 172 n.1 174 n.22, n.36, 176 n.65, 178 n.3, 180 n.35

Aesthetics, 4, 23–24, 93ff, 138, 164 n.34. *See also* Taste

Akenside, Mark, 93

Alfieri, Vittorio, Count, 128

Alison, Archibald, 24, 25, 170 n.33, 172 n.27, 177 n.73, 187 n. 10; as 'Pre-Romantic', 93ff

Amplification, 59–60, 70–72, 127, 144, 147, 170 n.41

Aristotle, 10, 11, 30, 38

Art of Poetry on a New Plan, The, 43, 152 n.4, 156 n.2, n.8, 157 n.21, 159 n.36, 161 n.26, n.37, 163 n.9, 163 n.18, n.21, 165 n.40, 166 n.46, n.48, n.55, 167 n.20, 168 n.26, 169 n.17, 171 n.2, n.6, 172 n.28

Art of Rhetorick, The, 153 n.15

'Art' *vs* 'Nature', 27–28, 52–53, 62–63, 75–76, 85–87, 90. *See also* Spontaneity

Association of ideas, Theory of, in Alison's aesthetics, 94ff; and function of tropes, 60, 169 n.33; and nature of poetic thought, 162 n.41; principle of connexion in poetic thought, 41; and problem of Taste, 24; in theory of invention, 33–35, 69–70

Atkins, J. W. H., 151 n.1

Baldwin, C. S., 152 n.6

Barnes, Thomas, on the distinguishing characteristics of poetry, 81–82

Bate, W. J., 151 n.2, 174 n.37

Beattie, James, 17, 35, 42, 54, 55, 78, 79, 85, 94, 156 n.7, 158 n.30, 159 n.33, 160 n.14, 161 n.35, 163 n.22, 164 nn.30–32, 165 n.35, 166 n.6, 167 n.14, n.20, n.22, 168 n.3, n.7, n.9, n.11, 169 n.18, n.22, 170 n.33, n.36, n.1, 174 n.37

Belsham, William, 17, 158 n.28, 161 n.28, 165 n.39, 171 n.16; criticism of Kames, 22–23

Blair, Hugh, 18, 23, 25, 42, 52–53, 56, 57, 61, 71, 78, 80, 85, 153 n.12, 155 n.28, 156 n.7, 157 n.18, n.20, n.24, 158 n.28, n.7, 161 n.26, n.28, n.31, n.33, 163 n.12, n.15, n.16, 164 n.26, n.27, n.30, n.32, 165 n.36, n.42, 166 n.55, n.1, n.6, 167 n.7, n.9, n.10, n.13, n.15, nn.20–22, 168 n.23, n.26, n.27, nn.2–4, n.12, 170 nn.35–37, 171 n.2, 172 n.24, n.26, n.28, 174 n.37

Boileau, Nicolas, 157 n.25

Boswell, James, 154 n.19

Brooks, Cleanth, 151 n.1, 154 n.22

Burke, Edmund, 14, 43, 55, 65, 160 n.15, 168 n.8, 187 n.11; as 'pre-Romantic', 90–92

Burke, Kenneth, 152 n.2

Butler, Samuel, *Hudibras*, 81

Byron, George Gordon, Lord, 133, 151 n.5, 178 n.4, 185 n.49